Re-Imagining Government: Part I

Re-Imagining Government: Part One
Copyright © 2018 by Christopher Wilson

No part of this publication may be reproduced, distributed, or transmitted in any form or by any means, including photocopying, recording, or other electronic or mechanical methods, without the prior written permission of the author, except in the case of brief quotations embodied in critical reviews and certain other non-commercial uses permitted by copyright law.

Tellwell Talent
www.tellwell.ca

ISBN
978-1-77370-697-9 (Hardcover)
978-1-77370-696-2 (Paperback)
978-1-77370-698-6 (eBook)

Re-Imagining Government

PART ONE

GOVERNMENTS
OVERWHELMED
and in
DISREPUTE

CHRISTOPHER WILSON

Other Books by Christopher Wilson

Intelligent Governance, Invenire Books, 2016 with Gilles Paquet

Stewardship: Collaborative Metagovernance and Inquiring Systems, Invenire Books, 2012, with Ruth Hubbard and Gilles Paquet

Table of Contents

Foreword 9

Preface 13
Time to re-imagine a different way of working together 22

Chapter 1: Democratic Governments Out of Sync 33

Chapter 2: Government in Disrepute 41

Government Shortcomings 42

    Health 42
    Security 43
    Infrastructure 44
    Employment 44
    Automation 45
    Social supports 47
    Climate change 48
    Evidenced-based policy 50
    Transparency 52
    Disreputable leaders 53

Disempowering elected representatives *54*
A partisan Public Service *54*
The decline of public debate *55*
An Outmoded Paradigm 57
Needs of complexity overshadow capacity for coordination *61*

Chapter 3: Government Ill-Suited for Tomorrow's Challenges 71

Issues in Pursuit of Collaborators 75

International cooperation to limit the effects of climate change *75*
Increasing human migration flows *75*
An escalating income gap *77*
Perpetual economic growth as the basis of the global economic order . . *78*
Access to basic resources *79*
Over-population *80*
Public sector liquidity *82*
Alternatives to government *83*
Working together *84*

Chapter 4: The Digital Era Will Profoundly Alter the Landscape of Governance and Government. 87

Creating more knowledge.. 90

Democratizing knowledge 93

Legal constraints on sharing 97

Increasing transparency 98

Creating more opportunities for self-organization and collaboration... 99

Facilitating greater access to more resources................... 101

Creating more communities..................................... 104

Increasing the self-sufficiency of citizens 107
Government overwhelmed. 108

Chapter 5: The Paradox of Populism and the Erosion of Democracy 113

What do we mean by populism? 115
Illustrations. 119

Donald Trump (the Needy Narcissist). *119*
Recep Tayyip Erdoğan (the Paternalistic Nationalist). *121*
Rodrigo Duterte (the Saviour / Punisher) *124*
Vladimir Putin (the Kleptocratic Tyrant) *127*

The costs of populism 134

Immediate costs. *134*
Opportunity costs *135*

Responding to the populists. 140

10 responses to populists. *140*

Chapter 6: The Emerging Dimensions of a Government Reimagined 145

No one's in charge 148

Leadership, not leaders, is the real problem *158*

From leadership to stewardship. 161

A different mechanism for social coordination. *165*
Glimpsing stewardship in action—hints of things to come *169*
Goldcorp Challenge. *170*
Brazil's HIV-AIDS strategy. *171*
Governance of technology start-ups. *173*
Stewardship and self-organization *174*
Re-emphasizing social coordination over redistribution. *178*

Focusing on scalable learning over scalable efficiency 181

Re-designing government around collaboration. 197
> Becoming a trusted platform for others to work together 199

Generating stewardship from process design 204

Conclusion 215
> Bad assumptions 216
> Distorted mechanisms 217
> Defective practices 218

Acknowledgements 219

Endnotes 221

Foreword

Re-imagining Government challenges the present world of governance and invites us to re-imagine how we should work together through collaboration and engagement. It is written in a pleasant, easy-going style, and is based on decades of academic and practical work by a very perceptive observer of the world of governance, and one of the founders of the Governance Project – an intellectual endeavor developed around www.optimumonline.ca. Some of the landmark papers of Christopher Wilson that were published there have been included in this book.

Even though Christopher has published widely and has done pioneering work on collaboration, he is first and foremost a seasoned professional. *Re-Imagining Government* is a two-volume book representing the first comprehensive effort to produce a revealing map of the present toxic government scene (Book 1), and of a provisional look at a re-imagined government of the future (Book 2) based on what Wilson has been able to derive from his own work and the work of his colleagues.

In Book 1, the current volume, this process unfolds in three stages: the first three chapters aim at exposing the government scene as out of sync; at illustrating how these shortcomings are spread over a vast range of issue areas; and at underlining the great difficulties governments have in coping with the fundamental pursuit of effective collaboration. The next two chapters (4 and 5) probe two major forces – the digital revolution and populism – that are both assets and hurdles to today's democratic governance as they challenge democratic governments to deliver on social coordination. Wilson tries to identify some of the ways that good governance may be screened from the possible contamination that these forces might bring to bear. The last portion of the book then sets the stage for the second volume by sorting out the important new pillars upon which a re-imagined government might be constructed.

Wilson's plan is quite wise but also quite bold: *wise*, because he has chosen to start with the thankless task of decontamination: unless the forces that have produced the current dysfunctional governmental arrangements are persuasively unmasked and explained, there is no way that citizens will accept gambling on shedding these 'Big G' Government arrangements or experimenting with the sort of modern collaborative governance mechanisms that are required; and *bold* in tackling head on the crippling mental prison that posits that "'Big G' is the only way to govern" by putting on the table alternative 'small-g' governance arrangements that have been shown to be both tractable conceptually and eminently practical. This is where Christopher's dual experience in both academe and the consulting world comes in handy, for it enriches significantly his arguments in both Volume I and II of *Re-Imagining Government*.

Christopher Wilson's two-volume work is a most valuable contribution to the significant body of work in governance that has emerged over the last twenty years, and it represents a significant and unique progress report on what this ambitious research program has accomplished.

However, one has to guard against unreasonable expectations. Christopher's Volume II of *Re-Imagining Government* should not be expected to provide a full-fledged version of the 'small-g' governance systems that are just in the process of emerging. It will take some time before these have fully materialized and before they are regarded by the citizenry as acceptable and workable. But, after demonstrating in Volume I, that the present arrangements are unbearably toxic, Wilson is well equipped to sketch out how one can imagine an acceptable and workable redesign of the 'Big-G' Government, one that can comfortably fit within a more generalized 'small-g' governance world and usefully complement it. His crucial contribution will be in providing the missing link between the present, unworkable 'Big G' regime and the collective governance world *en émergence*.

In fact, not only does Christopher's two-volume *Re-Imagining Government* do a particularly good job at debunking the mental prison of 'Big-G' Government, but it is also particularly effective at building connections with the emerging world that is increasingly dominated by collaborative, 'small-g' governance arrangements. This perspective is based on his innovative work as a pioneering member of the Governance Project over the years in Ottawa, and I am confident that his work on the missing link between the old institutions and the emerging regime built on the dynamics of collaboration, will prove to be a major step toward resolving the distributed governance problem. This is a problem that the members of the Governance Project have all been engaged in over the last decades – that is, designing *intelligent governance.*

As one who has been similarly engaged for decades in trying to refurbish the 'Big-G' Government citadel, as Wilson has undertaken in Volume I, and also in trying to persuade the circle of governance practitioners of the need for significant governance redesign to make it compatible and workable for a 'small-g' governance world, as Wilson does in Volume II, I can only add that I welcome Christopher Wilson's two-volume book warmly and that I recommend it in the strongest terms.

Gilles Paquet, C.M., M.S.R.C., F.R.S.A., M.A.
Animateur of La Maison Gouvernance in Ottawa
Former President of the Royal Society of Canada
April 2018

Preface

Take a moment and consider that today, in 2018, we have a system of collective governance that was designed and built for people who lived so long ago that none of them remain alive today—not even their great-grandchildren. That system of government was created in a time when most people were farmers; when education was rudimentary and rare; when science was only just beginning; and when transportation involved largely walking and horses (although, if you were very fortunate, you might take a ride on a steam train or a sailing ship). It was a time when doctors were not much more than butchers, and the ideas of antibiotics, vaccines and DNA were unknown. Cities were a social blight of overcrowding, poverty and sewage. Slavery had just officially ended in the US, but the practice was still prevalent in much of the world. It was a time when people rarely left their village or town, and had little sense of the world. Needless to say, there was no Internet or Facebook, no cellphones or computers, no TV or radio, no movies, no Disneyland and no summer vacations. There were no drones, no satellites, no rockets, no moon landings, no planes and no cars. There wasn't even electricity.

And yet, surprisingly, the system of democratic government that was designed for that time is presumed, by almost everyone, to still be the best form of social coordination we could possibly use today. That system is also assumed to require no significant adjustment for the obvious advances in knowledge and technology, or the behavioural and cultural changes that have occurred over a century and a half within the populace. This is not to say that the basic principles of democracy—"rule by the people"—have lost their lustre. Quite the contrary, the vast majority of people around the world persist in their commitment to democracy's basic tenets, even when the rules and mechanisms by which democracy is energized in society seem a bit dated.

Yet, despite being surrounded by relentless social change, there remains a strong cultural resistance to even considering changes to our system of governance, as if the social contract established over a century ago between citizens and their governments is so fragile that any amount of technical tinkering would bring the whole democratic edifice crashing down.

To some, democracy is no longer a living, breathing process, but a fragile museum piece that has taken on a rigid, canonical stature as if it had been etched in the ancient tablets given by God to Moses. And strangely enough, the more these sclerotic structures of democracy are challenged by the realities of everyday life, the tighter people hold on to them. They consistently and obstinately mistake the aging institutional *form* of democracy for the *spirit* of democracy.

Moreover, it is these same, persistent institutional failures that are eroding popular faith in the system of democracy itself. You would have had to have lived as a hermit over the last decade not to have heard something along the lines of: governments are ineffective; government institutions are not satisfying the needs of citizens; government leaders are corrupt or out of touch; government bureaucracies are too slow or too stupid; governments no longer represent their electors; governments are no longer perceived as fair, or they are just incapable of looking out for the common good.

While all these shortcomings are invariably placed at the feet of political and organizational leaders of different stripes, in my opinion, this is erroneous—even though it is quite clear some leaders are assuredly better than others. The bigger problem is that our governance system has not evolved at the same pace as society, and this has created an inevitable disconnect that *no* leader, no matter how brilliant or well meaning, can ever bridge. It's like trying to run today's *Call of Duty: Infinite Warfare* on an ancient Atari 2600 console. It doesn't matter what the skill of the player is, it just won't work.

Preface

This book is my attempt to understand the degree of disconnection that exists between the structures of our existing government and the roles government is being called on to play—both now and in the near future. This will help to identify where the biggest misalignments are, in order to help us focus on what needs to be transformed and how to have the biggest impact. The sequel to this volume, *Re-Imagining Government Part II*, will attempt to sketch out how our governance system might be redesigned to make it more effective in a modern-day context.

This work is the culmination of almost 20 years of research and experience—work frequently done in conjunction with colleagues at the University of Ottawa, which, in various ways, has concerned itself with learning how to get people to work together better. It is also the product of work done with a host of public, private and civic clients and partners who have been forced to consider new ways of working together to address issues of urgent concern to them. Their insights and innovations have been both marvellous and inspiring.

To begin with then, we should be clear that government is fundamentally about social coordination. Most simply, it's about how we try to prevent tripping over each other as we go about our lives in close proximity to one another. But government is also how we organize ourselves to accomplish things collectively that we could never do alone.

Over the years, however, I have observed that while most people will freely admit that they can probably accomplish more together than they can separately, they are generally not very good at it—working together, that is. All too frequently you hear complaints about how "it's too difficult"; "you can't trust people"; "too many cooks"; "if everyone's accountable, no one is"; and so on, and so forth. Consequently, most people tend to shy away from situations that require them to collaborate or work in partnership with others—especially in government—unless there's no other choice for them. Unfortunately for them, in today's world, *there is no longer any other sane choice but to learn to cooperate.*

Furthermore, most people continue to be obsessed with the idea of the heroic leader, "the saviour," who they believe will protect them from all manner of shortcomings, relieve them of the burden of having to work things out with their neighbours themselves, and do so while magically ensuring that all of their preferences will be met regardless of everyone else's. These "leaders" prey on our immense sense of entitlement. Government, for instance, should absolutely protect me against the costs of falling sick, but I shouldn't have to pay taxes to protect someone else. Government should ensure that my outdated job of digging coal is protected, but government should not collect taxes to help create new jobs in the clean energy economy of tomorrow. Amazingly, many people defer to these heroic leaders even when it comes at the cost of their own best interests and well-being. From an economics point of view, these attitudes go totally against the commonplace idea that people are "rational actors." Instead, it's a form of collective irrationality.

Inevitably, the narrative of this "great man" (and it's almost invariably a man) involves him being bold enough, confident enough, or stupid enough to make choices that others would normally run away from. For example, in his acceptance speech to the US Republican National Convention in 2016, political novice Donald Trump said, "Nobody knows the system better than me, which is why *I alone can fix it.*"[1] Such hubris! Often without any regard to their rationality, the decisions of the "great man" are then imposed on others, usually with religious-like fanfare, but inevitably favouring one person, one group, or one organization at the expense of all others in a "win-lose" scenario reminiscent of medieval conflicts. In fact, the degree to which such inequitable decisions are successfully imposed is often seen as a proxy measure of the leader's "greatness."

Thus, our modern history of organizational and political interactions has tended to play out like a real-life *Game of Thrones*, serial performances of zero-sum games that involve a revolving cast of "white knight" leaders acting as deciders and arbitrators of who wins and who loses. The "great man" is the one with the courage to make tough decisions when others might pause to think things through.

In a recent survey of 38 countries conducted by the Pew Research Centre, while "more than half in each of the nations polled consider representative democracy a very or somewhat good way to govern their country, in all countries, pro-democracy attitudes coexist, to varying degrees, with openness to nondemocratic forms of governance, including rule by experts, a strong leader or the military."

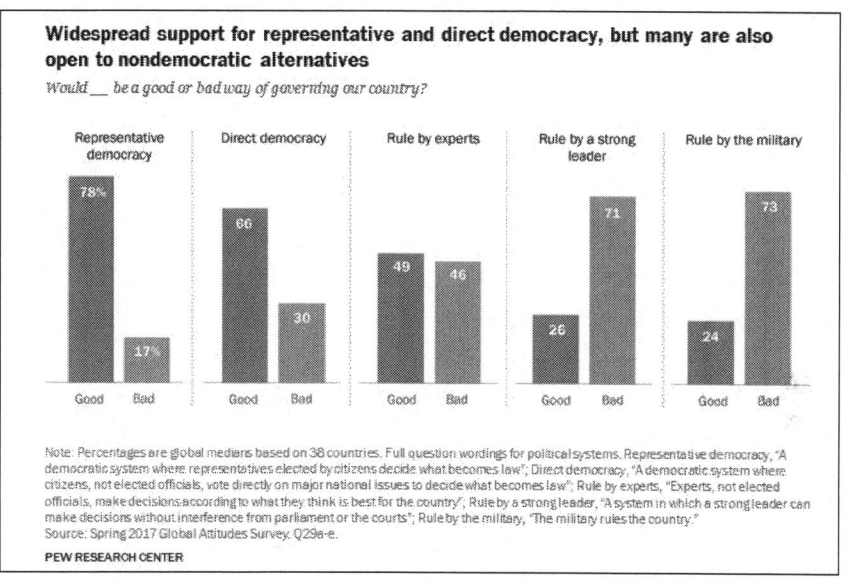

Source: Richard Wike, et.al.. 2017. "Globally, Broad Support for Representative and Direct Democracy", *Global Attitudes Survey*, Pew Research Centre, October 16. Accessed at: http://www.pewglobal.org/2017/10/16/globally-broad-support-for-representative-and-direct-democracy/

Our tolerance and acceptance of this "great man" myth is not the product of informed rational choice, but it is more a cultural legacy whose roots have long ago passed out of memory. Everybody just knows that some one must be in charge. Not only do such cultural relics fail to guarantee any current usefulness or efficacy, but they are generally significant impediments to collective learning, social adaptation and evolution.

Richard Rochefort, founder and former Senior Director General of Service Canada College, once illustrated this phenomenon to students in one of my classes. He described some social science research in which six chimps were put in a cage and then fed bananas. Naturally the chimps went for them. But when they did, a loud obnoxious sound was introduced, frightening them, and causing them to back away. After a several experiences like this, the chimps learned not to go for the bananas and the loud noise was never used again.

Re-Imagining Government - Part 1

Then the researchers started replacing the chimps one by one, taking the original ones out of the cage and putting new ones in. Each time a new chimp came in, bananas were once again introduced, and naturally the new chimp tried to go for them, but each time it did, the older chimps would beat it back until it, too, stopped going for the bananas. The loud noise was never heard by the new chimps. Eventually all the original chimps were replaced, but their replacements would still not go after the bananas. Even though none of the remaining chimps had ever experienced the obnoxious sound. They had all learned to go against their basic nature and not eat the bananas. Rochefort pointed out that this phenomenon of socially learned behaviour is similar to our cultures in organizations and in society. None of us really challenge why we accept unquestionably the assumption that "someone has to be in charge." We simply follow it out of blind habit and Pavlovian peer pressure.

Additionally, the perpetuation of the "great man" myth buttresses our need to find justification for our own abdication of social responsibility. We don't want to be inconvenienced by our democratic responsibilities, so we're all too willing to delegate the job to others who say they will do it for us. We choose to believe these agents are "great men" who can look after things on our behalf because: we imagine they know nearly everything; that they have special and uncommon insights; and that they have superior capacities that are unknown to us—beliefs which, of course, they do everything in their power to encourage. Yet in today's world, the hard truth is that *no one* has all the knowledge, resources or power to do anything of significance in society— least of all address any of the complex concerns currently of importance to citizens.

When, for instance, have our elected leaders responded to questions about a problem by saying, "I really don't know; let's find out together"? They don't do this because, as US President Truman once remarked, not having an answer is tantamount to admitting that you're not an expert and that you don't have the "right stuff" to be a "great man." Accordingly, "great men" have become particularly adept at evading, dissembling, hedging, spouting vagaries and outright lying in order to maintain the public fantasy of their superiority— although in truth, the only secret they hold is usually that they just don't know. A humble leader, willing to learn from others, is in fact an absolute rarity.

Equally rare, especially politically, are those leaders who can bring together all the diverse voices of their community or society and inspire their collective creativity and wisdom. This is the social equivalent of being a conductor of an orchestra, bringing all the varied contributions of different people together to orchestrate social cooperation and collective impact. Instead, what's usually on order are wannabe generals, playing politics as partisan warfare, pitting one group against another, where winning or losing is the only possible outcome, and where collective learning is rarely, if ever, on the agenda.

When confronted by complex or wicked problems, "great men" prefer familiar, black-and-white answers to issues they over-simplify. This enables them to communicate to the media in friendly "sound bites," and to demonstrate their brilliance and effectiveness with quick instinctive decisions. Instead of having to take the time to understand a problem's complexity, or to attend to a variety of perspectives, or to assemble the collective learning and shared commitments necessary to resolve it, they just wing it. It's laziness, pure and simple; at best, it's a recipe for institutionalized mediocrity.

This combination of incomplete understanding and quick decision-making, not only leads to ineffective action, but it also produces rich fodder for all those rebellious critics who inevitably resist a leader's claim to being "the one true patriarch," invariably with the aim of replacing the existing "patriarch" with themselves. Under the universally mistaken assumption that a government's past shortcomings can be wholly attributed to one person—regardless of the system in which they operate—the failures of one leader become fertile ground for more "great men" to arise, like weeds. In such an environment, important practical concerns, such as avoiding the possibility of operating with incomplete understanding, or with limited creativity, or with weak implementation capacity, are never addressed because they are always assumed to be a function of the leader's "greatness."

In contrast to popular belief, however, the complex, socio-economic challenges of today's world do not respond well to the simple, linear solutions of "great men." Nor is trying to funnel society's creative capacity through a handful of individuals even the best way to marshal society's collective potential. As we hear from a growing chorus of actors from all sectors of society, there is an urgent need to find better ways to cooperatively utilize our vast collective resources—both tangible and intangible. Yet, this ambition remains largely unrealized because "great men" and cooperation have proven so far to be antithetical.

Over the years, I have researched, participated in, and evaluated partnerships of various descriptions, and one other thing has repeatedly stood out. Most people, but most especially managers and organizational leaders, know very little about collaboration or partnership. They assume that because they may be a subject matter expert, or because they hold a leadership position in an organization, they automatically know how to behave in a collaborative setting. Unfortunately, when actual cooperation is demanded of them, they default to their MBA knowledge, or whatever else they picked up in some leadership training course, which amounts to just about nothing of real value as far as collaboration is concerned!

Therefore, when they try to shoehorn those well-worn management rules and best practices into their collaboration work, they quickly discover that they are producing entirely the wrong impact. Consequently, they begin to feel discomforted, in over their head, and unsure of themselves, while still trying to present the obligatory pretense of confidence and being in control. Then, instead of seeing collaboration as the incredible learning and creative opportunity that it is, they fret about their loss of control, about time wasted in group meetings, about partners shirking their commitments, about a lack of accountability, and a host of other complaints. Not surprisingly, many just get fed up and quit.

Yet, there have also been times, when the need to resolve an issue was particularly acute, so strong in fact that the participants were willing to go off the beaten path and invent entirely new rules and behaviours to allow themselves to get where they needed to go. In the end, for those who stuck with trying to work together, this innovative practice was perceived as a very rewarding journey, both professionally and personally. In fact, my experience has shown that successful collaborators have consistently identified their participation in the collaborative process as being one of their most important accomplishments. And almost invariably, that participation has encouraged them to seek out new opportunities, to expand their scope of working together, and to embrace larger, more complex concerns. It is an attitude that is reflected by the idea that, "If we can do this together, then what else can we do?"

Nevertheless, I have often asked myself, why must the wheel be repeatedly reinvented each time groups and organizations choose to cooperate? Why do we not understand collaboration as well as we understand, say, management?

The answer to this is both cultural and paradigmatic. Our Western culture lionizes individual over collective achievement, even when those supposedly "individual" achievements would clearly never have happened in the first place without significant collective input. It's the army that wins the war, but it's the general who takes the credit. This age-old cultural bias is now reinforced by mechanistic and industrial management paradigms which presume that only an elite few have the wisdom, creativity and energy to make things happen. Employees are just so much undifferentiated raw material, and from the perspective of many organizational leaders, they are simply interchangeable widgets to be manipulated by those "enlightened" few. Among most practitioners, top-down is still perceived to be the only way to coordinate among a variety of organizational capacities.

That said, things are beginning to change. For instance, it should be obvious to everyone that because of universal education and universal (or nearly so) connectivity and access to knowledge, any reliance or dependence on a select few is both naïve and hugely problematic, not only for solving the tough complex problems of the day, but also for a healthy democracy. Limiting the task of social coordination to the capacities of a few individuals seriously constrains both understanding and innovation, while simultaneously encouraging authoritarianism and a population guided by entitlement and bribery, in lieu of their shared ownership.

Time to re-imagine a different way of working together

So here we are today, almost a century after the advent of universal education and decades after the foundation of the global Internet, with many of our democratic institutions under attack for being quaint, ineffective, or at worst counterproductive to the needs of the time. In truth, we have witnessed the emergence of ideas like *multi-stakeholderism, cross-agency working, cross-sectoral collaboration* and *participatory democracy*—not because someone at the top felt inclined to be generous or inclusive—but because they have been understood as pre-conditions for social coordination and progress. Unfortunately, our public institutions generally show little progress on these fronts, beyond an ample amount of empty rhetoric.

Simultaneously, governments increasingly find themselves without all the knowledge, resources or power they need to fulfill their intents. This is because the issues they face require input nationally, regionally and locally. They also require input from many different disciplines and many different stakeholders. *No single government body*—no matter how extensive its legislative or taxing capacity—can be successful simply by working alone; that is, of course, if the measure of success is producing positive results in society.

While siloed governments were a standard feature of Westminster-style models of top-down government, today these structures are viewed with great distrust and suspicion due to their being overly bureaucratic and incapable of producing the results that their citizens want. They represent a design *malefit* that has contributed inexorably to an ongoing, de-legitimization of the State as a valid mechanism for social coordination, and to surreptitiously encouraging alternatives to government to compensate for the State's repeated failures.

Since the 1970s, for instance, voting participation has steadily declined in every Western country*, and is coincident with a dramatic decline in the public's confidence and trust in both their governments and their leaders. Not surprisingly, there are a growing number of substitutes for government,

---

* Except where voting has been made legally compulsory, such as Australia or Belgium

including both community-based and online collaborations, in which new mechanisms for social coordination are being experimented with. Even within governments, the old rhetoric around "streamlined silos" is out of fashion. In its place, there is talk of "integrated government," "horizontal government," and "whole of government" methodologies.

Yet, despite the rhetoric, governments remain deeply entrenched in their old "top-down" approaches. Read anything about government reform, and the first prerequisite for successful change that is identified is "support from the top." Governments are woefully lacking in the frameworks, skills and mechanisms that would enable them to affect the more cooperative behaviours that underlie these more integrative styles of operating.

The traditional paradigm of government says that "government is about some combination of coordination, stabilization, redistribution and pedagogy while the primary function of the bureaucracy is to protect and preserve administrative institutions consistent with constitutional processes, traditions, values and beliefs"[2]. But if one pulls back a bit from the specifics of what government does—making rules and laws, delivering services, operating multiple business lines, generating revenues and providing protection—the basic *raison d'être* of government is coordination. Stabilization and redistribution are essentially tools governments use when their efforts at social coordination fail, and while administrative preservation is a device to pass on institutional learning, it is also a device to insure against periodic hijackings of government by groups of citizens fomenting non-cooperation in society.

Governments coordinate among groups and individuals in society; they coordinate between people and organizations, and they coordinate between governments. Laws, regulation, policy making—even taxation—are mechanisms through which governments potentially reduce the friction between people and organizations, and therefore promote less social conflict and greater social stability. Governments also coordinate among societal actors in order to foster social innovation, either to solve problems or to take advantage of new opportunities. And, until recently, governments have represented the principal (if not the exclusive) social organizing power within society.

The basis of all this coordination has been government's traditional monopoly on coercion and its *perceived power* to punish or reward. This is a legacy of ancient, autocratic kings. More recently, in the last few centuries, this *perceived power* of governments has been augmented by the *legitimate authority* that has been conferred on them by citizens in democratic societies who have elected them to deal with issues of social concern and public interest. Over time, governments, empowered by these two sources of power, have co-evolved along with their increasingly more diverse societies to become a tremendous force for social coordination—albeit in a centralized, top-down fashion—one that was ultimately embodied in the notion of the Welfare State.

Yet a quick scan of recent media readily reveals evidence of an erosion of both the government's *legitimate authority* as well as its coercive, or *perceived power*. The perception that government leaders are ineffective and/or unethical is wearing away at the former, while technical innovation is eating into the latter. Whether it is highly regarded public officials being charged with "gangsterism"[3], or the obvious inability of any government to direct its economy as it responds to global forces beyond its borders[4], the perception is growing that governments cannot be relied upon to get the job done. Simultaneously, emerging technical innovations like "Bitcoin," which operate independent of government monetary control,[5] or the repeated and intrusive hacks by small groups or individuals into government electronic infrastructures* suggest that governments are no longer in control.

Take away both of these enabling tools—*legitimate authority* and *perceived power*—it then becomes questionable as to whether governments can continue to be trusted to fulfill their traditional role as the principal coordinator of society. For some governments, like, for instance, Canada's federal government, the task of providing social coordination has simply been vacated,[6] in favour of a focus on redistribution to mitigate the impacts of its coordination failures.

Restoring the ability of governments to once again effectively orchestrate social coordination lies somewhere between two collaborative maxims: *be helpful* to others, and *don't take all the credit* for someone else's work. Instead of seeking the kind of legitimacy derived from being able to impose

---

* Like the Russian hack identified by the CIA of the Democratic National Convention during the 2016 US presidential election

solutions on others, governments today are more likely to garner legitimacy by helping others to solve their own problems in their own way.

For instance, it has been amply demonstrated that the standardized solutions characteristic of the Welfare State do not work for everyone, everywhere. Often these solutions are found to be palliative at best. However, being able to help those most affected by a problem to help themselves—with contributions of knowledge, resources or influence—dramatically increases the likelihood that those local solutions will actually work. When governments can act in this way as effective brokers or helpful partners, their reputations in communities soar. Those partners who are helped quite naturally tend to acknowledge the support provided by government, and in the end, there is no greater legitimacy than that which is bestowed upon you by others. If, therefore, governments can foster reputations that flow from their *perceived generosity*, then they will acquire a new place of respect and trust among the citizenry. But we are far from there.

A colleague and former federal deputy minister, Ruth Hubbard, once told me that governments will pay any price to be viewed as legitimate in the eyes of their constituents. In fact, legitimacy is the true currency of government. And while there is always some legitimacy to be derived from being able to punish people or enact laws, it pales beside the legitimacy generated from *perceived generosity*. Such legitimacy is naturally attractive: people *want* to work with you, they *want* you to work with them, as opposed to being forced to work with you or for you. It showers its recipients with a collective power that is willingly bestowed by others, as opposed to the power that governments have traditionally just taken for themselves. Unfortunately, this notion of *perceived generosity* is clearly lacking among today's leaders of government, because they remain stuck in an inherently feudal mindset of government by control.

Former Canadian Prime Minister Joe Clark, who once described Canada as a "community of communities," recently commented, "I think the greatest threat to Canada is not some disease that will come, not some attack that will come. But we will just grow sufficiently indifferent [to each other] that instead of finding national reasons to come together, to be our best, to be excited about our whole country, we sort of slip off into our gated communities and stay there and watch the world go by."[7]

By being indifferent to each other, or retreating into a mean-spirited and isolationist "us-them" mentality, we risk losing our sense of wholeness as an inspiration for national creativity and strength. Without it, we enable the foundations of fear and terror to emerge from our continuous exposure to a world full of differences and uncertainties.

Those leaders who seek to separate us, or diminish our diversity, or who would have people turn against one another are inherently weak, often narcissistic and uncreative people. They are incapable of seeing beyond the most obvious limitations, or of productively utilizing life's great gift of diversity. In that light, the long decline in public sector legitimacy may also be tied to the inability of its leaders to connect with society's rich tapestry of people, or their inability to articulate the wholeness which emerges from them all. And without that sense of wholeness, the task of governing for everyone has become immensely more difficult, if not impossible.

Who then, if not the leaders of government, is best equipped to change government and make it more cognizant of the whole and more adaptable to an ever-evolving environment? The only plausible answer to that question is: those who are the actual owners of government—*the citizens*. But then, how could I, as a citizen, go about doing that?

First and foremost, I believe we must be able to imagine and give expression to a future in which we are all willing to share. That means developing a collective "capacity to imagine" that possible future and an ability to share it. Believing that my future can come only at the expense of another's is a tried and true recipe for great tragedy. Similarly, believing that the future must be like the past is a ludicrous invitation to recreating the shortcomings of the past in the future. There is no more certainty to be gained from trying to impose the past on the future, than there is in trying to use the knowledge of horse-drawn buggies as a guide for space travel. Finally, the claims that the tools and structures that worked so well in the past, must *always* be good enough for the future is completely groundless. If new tools are available, we should use them. The past is past, so leave it there—no matter what the populists would like you to believe.

Preface

Without trying to make specific predictions of the future, or being able to explicitly identify all the tools we will need to create the future we want, this book and its sequel are meant to try and read the tea leaves and lay out some of the broad strokes of what isn't working and what is likely to be needed. With these in mind, we can consider what might be possible and then we might imagine the types of governing tools we should be looking for to get us to where we need to go.

Consider this book like a "kernel" of software code. There are many others around the world who are also making valuable contributions in this area and maybe together we can come up with something truly transformative. Hopefully, this book and its sequel can offer enough detail that others can imagine their own possibilities based on it and then add or enlarge upon it. Therefore in an iterative way, we—you the reader, myself and many others—can begin shaping a new model of co-governance that can practically shape social coordination for the tomorrow we would like to live into, one that might ultimately encompass the totality of our human connectivity, our shared knowledge, and our collective power—not to mention our shared aspirations for the future of our children, our communities, and for all of humanity.

It is no accident that the growing connectivity of the Internet has led to a reflective process that is beginning to question the very foundations upon which our governments were built—notions like representative government, the use of expert decision makers, and the obsession of equality over basic fairness. More access to information has given rise to the greater likelihood that people will ask questions. And with more than half the world's population now using smart phones and able to connect with one another, it's not just the world's most repressive regimes that are being questioned, but the world's most democratic ones as well. In light of all this global scrutiny, it's no longer enough to be content with simply reforming existing governments—that is, fiddling around their edges[8], adopting, say, a newer, friendlier language of cooperation, while keeping the same old structures and operational assumptions alive. People are beginning to look for significant change—they just don't know yet what form it should take.

In **Chapter 1**, I examine how governments—even the fundamental notion of democracy itself—seem to have fallen out of alignment with the needs of their citizens, resulting in an ongoing decline in public confidence that governments can act as a credible source of coordination in society. Yet, serious discussions to bring our systems of collective governance up-to-date, or any of their institutions, remain by and large a taboo topic. The idea of possibly walking away from our Westminster or republican models of government is considered heresy, not only among those involved in the public sector, but also by a public brainwashed into believing this man-made process has now gained the status of something sacred and inviolable—despite its obvious dysfunctionality.

For instance, the original design assumptions of our legacy system of representative democracy no longer exist. The monopoly that governments once had on social coordination has ended—and an increasing number of alternatives to government exist. The traditional Western models of government have been largely hollowed out in practice by both extreme partisanship and cult leadership, becoming little more than a husk of their former selves. Finally, the legitimacy of both our governments and their leaders is continually being undermined by both unethical behaviour and overall ineffectiveness. In fact, an entire generation of people from around the world is beginning to lose faith in democracy altogether[9].

Chapter 2 looks at the extent to which our system of governance has become ineffective in dealing with the needs and realities of today. In the press, we can witness a litany of protracted public concerns involving: the provision of quality health care; the reduction of poverty; issues around indigenous peoples; climate change; the balancing of privacy and security; the growing unaffordability of education; the increasing infrastructure deficit; and government's overall incapacity to manage the economy. The very chronic nature of these concerns should flag the fact that these problems, together with their solutions, are systemic in nature, requiring contributions from many different people and groups, often crossing the lines between business, government and civil society.

Against this backdrop of ineffectiveness, there are a significant number of emerging policy challenges which demand unconditionally that governments operate in a more open and collaborative way. Until now, governments were designed primarily as mechanisms to achieve coordination via control, whereas these emerging policy challenges require governments to be primarily effective learners and collaborators. **Chapter 3,** therefore, presents this emerging public policy background to underscore the critical need for governments to function differently in the future.

As complex as current files may seem, these future challenges appear to be even more fundamental, existential even, yet they are receiving much less popular attention. These include concerns such as: the global viability of perpetual economic growth; the future of human work in an era of ubiquitous technology; the growing risk to humanity of unrestrained and democratized technological advancement; the global impact of unconstrained population growth; the growing threats to accessing basic resources (such as water, food, housing, and security); the inequitable distribution of society's wealth; the destabilizing threats of mass migration; and the continued solvency of governments addicted to debt.

These profound public policy concerns are further complicated by the Internet and the tools of the digital era. **Chapter 4** raises new challenges that stem directly from these new technologies: from trying to make sense of all the added information, in order to foster social innovation, to finding the necessary resources to implement change and ensuring that technology helps create healthier human communities—all while mitigating the possible impacts of putting this tremendous knowledge in the hands of everyone, including a few very disturbed individuals.

What all of these unresolved and fundamental concerns have in common is their complexity and their inherent "unknowableness." More important, however, they all represent shared problems. That is, we each contribute to the problem and therefore we can contribute to its solution. Furthermore, they are all coming to the fore simultaneously, adding to the complexity of the challenge to government. In addressing them, governments can no longer lay claim to having all the answers, the knowledge, the resources, or the power they will need to affect solutions on behalf of their citizens. Governance has thus become a function that is widely distributed, requiring many people, many minds and hearts, and many organizations in and out of government to cooperate and coordinate amongst themselves.

The added social complexity that is generated by this growing diversity and distribution of governance has also given rise to fear and uncertainty in the minds of many, opening them to the "siren" promises of populists and demagogues. **Chapter 5** looks at this rise of populism that is stirring around the world as a symptom of this misalignment between democratic governments and their ability to fulfill the needs of their citizens.

What is particularly unique and somewhat remarkable in human civilization today is that there are now more than just two options for resolving governments' coordination challenges. Historically, leaders of government have often met these types of challenges either by *reducing social diversity* (and all the harshness and violence that implies) or by imposing more comprehensive and severe *systems of control*. **Chapter 6** explores the outlines of a different approach by imagining the dimensions of a government that may be more consistent with the times.

The chronic inability of governments to meet the needs of their citizens has already given rise to a host of new, creative behaviours—behaviours that are occurring on the margins of government or external to it. These changes tend to embody one or more of the following five mental shifts or metanoia:

- Recognizing that no one's in charge;
- Shifting from leadership to stewardship;
- Focusing on scalable learning as opposed to scalable efficiency;
- Redesigning government around collaboration; and
- Generating stewardship from process design.

These five shifts have been observed as elements of an emerging *evolutionary* model of organization[10], one that is likely to become more central to a modernized form of democratic government. With these shifts in mind, we can begin to imagine what government might look like in the future.

But just the act of "imagining what might be" represents a clear break from traditional thinking that assumes the future of government must always be like the past, only slightly different. I believe the collaborative challenges of our times are sufficiently great that we need people, lots and lots of people, thinking about what might be, and having the courage and enough skin in the game to be willing to embrace change, so that we can bring into being that which they can imagine. Our greatest challenges are shared, thus necessitating that the source of our respective solutions must also be shared.

Therefore, the **Concluding Chapter** is less a *call to arms* than it is a *call to imagine*—something requiring only a sense of ownership and a willingness to be open. In attempting to re-imagine government, I will try bringing all the pieces together to envision the possible contours of what a new model of government might be. This will set the stage for this book's sequel, *Re-Imagining Government Part II*.

While to some, engaged as they are in the day-to-day activities of government, the very idea of transforming this giant behemoth of government organization may seem impossible or unimaginable, it really isn't. It's already being done. At the core of this transformation is a simple psychological shift from "Thou shalt do this" to "How can we help?" Beyond this, very little new needs to be invented. The tools are all basically there. Even the new social technologies that facilitate collaboration might be no more than those employed among healthy families and networks of friends. Therefore, it's not good enough to claim that "I can't," because "you can." You can certainly do what you can do, and together "we can" do something which is much greater.

However, each person must make a choice. You must begin by choosing the future that you want for yourself and your children—that is, if you want to avoid someone else's future being thrust upon you unwillingly.

Chapter I
Democratic Governments Out of Sync

"Democracy as we know it is failing."

—Yaneer Bar-Yam, President,
New England Complex Systems Institute, MIT

Around the world in many countries, democratic government is increasingly under attack. Their leaders are all too frequently caught up in scandal or corrupt practices, and their capacity to solve the problems that actually matter to people seems at best a matter more of chance and coincidence, rather than design or skill. Most often those leaders seem in over their heads. In place of democracy, we see an upsurge in authoritarianism. In places like Poland, the Czech Republic, the Philippines, Hungary, Romania, Kenya, Thailand, Venezuela, Nicaragua, Bolivia, Ecuador, Botswana, and Turkey, we see countries that have become democracies in name only. In addition, well-established authoritarian regimes such as Russia, China, Iran, and Saudi Arabia are seeing the shadow of their influence in the world steadily grow. The United States, once the world's foremost bastion of democracy, seems intent on retreating from the world and from its founding democratic principles.

Once, it seemed that having a successful democratic government was something that all peoples aspired to. By the late 1990s, the once mighty communist Soviet Union became economically and intellectually bankrupted and fell by the wayside. By 2000, the military juntas of South America had been replaced by popular democracies. But for over a decade now, the idea of democracy has fallen out of fashion. According to Larry Diamond[11], the expansion of democracy in the world came to a grinding halt around 2006, with no net expansion in the number of democratic states since then. And given that "rule by the people" is closely associated with the vitality of civil liberties, it should come as no surprise that these, too, have steadily deteriorated around the world since 2006.

Paradoxically, the decline of democracy and the shift to authoritarianism has often been ushered in by democratic choice. When faced with the discomfort and fear engendered by constant and ever-increasing change, many citizens seem more than willing to trade their civil liberties for an illusion of certainty and predictability. It seems easier to choose a populist, authoritarian "leader" shilling over-simplified, improbable solutions, than it is to become authentically engaged oneself in understanding a host of complex issues. If reality is uncertain and uncomfortable, then the simple fix is to replace existing "elites" and "know-it-alls" and gamble on inexperienced newbies to "shake things up" a little.

The perennial assumption is always that the problem is the leader, and not that the issues themselves may be complex and hard to resolve. And whatever is done, don't ask people to either give up their entitlements or to take time to act as informed, rightful owners in a system of shared self-governance. For many, simplicity is better than uncertainty or the inconvenience of responsibility. As a result, populations have proven all too susceptible to the siren calls of populist leaders claiming a fictional ability to control, and promising to return them to the "good old golden days" of more certainty.

Around the world, even in well-established democracies, countries are struggling with the resurgence of regressive, or what Fukuyama calls "neo-patrimonial," tendencies from bygone eras. "Leaders who think that they can get away with it are eroding democratic checks and balances, overriding term limits and normative restraints, violating opposition rights, and accumulating power and wealth for themselves and their families, cronies, clients, and parties."[12] In the past, these "strongman" tendencies were kept in check by a watchful media and the back and forth of an open

Chapter I

and vigorous democratic process. However, as democratic governments have consistently failed to deliver on a host of issues of importance to their citizens, a climate of failed public expectations has grown, followed by a culture of distrust in established leaders, creating a fertile ground for these bad governance practices to take root.

Old precedents and behaviours are being blatantly discarded, and new norms are developing in the political classes. For instance, in contrast to a century of policy making that has tried to be evidence-based, Trump spokeswoman Scottie Nell Hughes[13] claimed on National Public Radio that, "There's no such thing as facts anymore"—besides, said Republican House Speaker, Paul Ryan, "Who cares?"[14]

Says Diamond, "Democracies fail when people lose faith in them."[15] As we witnessed in the 2016 US presidential election, when a country's leaders can no longer command their citizens' confidence—either because they are seen as *"unethical"* (that is, they are not seen to be operating for the collective good); or they are perceived as *"ineffective"* (that is, they are incapable of producing the desired results)—citizens may react by trying to remove the leadership class entirely in order to underscore their displeasure.

In this environment, "outsiders"—those not established in well-worn democratic precedents, tradition and accepted rules of behaviour—become favoured. And while the ability to "throw the bums out" is considered a laudable feature of democracy, doing so does not always guarantee a change to the system under which the new leaders will operate. And it sometimes leaves the door open to leadership aspirants who are willing to make fundamental changes that are in their interest alone, subverting even the very nature of democracy itself.

In this light, 2016 may go down as a watershed year for the practice of democratic government. First, in June, there was the surprise referendum decision in the UK to leave the European Union, the so-called Brexit decision. Also in June was the election of strongman Rodrigo Duterte to the Philippine presidency, making the country the poster child for democracy's disintegration in Southeast Asia. Then later in July we saw the attempted coup in Turkey and the subsequent crackdown on any and all opponents of Turkey's President Recep Tayyip Erdoğan*. Finally, the fall was witness to the election of populist Donald Trump to the US presidency. While each of these countries have historically been seen as defenders of democracy in their own sphere, each has now been caught up in groundswell reactions to the systemic failures of their democratic institutions in addressing issues of importance to their citizens.

In the case of the UK, feeling threatened by potential waves of refugees, by a sense of being left out of the benefits of a global economy, and by a perceived loss of national autonomy in a European Parliament dominated by non-Britons, a majority of Britons opted to leave the EU. It is interesting to note that those wishing to remain in the EU tended to be those most comfortable with change and diversity, including cosmopolitan Londoners, the Scots and Northern Irish, the young, as well as the well-educated.

In the Philippines, the shift was driven by rampant and systemic corruption, while in Turkey the instigator was the security issue that arose from an attempted coup and persistent concerns about ISIL. In each case, the fears of citizens were channeled into the hands of those who made the most forceful claim of being in control.

Similarly, in November 2016, Americans voted to make businessman and reality TV star Donald Trump—a narcissistic serial liar, xenophobe, racist, misogynist and government novice[16]—their next president. Trump's key message was that America was in decline. He laid blame for that at the doorstep of an assortment "others": educated but ineffective "elites" (both Democratic and Republican); too many immigrants; biased journalists; bad trade deals; a weak military; too much taxation; and an overreaching government bureaucracy. And like the many populists who have preceded him, Trump was quick to target those who were visibly "others"—referring in his campaign to Mexicans as "rapists" and "criminals," and repeatedly pledging to ban all Muslims from entering the US while forcibly removing

---

* Four years ago, Turkey's democracy was held up by the West as a secular model for the Muslim world: a democracy that was negotiating EU membership and advancing towards a peace settlement with its Kurdish minority. Now, the government of President Recep Tayyip Erdoğan is for all intents and purposes an elected dictatorship.

Chapter I

11 million illegal aliens. His was the classic populist narrative of "us" versus the scary "them."

"Donald Trump's message resonates in the most forgotten corners of the US," says Chris Arnade, "because viewed from these places, America no longer seems a great country."[17] Of the 11 national polls taken in the US between November 3rd and 28th, on average, only one quarter of Americans felt their country was headed in the right direction[18]. The Oscar-winning filmmaker Michael Moore put it succinctly in a tweet: "In June, Britain voted to leave Europe. Yesterday, America voted to leave America."[19]

While the USA has long considered itself to be the world's standard-bearer of democracy, it has now been classified as a "flawed democracy," according to the Economist Intelligence Unit[20]. Its 2016 score in the annual *Democracy Index* fell to 7.98 from 8.05 in 2015, just below the threshold of 8.00 for a "full democracy." The researchers suggested this downgrade was caused by a continued erosion of trust in government and in elected officials, which the index measures using data from multiple global surveys. This decline in democracy is not unique to the USA. A similar pattern of declining popular confidence in political elites and institutions has been evident in many other countries as well. More than 70 countries on the *Democracy Index* have declined since 2015.

The problem is also not limited to nation states, as the latest *Election Integrity Report*[21] makes clear. In this report, North Carolina along with a dozen other American states had an overall electoral integrity score of 58/100 or less for the 2016 election, a ranking that puts them alongside authoritarian states and pseudo-democracies like Cuba, Indonesia, Sierra Leone, Mali, Algeria and Kenya. What does it mean when the US nationally, as well as 25% of American states can no longer be considered fully functioning democracies?

Saying that democratic governments are out of sync with reality and not producing the results expected by their citizens is, however, not the same thing as saying that the principle of democracy itself has failed—only that the version of democracy that we have come to know has. Our institutions are outdated. Their design was shaped by physical and social technologies that were present in society over 150 years ago. They have also been shaped by a cultural legacy of feudalism that presumed that *someone must always be in charge*.

Furthermore, human society has become immensely more complex— ironically due principally to the widespread success of democracy. If anything, therefore, what the world needs today is more democracy not less. Nevertheless, according to a recent Harvard study[22], many young people the world over have "become more cynical about the value of democracy as a political system, less hopeful that anything they do might influence public policy, and more willing to express support for authoritarian alternatives."

My home country, Canada, has not been immune to these anti-democratic tendencies. At one point, the cover of Canada's national newsmagazine, *Macleans,* screamed[23], "The House of Commons is a Sham." More recently, the *Ottawa Citizen* claimed Canada's Parliament was "close to a point of no return"[24], and becoming simply a ceremonial body instead of being the central pillar of Canadian democracy. Unfortunately, this decline is not a condition that will be eliminated with the election of a selfie-friendly Prime Minister. In the past, opinion makers referred to Canada as the "friendly dictatorship"[25], and people thought it was a clever turn of phrase. Yet, one after the other, Canada's political leaders have continued to flaunt their distaste for the inconvenience of Parliament[26], its institutions[27] and its traditions.

Typically, public reaction to some flagrant disdain of democratic institutions is written off as so much media hype and dutifully ignored by a Canadian public famous for its politeness and unwillingness to become excited about anything but hockey. However, such "neo-patrimonial" behaviour is becoming the new norm among governments that see themselves as being free from democratic precedent, and even from the need to hold debate among the country's elected representatives. Instead, successive governments are shifting towards the media optics and the expediency of decision making, in order to validate their leadership credentials with little regard to whether a decision itself may be right, wise* or even cost-effective. Political calculus demands that governments must, at all times, *appear* to know what they are doing[28] – even when they don't.

In Canada, for instance, our federal parties tend to make a big show of being "global peacekeepers" as part of the "Canadian brand," and yet our involvement in UN peacekeeping missions abroad has dwindled to one-tenth of what it was in just 1992.[29] In addition, successive Canadian governments of every stripe have been unable to purchase any significant new equipment to "protect our troops" in over 30 years,[30] leaving those troops with antiquated naval ships, airplanes, helicopters, and army vehicles operating well past their "best-before" dates. Much smaller Third World countries do better. Moreover, despite well publicized declarations of their "allegiance to the troops," they have consistently underfunded assistance to Canada's veterans that would help them heal their wounded bodies and minds[31]. And after years of purchasing obfuscation by a previous Conservative government, it came to light that the federal government kept two sets of books—one for themselves, and the other for public consumption[32]. "As a saga of institutional manipulation and mendacity," says journalist and author Michael Harris, "it is unparalleled in modern Canadian politics."[33]

The old government delivery model for identifying problems, designing and implementing solutions, and providing support, is in much need of repair according to none other than Michael Wernick, Canada's Clerk of the Privy Council and head of the federal public service.[34] He admits "It's a bit of a fixer-upper." The structure of government necessitates some serious redesign and not just some patching up around the edges.

But if the old bargains and norms can now be so easily abrogated[35], then what is being put in their place? In Canada, most decisions, even minor ones, are now made in the Prime Minister's Office. Despite superficially having a Westminster-style government, it is no longer relevant what MPs, or even members of cabinet for that matter, think or believe—other than

---

* In 2014, a Canadian Finance Minister simply announced a $550 million tax break for small businesses without any internal study by his own ministry officials. In the US, the President announced that transgendered members of the military would be let go, without consulting with the military's top brass.

Re-Imagining Government - Part 1

they should not embarrass the Prime Minister that is. Their job is merely to keep to their talking points and do what they are told and to represent the government to the people.

According to Jason Kenney, former Canadian Defence Minister and now leader of the Conservative party in Alberta, there is a risk that too much power is being concentrated among a handful of people, thus jeopardizing democracy. "The prime minister, who acts in the name of The Crown, has become a modern monarch for all intents and purposes."[36] If so, then what stands in the way of an even broader return to feudal practice? What guarantees do today's citizens have that they will benefit from these new behaviours of their elected representatives, more so than long-established precedents and the "old ways"?

Incredible as it is to say, we in the West must now take seriously the possibility of authoritarian regimes emerging in such democratic strongholds as the US, the UK, the EU and, yes, even Canada.

With this possibility in mind, is this not sufficient motivation for those in and out of government to work at getting the institutions of government right and working for everyone?

Chapter 2
Government in Disrepute

> *"Canadians are more likely **not** to have confidence [in their leaders], and the sad thing is, that confidence relates to many issues that are very, very important to them. I think it's almost a public policy despair."*
>
> —pollster Nik Nanos[37]

Even if we, as citizens, still enjoy some relative confidence in the quality of our democracy (with Western countries ranking among the most democratic), shouldn't we at least be paying better attention to what our governments are actually doing (or not doing)? Shouldn't we be asking ourselves, if they're consistently not producing results, then why not?

What's so different about governments today compared to 50 years ago when confidence in governments was so much higher? Is it simply that we're not producing good political leaders anymore? Or is it some other reason?

Let's look at a few areas where governments and policy making seem to be falling short.

Government Shortcomings

Health

Universal healthcare is proving to be either too costly to provide, or too narrow in coverage, and declining in quality. It has been revealed, for example, that at current rates of increase, the cost of health care for Canada's provinces will equal 103% of their total revenues by 2037, according to the Canadian Institute of Actuaries[38]. Let me restate that. Without radical reform to the Canadian health care system, all the provinces in twenty years will be spending more on *just health care*, than all the money they are expected to collect in taxes. That means no money for education, for infrastructure, for policing and the judiciary, for jobs development—nothing, unless we consider unsustainable levels of debt as a short-term option.

Quite obviously, we can expect significant cuts to health care in the near future, regardless of what any politician might say. With the American Health Care Act, the US GOP seems to be on track to do just this by significantly cutting back on health care costs, denying health coverage to some 24 million Americans according to the Congressional Budget Office, and increasing premiums from anywhere from 15 to 20%[39].

To begin addressing this impending budget shortfall, Canadian provinces have begun undertaking similar cutbacks to reign in their health spending (i.e. cut services), by limiting increases in their health care budgets to roughly 1% per year[40]. This constraint exists despite 6% annual increases in health care transfers from the federal government to the provinces that have been held constant since the Canadian Health Accord was signed in 2004. Yet as a recent survey by the Fraser Institute[41] found, provincial health ministries continue to be squeezed, resulting in the median wait times across Canada for "medically necessary" treatments and procedures rising to 20 weeks in 2016—the longest-recorded wait times since the think tank began tracking them in 1993*. It appears the 5% difference between increases provided by federal health transfers and actual increases in provincial health spending

---

* It was growing health care wait times that was the initial trigger for the federal government to support the provinces in 2004.

now goes directly into the provinces' general revenues. Yet even despite this windfall, the provinces are still adding approximately $16.3 billion[42] annually in their collective deficits.

Nevertheless, a meaningful public conversation on health care in Canada remains largely off the table. Health care, it is said, is part of the Canadian identity and therefore any attempt to modify it would amount to sacrilege. Both the media and politicians regularly encourage the myth that Canada has the best health care system in the world, implying there's no need to change. This is in clear contradiction to long standing evidence[43] that Canadian health care ranks near the bottom of developed countries.* However, challenging this popular myth remains a taboo topic in government circles, largely because there is no political advantage in entertaining it. Nobody has any clear-cut idea of how to improve the health of Canadians, while simultaneously making it more affordable to deliver health care, so the discussion is avoided altogether, because nobody can claim political credit.

Security

On a different front, we are continuously beset with a mind-numbing assortment of threats from all sorts of places—from Islamic terrorists abroad to homegrown ones; from rogue kleptocracies like Russia; from disease pandemics like Ebola; from state-sponsored hackers, like China; a wide assortment of cyber-criminals and ransomware seekers; and from anthropomorphically induced natural disasters like climate change. Yet according to Canada's most prestigious business organization, the Conference Board of Canada, the biggest threat to public safety in Canada is "governance"[44]. Specifically, they refer to the inability of our governments and government agencies to effectively cooperate amongst themselves and other stakeholders to protect and respond to such a complex assortment of threats. This is seen as a much bigger problem than that posed by any of these threats taken separately. It should be a scandal. It isn't even in the news.

---

* Actually, Canada is ranked 10th out of 11 countries according to the Commonwealth Fund.

Infrastructure

As every Canadian citizen is reminded of on an almost a daily basis, as they drive on Canada's crumbling roads and highways, our municipal infrastructure deficit (defined as infrastructure being in fair to poor condition) now stands in excess of $172 billion[45] with almost no hope that it will be reduced—*ever*—due to the ongoing rate of asset depreciation and a declining appetite for public spending.

Yet when governments do make the attempt, as they did in the province of Quebec, it was revealed by the Charbonneau Commission, in a manner reminiscent of a reality TV show, that the efforts of government were frequently intertwined with corrupt practices that both raised the costs and reduced the quality of that new infrastructure, because public resources were being siphoned off into the hands of corrupt politicians and mobsters. "The Charbonneau Commission has been an indictment not just of Quebec's Liberal Party but of the political class in general."[46] Yet from the public's perspective, this was just another example of the standard operating procedure for government.

Employment

Youth unemployment in Canada now hovers around 13%, although in some areas of the country it is much higher, and it is expected to remain high for at least the foreseeable future over the next 20 years. A growing chorus of analysts and commentators, meanwhile, have pointed out that the continuing erosion of jobs is not due to an outsourcing of jobs overseas, but to robotics and advanced technology. According to the Mowat Centre at the University of Toronto, this decline may amount to as much as 42% of existing jobs[47] while others suggest this may be as high as 85% of the current job inventory[48].

In an attempt to resuscitate employment, the former Conservative government announced the *Canada Jobs Grant* in 2013. "The fact is" they admitted, "that previous investments in skills training were not as effective as they could be, resulting in a skills mismatch with too many jobs without people and too many people without jobs."[49] It was interesting that after seven years

Chapter 2

at the helm, the sitting government was admitting that they had not been effective at job creation, and therefore they had to start all over.

Initially, the 13 provincial and territorial leaders unanimously rejected the federal *Jobs Grant* proposal, saying it would jeopardize existing programs, while they complained about a lack of provincial consultation on the matter. Then after a little negotiation, 10 out the 13 reached an agreement and signed on. Not coincidently, these were essentially the same parties that oversaw the previous "skills mismatch."

That said, what successive governments going back decades have all assumed about job creation, is that the demand for skills evolves slowly, so slowly in fact that once a shortage has been identified, programs can be designed, and workers can be trained to fulfill a specific employer requirement before the skills market actually changes. In reality, changes in the skills market can occur quite quickly, in just a matter of months, much faster than any training program can be designed or delivered by government. This antiquated, Soviet-style thinking within governments has been an ongoing handicap to employment and training policy for decades—regardless of which party was in power or the level of government involved. Nevertheless, governments continue to believe they can keep doing the same old things and expect different things to happen.

Automation

This inability to think innovatively and act long term on the employment front is likely to prove much more problematic—dangerous even! This is because the problems are no longer just about having adequate training programs, or seeing manufacturing jobs offshored, or being able to integrate immigrant workers. The critical problem on the horizon today is that machines will be doing more and more of the work previously done by humans, and doing it more cheaply and reliably. According to the *Washington Post*[50], *"There won't be much work for human beings. Self-driving cars will be commercially available by the end of this decade** and they will eventually displace human drivers—just as automobiles once displaced the horse and buggy—and they will eliminate the jobs of taxi, bus, and truck drivers. Drones will take over the jobs of postmen and delivery people. [One of] the debates of the next decade will be about whether we should allow human beings to drive at all on public roads. The pesky humans crash into each other, suffer from road rage, rush headlong into traffic jams, and need to be monitored by traffic police. Oh yes, we won't need traffic cops either."

Figure 1: A robot traffic cop at work on Triomphal Boulevard in Kinshasa, Democratic Republic of Congo. Source: Alan Taylor, "Robots at Work and Play," *The Atlantic*, 19 Nov 2014

As for those workers in "developing" countries who are supposedly taking manufacturing jobs away from North American workers, robots are already replacing them. For instance, the Taiwanese manufacturer Foxconn (maker

---

* Ford, for instance, has announced its intent to have fully autonomous vehicles in commercial operation by 2021 (FIELDS, Mark. 2016. *Ford's Road to Full Autonomy*. 16 August. Accessed at: https://www.linkedin.com/pulse/fords-road-full-autonomy-mark-fields), while Uber has already launched self driving cars in Pittsburgh (KANG, Dake. 2016. "Uber Launches Self-Driving Cars In Pittsburgh, Vaulting Humanity Into The Future", *Huffington Post Canada*, 14 September. Accessed at: http://www.huffingtonpost.ca/2016/09/14/uber-self-driving-cars_n_12011376.html

of many of Apple's products) has made a commitment to introduce enough robots to replace over a million workers[51]. The robots can work 24 hours a day and they require minimal maintenance. Already robots are taking over the jobs of law clerks, farmers, hotel staff, pharmacists, hospital staff, journalists, surgeons, waiters, security, manufacturing and grocery clerks. This is the real reason why there has been a largely a jobless recovery since the 2008–2009 recession. Machines are increasingly doing the work that humans once did. Using similar lines of reasoning, robots in the future are likely to take over any work that is routine. On the one hand, this sounds great. More free time for people (but less paid time). But who's benefitting from this transition, and what do all these unemployed people do with their "free" time?

Social supports

If the trend in automation continues, as everyone expects it will, then what becomes of all those people not working? Do they still share in the economy? What becomes of the upwards of 85% of the population who may be displaced from their current jobs and are no longer able to find employment in the future? Why invest in an expensive education if you can't find a job—a question many students on campus are already asking themselves? Already the 1.4 trillion dollar level of student loans in the US is reaching a crisis point.[52]

If machines eliminate the need for "working to live," then what do all those unemployed people do with their time? Who do companies sell their goods and services to if these people have no income? What happens to the government's revenue base? Does citizenship become a function of your ability to contribute taxes? If most people become unemployed in the traditional sense, do we start requiring robots to pay income tax?* This is an issue with tremendous economic, social and moral implications for our collective futures, but it remains largely absent from public discourse.

---

* This has already been suggested by former Microsoft CEO Bill Gates. TITCOMB, James. 2017. "Robots that take people's jobs should pay taxes, says Bill Gates", *The Telegraph*, 20 February. Accessed at: http://www.telegraph.co.uk/technology/2017/02/20/robots-take-peoples-jobs-should-pay-taxes-says-bill-gates/

Finland, for instance, is currently experimenting with a scheme to provide its citizens with a universal basic income or UBI, regardless of employment. The two-year pilot will provide 2,000 unemployed Finnish citizens, aged between 25 and 58, with a monthly basic income of 560 euros that will replace their other social benefits[53]. These citizens will continue to receive the basic income even if they find work. Other countries that have been considering this include Canada, Holland, the UK and the USA.

Climate change

There is no other public issue that better demonstrates the chronically debilitating impact of short-term thinking and an inability to cooperate than that of climate change. While virtually 100% of the world's climate scientists believe that human behaviour has a warming effect on the planet's temperature[54], and therefore poses significant risks to human society, roughly half the people in the Canada, United States, and Britain do not believe the experts are right[55]. That's like half the people saying they don't believe in gravity.

In December 2016, President Trump appointed Scott Pruitt[56], a strong climate change denier, as head of the Environmental Protection Agency, the lead US agency on the issue. In May of 2017, Trump announced the US will withdraw from the Paris climate agreement the US signed in 2015 and is defunding crucial climate data gathering functions at NASA and in academe. He has also said the use of burning of oil and coal will once again be encouraged to help those who have been unable to transition away from jobs in the fossil fuel industry—despite clear evidence that solar power is now cheaper to produce than that of fossil fuels[57].

In Canada, the response of the previous federal government to climate change was at first to deny it, then to ignore it, and then to hinder access to credible evidence on the subject in order to encourage public naivety. The National Roundtable on the Environment and the Economy was shut down; federal scientists were muzzled; federal research funding for the world renowned Experimental Lakes Area was withdrawn; environmental organizations were harassed via Revenue Canada; and eleven libraries in the Department of Fisheries and Oceans were closed, their contents thrown into dumpsters. The Ottawa-based Canadian Foundation for Climate and Atmospheric Sciences was also defunded, resulting in the closure of such facilities as the Polar Environment Atmospheric Research Laboratory (PEARL) in Nunavut, which was responsible for making key measurements needed to detect and analyze the rate of global environmental changes, which tend to occur first in the Arctic. It would appear that the Canadian government was intent on purposely killing the canary in the coal mine, as if that would stave off harm.

The previous government also employed misleading language to reassure the public that the issue of climate change was under control by suggesting the opposite of reality, as it did when the federal Environment Minister said that by 2020 Canada's CO_2 emissions will have declined to 720 megatonnes a year[58]. In fact, the 720 amount (let alone its revised 734 MT amount) was actually *higher* than 2009 levels and nowhere near the 607 MT levels Canada had agreed to in Copenhagen as its target for 2020[59].

More recently, a new Liberal federal government, in agreement with provincial premiers, promised "dramatic" action on climate change ... by studying the issue further. In April 2016[60] the new government ratified the international Paris climate agreement to reduce greenhouse gas emissions by 30% from 2005 levels by 2030—a goal set by the previous Conservative government. In October 2016, the Liberals announced targets for a carbon pricing scheme that they believed would allow Canada to achieve its emission goals. On the plus side, while the federal government committed to having a carbon pricing scheme in place by 2018, it left the specific solution up to each province to decide, rather than imposing a single centralized solution on everyone.

When Donald Trump was elected to the US Presidency and began a renegotiation of the NAFTA agreement, Canadian climate plans were largely put on hold, so as to ensure Canadian companies remained competitive with their American counterparts. These types of short-term wins come at the expense of long-term tragedies, demonstrating the narrow thinking that seems to dominate political calculus.

Evidenced-based policy

There are always many issues of concern to citizens, but since the Second World War it has generally been assumed that decision makers of every generation would rely on objective evidence to make choices between policy options. This practice of *evidence-based policy making* evolved as a means for overcoming the inevitable conflicts of belief and incomplete knowledge arising from multiple stakeholders. It relied on a professional public service to collect and analyze data in a non-partisan way so as to provide independent apolitical advice to political decision makers.

However, this long-established practice of basing decisions on "objective" facts has given way to *policy-based evidence making*, as one senior government executive described it to me. What she meant was, instead of letting evidence guide policy development, today's policy makers look only for data that supports their established view. Today, decisions come first and then the collection of data to support it follows. Contrary data, which might prove critical of that decision, must then be suppressed and restricted either by the elimination of problematic data sources or by restrictions imposed on an independent media. Such tunnel vision is ultimately quite dangerous in today's world, when no one has complete knowledge to deal with any issue and yet wishes to pretend as if they did.

Unfortunately, fiction is now the bread and butter of political discourse. For instance, Russia's President Putin doesn't need to tell the truth or even have a more convincing story than his opponents, he just has to point out that *everyone lies*. When Putin lies brazenly, he wants the West to point out that he lies, says Bulgarian political scientist Ivan Krastev[61], "so he can point back and say, 'but you lie too.'" And if everyone is lying, then anything goes; there is no such thing as objective truth that can be agreed upon, whether in your personal life or in the invasion of a foreign country.

Surprisingly, this notion that there is no such thing as objective evidence is supported by senior officials in the White House. According to Scottie Nell Hughes, a spokeswoman for President Trump, "One thing that's been interesting to watch is that people say that facts are facts. They're not really facts. Everybody has a way of interpreting them to be the truth or not true. There's no such thing, unfortunately, anymore as facts."[62] So when the US

President says that millions of votes in the last election were cast illegally, despite there being absolutely no evidence of this, it must now be considered on par with empirically, scientifically or statistically generated evidence.

In addition, public media, who say they claim to be balanced in their reporting in order to retain their legitimacy, now disseminate truth and lies as if they were on equal footing. As a further indication of the decline of evidence over fiction as the new norm of policy making, US House Speaker Paul Ryan was quoted as saying that if the President circulates false information on social media, it is not a concern to him. "Who cares what he tweeted?"[63]

Similarly, the former Canadian PM, Stephen Harper, urged voters to ignore the statistical evidence of declining crime rates, and follow the truth of "your personal experiences and impressions"[64] (fuelled, of course, by an overhyped media and Hollywood storytelling) that crime is indeed increasing. From his point of view, the growth of crime was such a simple, obvious problem, it was "common sense" to know that crime is increasing—even if the objective evidence presented by academics or experts said otherwise[65].

When criticized for ignoring objective evidence, former Justice Minister Rob Nicholson asserted, "We are not governing by statistics. We are governing by what we promised Canadians in the last election and what Canadians have told us."[66] However, if we're not governing by evidence, then we're either governing by fiat, or by stupid, or both—something that we had hoped that the Renaissance and the early scientific periods had put an end to.

The former conservative pollster, Allan Gregg, recently lambasted the previous Conservative government for its "assault on reason," for curtailing open debate on issues, and especially for its "Orwellian" attacks on scientists and environmental policy advocates[67]. At the same time, Gregg linked the popular acceptance of this behaviour with the decades-old decline of deference to authority, and the rise of the most authority-phobic generation in history, which he said has contributed to the most anti-elitist, anti-science, anti-knowledge governments in Canadian history.

Gone then is the cornerstone idea of the "Enlightenment" era that in a world of incomplete knowledge, let alone a world of so many competing opinions, objective evidence should be the foundation of shared learning and of diffusing conflicts. Its very objectivity was something that everyone could agree on. This did not mean that different interpretations of the facts did not or should not exist, only that the facts themselves should not be in question. Today's embrace of fiction as the equal to fact removes a principal pathway for achieving social consensus and cooperation. The risk, of course, is a return to the old feudal practice of governing by subjective decree, and the violent imposition of one belief over another, instead of achieving consensus around evidence and moving forward by learning together.

Transparency

In most democracies, the citizen's right to information has been recognized alongside the citizen's right to vote. The assumption is that a citizen can't make a proper choice if they are not adequately informed. For instance, in Canada, as in many countries, this right to be informed has been recognized and enshrined in the Access to Information Act and its provincial equivalents. Yet while Canadian governments openly claim that they are making data more available to the public in the name of transparency, accountability, innovation and economic growth, their actions tell a different story.

"Freedom of information" has been reinterpreted to refer to data that is released only when a government chooses to release it, and only after being carefully vetted and sanitized for public consumption. Information that may prove critical of a government must be suppressed at all costs. Transparency and accountability are now attributes that apply only to political competitors and not to a sitting government. In many countries, including Canada, through a series of small, steady steps, the practice of openness and transparency is being transformed into the obliteration of a citizen's right to know— anything[68].

According to the Canadian Newspaper Association (CNA), which audits how well Canadian governments adhere to their Access to Information laws, "The one thing users all across the country tend to agree on is their belief that governments go out of their way to slow down or block the release of contentious information with the potential to embarrass officials or damage the re-election prospects of political leaders."[69] The impediments put up include extremely high access fees, delays of months or years, inappropriate electronic formats, and just plain obstinacy.

Canada's Privy Council Office, for instance, recently suggested during the CNA's 2014 audit that the PCO simply does not have to release electronic records. Despite being reminded of its obligation under the FOI Act to do so, the agency has refused to relent, declaring it would release records, but only in paper format. In this way, the PCO could claim transparency and adherence to the law, while simultaneously obstructing the provision of usable information. According to the Access to Information Commissioner, the ATI process is so seriously flawed, that it threatens "to render the entire access regime irrelevant"[70].

Disreputable leaders

To the electorate, policy solutions are always pitched as a direct consequence of the character and "greatness" of the person in the leadership position. Political campaigns and all manner of political debate are couched more often in personal attacks rather than substantive argument. That said, in all of Canadian history, the recent spate of firings, resignations and criminal indictments against MPs, Senators, Cabinet Ministers, Chiefs of Staff, Premiers, and Mayors on everything from unethical behaviour to campaign over-spending to fraud to "gangsterism" is absolutely unprecedented. When the behaviour of a self-confessed alcoholic, drug-using, misogynist bully of a politician like Toronto's former Mayor, Rob Ford, can set the standard for acceptable behaviour among our elected agents, surely we have to know something isn't right?

But even if we believed that there are only "a few bad apples" who we can still throw out at election time, how does an ordinary citizen interacting with politicians only at great distances tell the difference between an ethical politician and an unethical one? "The problem is," according to Postmedia journalist Andrew Coyne, "that nobody is inclined to believe any of them any more, the honest politicians along with the dirty liars."[71] This leaves citizens in a position where they cannot trust their leaders. As James Travers, the former editor of the *Toronto Star*, once described, "Democracy is too important to delegate to politicians."[72] But what's the alternative? Strongman populist dictators? A society run by artificial intelligences?

Disempowering elected representatives

While traditional Canadian democracy has always embodied at its core the back and forth of political debate—both in developing effective policy and in holding sitting governments to account—today's rabid partisanship does neither. In fact, it has subverted parliamentary democracy altogether. Elected representatives, who were once the voice of their constituencies, now act like trained seals, barking whatever nonsense is forced upon them by their party bosses. Where once there were 300+ voices in Parliament willing to discuss and debate and learn, now there are but four or five voices in hostile competition.

It's a situation that led the former Conservative-led Canadian Government to become the first in Commonwealth history to be found in contempt of its own Parliament.[73] And in a manner similar to the tin-pot, authoritarian regimes we say we so despise elsewhere in the world, any criticism of government is regarded as "treason,"[74] and those who are critical of the government, whether they be citizens, scientists, journalists, academics or elected representatives, are deemed to be "radicals"[75] or even "enemies of the people."[76]

A partisan Public Service

In the traditional model of Westminster government, the public service, in particular senior executives and deputy ministers, are supposed to act as loyal implementers of government policy, "speaking truth to power" and acting as watchdogs of the public interest, thus ensuring an appropriate balance can be struck between the interests of citizens and those of political partisans. No longer.

Today the number one job of senior mandarins is protecting their minister and the prime minister from political controversy. Rather than cultivating a culture of stewardship on behalf of all Canadians, the senior ranks have cultivated plausible deniability, intellectual laziness, learning disabilities, and a lack of collaborative behaviours[77] in direct opposition to the capacities that would seem to be most needed. Green Party Leader Elizabeth May has observed that, "public policy making is now only a shadow of good government. The outward appearance of a functional Cabinet government supported by a non-partisan civil service is being maintained, but the reality is that nothing is normal."[78]

The decline of public debate

What do all these things have in common? The growing perception of illegitimacy surrounding our public institutions. This is precisely what Donald Trump tapped into in the last US election, what fueled the Brexit decision, and what Canada's federal Liberals capitalized on in their victory in 2015. There is a "feeling of disconnection with . . . authority that has grown while the powers of Parliament have declined."[79]

Today it is all too easy to think of government as something that does not represent "us," (whoever "us" is). Despite being part of very diverse modern societies, over and over citizens are compelled to endure stereotype depictions by governments that pretend as if these differences did not or should not exist, that presume that everyone shares the same values, and that what is "right and good" for one, is "right and good" for all.

And then there is its corollary—if it's not good for all, it should be opposed. The result has been a politics based on the lowest common denominator, and rather than leading society forward, the policy process leads neither to innovative solutions, or to the enablement of shared possibilities, but to undifferentiated, ineffective, policy pabulum. How can anyone begin to see themselves in that?

And somewhere in all these banal and unproductive efforts that avoid conflict by suppressing any appearance of difference, a *coup* has taken place unnoticed—we no longer elect agents to represent us to government; we elect them to represent the government to us.

Re-Imagining Government - Part 1

In Canada, for instance, the regular curtailment of parliamentary debate time, the abuse of omnibus budget bills to further avoid debate on multiple issues, the rabid partisanship, the abdication of the fundamental role of elected representatives to represent their constituents and to hold the government to account—all of these have contributed to a degradation in the quality of public discourse. Instead of informed debate, elected representatives perform like automatons, mindlessly repeating their party's message regardless of how inane it might sound.

In the previous Federal Government of Canada, Conservative MP Paul Calandra was the all-party champion in the House of Commons for this type of inanity with his relentless stories about his father's pizza store, his daughter's lemonade stand, his Philippine driver, and his stories about skunks and Santa Claus—all in response to legitimate questions from opposition members.

Likewise, the Government's House Leader, Peter Van Loan, was on record about his frustration with parliamentary debate—not about its quality—but that it should have to take place at all. He asserted that "debate is not mandatory and there's simply no time for it."[80] Imagine, democracy being too messy and too inefficient to give time for public debate! It's no wonder that Canadians live in a so-called "democracy" where the elected government writes a covert manual to sabotage the workings of its legislative committees[81] in order to limit the constitutional authority of Parliament to hold the government to account.

Trying to understand the often childish behaviour that presents itself as political discourse can also be hard for most ordinary citizens to comprehend, given the romanticized notions of government that they learned in school. Unfortunately, such base behaviour is common in most leader-centric organizations. "The best politicians are ... gang leaders. They are polarizing figures, ruthless at pursuing the interests of their tribe at the expense of others."[82] But is that who we want running our governments—gang leaders?

On the other hand, to some the best government is no government at all, to paraphrase former Prime Minister Stephen Harper[83]. "You know", he said, "there's two schools in economics. One is that there are some good taxes, and

Chapter 2

the other is that no taxes are good taxes*. I'm in the latter category. I don't believe any taxes are good taxes." No taxes means no government. And if the former Prime Minister had really believed in no government, then he would not have sought election as Prime Minister, or immediately resigned once he had been elected, or, at minimum, enlightened Canadians as to how social coordination could take place without any governmental action.

Instead, what he appeared to believe in were institutions which he could control without the inconvenience of being criticized or being called to account. This is authoritarianism plain and simple, and there is an old word for this—"tyranny." The "bromance" expressed by President Trump for Russian President Putin, or the fondness Canadian Prime Minister Trudeau has expressed for former Cuban President Castro and Chinese leaders reflect a similar appreciation for autocracy.

An Outmoded Paradigm

Why have modern democratic governments fallen into such a discreditable state? Who's to blame for all of this? Presidents and prime ministers, governors and premiers, the government parties, the opposition parties and their leaders, the public service, the media, academe, citizens? The complex answer is no one—and everyone.

Government is a system of institutions, mechanisms, rules and behaviours which, when applied to society, help (or help in theory at least) to ensure coordination, not only among the various individual members of society, but also between them and the numerous private and civic organizations in society. However, the mechanisms of government have evolved, and continue to evolve over time. Across millennia, that system of coordination has become increasingly more diversified and complex.

In response to societal changes, governments have continuously adapted, developing ever more sophisticated mechanisms of cooperation to allow citizens to benefit from their increasingly complex society, while trying to

---

* There is no such division among economists, which he as a trained economist would have supposedly known.

mitigate the potential conflicts that inevitably come with those changes. Governments have moved from organizational models that were totally leader-centric during humanity's early tribal eras, to the large conformist organizations that dominated much of the early period of nation building, to the modern meritocracies where evidence and expertise were the driving forces behind the use of power and authority.

This latter paradigm dominated Western governments, including Canada, for the last century. It was grounded in the Newtonian presumption that issues were rational and predictable, requiring the knowledge of experts to tease out cause and effect. It used centralized decision-making processes to guide and coordinate the actions of governments based on modest flows of information that moved slowly up and down hierarchical organizations. And once those decisions were finally taken, they flowed downwards through those same hierarchies under the exercise of rule-based controls and coercion. Stability was based on long adaptive periods with little need to rush, leading to deep-seated adherence to tradition, together with a strong deference and respect for authority.

When first applied, this model allowed one person (or a small group of people) to control the behaviour of many others who were not all that dissimilar in terms of knowledge, capacity, background, interests and beliefs. However, over time, its very success encouraged society to become even more diversified and complex, meaning that those at the top became less and less likely to understand the full implication of the interactions between everyone. As Yaneer Bar-Yam, president of the New England Complex Systems Institute at MIT has suggested, these "hierarchical organizations are failing in the response to decision-making challenges. Representative democracies still focus power in one or few individuals. And that concentration of control and decision-making makes those systems ineffective."[84]

In the traditional government paradigm,[85] humans were seen as separate, self-contained autonomous units which led governments to emphasize individualism, mutual exclusivity and the minimization of "community." It reflected a "cause and effect" presumption that human behaviour was pre-set, controllable, and governable by the same set of knowable laws (i.e. nobody operated from alternative values or behaviours).

Chapter 2

Because no one was unique, each person was completely interchangeable. Consequently, given the right knowledge, all future human events were assumed to be predictable, leading to public policy being centred around the optimization of rational alternatives that emphasized both *equality* and *conformity**. For example, since everyone was assumed to be the same, good outcomes resulted from governments treating everyone in exactly the same way.

Also, since the primary mode of human interaction was assumed to be conflict and individualism was believed to be something in need of protection, social interests were simply defined as an aggregation of individual interests. This led to a principal role of government being the defence of individual property rights and the social coordination powers of government centring on supporting the ability of individuals to defend and control their possessions.

With the advancement of the scientific world view, "*objective knowledge*" was considered the most reliable source of wisdom and it became the cornerstone of modern governments. Objective knowledge was supposed to be "universal" and "value-free." Our system of *representative democracy* was constructed so that social coordination could be achieved by delegating decision making to a few virtuous people who were steeped in objective knowledge and who could then work objectively and free of vested interests, on behalf of those lacking that knowledge.

This led to the creation of mechanistic bureaucracies in order to scale efficiencies, pursue equality and conformity, and enhance power and control across large, far-flung organizations and diverse jurisdictions. Regional and local concerns were de-emphasised in favour of national approaches that were enacted from the "centre" in order to guarantee standardization and equal treatment—regardless of outcome.

Lastly, it was expected that given the lack of uniqueness among people, they would all predictably act "rationally" in their own self-interest under the same stimulus. As a consequence, all relations with government were

---

* It should be noted that equality does not imply equity or fairness, and conformity refers to a state bias against diversity and change.

expected to be additive, resulting from the combined push-pull actions each member or organization of society. For example, the still popular but discredited notion of a "trickle down" economy suggests that when governments can instill success among a few citizens, the whole economy will ultimately benefit because the benefits to the few eventually trickle down to every citizen.

The perfection of public policy was assumed to be the result of optimal adjustment and balance between all of the social forces at play. The ideal policy would have equal numbers of people "for" and "against" it. The need to continually and dynamically adjust to these social forces was therefore seen as the *raison d'être* of *interventionist governments* with stability being the ultimate goal. This bias for stability was often expressed as institutional resistance to change, as opposed to showing adaptation in the face of changing environments.

Within the constraints of its jurisdiction, any government operating within this traditional paradigm was believed to be essentially an all-powerful and all-knowing entity. Since it was also assumed that knowledge was basically fixed and didn't change much, it was also presumed that full knowledge was obtainable simply by hiring a sufficient number of "experts" as part of an assemblage of public servants.

Over the years, governments began to employ diplomatic experts, transportation experts, military experts, Aboriginal experts, agricultural experts, mining experts, labour experts, etc., all of whom filled the appropriate government ministries, departments and agencies. At first, the number of these experts was small, but as the overall knowledge in society grew, so did the need for experts. In Canada, for instance, before 1918 the federal public service consisted of less than 5,000 workers, comprising less than 0.05% of the Canadian population, but by 2013 it had grown to 262,817 employees (or 0.75% of the Canadian population)—a growth rate over 12 times greater than that of the population.

Initially, stakeholder groups were relatively few and easily identifiable, allowing for clear trade-offs to take place between group representatives with the expectation that their followers would adhere to any agreements their representatives could hammer out. Information flowed slowly through well-defined and well-understood channels that were based largely on personal relationships that changed very slowly. For instance, government officials might remain in a department for decades acquiring both content expertise and significant relational capital. And once agreements were in place, governments could legitimately and effectively wield their coercive power to enforce compliance with any established rule.

Unfortunately, this paradigm of government no longer fits with reality.

Needs of complexity overshadow capacity for coordination

In his recent book, Canadian political pundit Donald Savoie poses the question "What is government good at?" On the one hand, he says[86] that senior politicians and public servants "*are good at* generating blame, avoiding blame, blaming others, playing to a segment of the population to win the next election, avoiding risks, embracing and defending the status quo, adding management layers and staff, keeping ministers out of trouble in the media, responding to the demands from the prime minister and his office, and managing a complex, multi-objective prime ministerial centric large organization operating in a politically volatile environment."

On the other hand, he says, "they *are not as good at* defining the broader public interest, providing and recognizing evidence-based policy advice, implementing policy, managing human and financial resources with efficiency and frugality, innovating and reforming themselves, making expenditure reductions unless the prime minister in a majority government decides that the time has come, being accountable to Parliament and to citizens, dealing with non-performers, paying sufficient attention to service delivery and frontline workers, and evaluating the impact of policies and programs."

In short, according to Savoie, governments are good at being self-serving, but they are no longer good at delivering on the things that matter to citizens. Is it any wonder, therefore, that frustration and resentment towards government has continued to build, as it fails in its central coordinating function in society?

What happened? Why are those public institutions that brought us so much relative peace and prosperity, particularly in the latter half of the 20th century, suddenly not working? According to Joseph Tainter, the traditional paradigm, and the structures of government that are based on it, has suffered from what he has taciturnly described as "decreasing returns to complexity."[87] In fact, they are teetering on the verge of collapse. The persistent failure of governments to address social complexity and the accompanying decline of capitalism is leading to "a prolonged period of social entropy or disorder," according to Wolfgang Streeck[88], director emeritus at the Max Planck Institute for the Study of Societies.

Knowledge today is growing so fast that it now exists largely outside of the public service domain. Given the government's insatiable appetite for knowledge, public service unions have developed significant power as knowledge suppliers. But governments have no hope of hiring all the experts they need, even if they could afford to, giving rise to a growing number of public service and political blind spots. The notion that governments are run by experts is therefore becoming antiquated and quaint.

Stakeholders have also become legion and they come now with multiple allegiances—so much so that the negotiating power of established elites has been largely eliminated. Today, information in society flows through an untold number of different channels and networks, particularly over the Internet. However, information flowing from government is often regarded as the least complete and relevant, and it is also considered to be the least trusted because it is presumed to have been manipulated or sanitized*.

Furthermore, the coercive power of government to control the behaviours of its citizens is continually being eroded by new technologies that are emerging faster than governments can understand them. Take, for instance, the example of Uber, which is in the process of replacing traditional taxis and other forms of public transit. As much as governments would like to curtail it, because it operates largely outside of their control, it continues to grow and grab market share. It remains cheaper and more convenient, all

---

* One could arguably count President Trump's disregard of the claim by multiple US intelligence services that Russia hacked the computers of the Democratic National Convention as evidence of this discounting of government knowledge.

the while coasting on government policies that promote ride-sharing. It may seem like a frivolous metaphor, but the truth is that traditional governments were structured for an analog world, not a digital one.

The reality is that the hierarchical model of coordination employed by all governments and which works well in environments of low complexity, simply breaks down in environments that demonstrate high complexity and interdependence. These environments may be characterized by:

- many actors, all with some knowledge, resources or power to contribute;
- many interdependencies;
- a speed of interaction that is much greater today than when our structures of government were first invented;
- a lack of clear understanding of the whole;
- nonlinearity and the presence of paradoxes, contradictory elements and logics; and
- a need for experimentation, self-organization and evolution over time.

Increasingly, to many people—outside of government, that is—top-down leadership has lost its edge. Widely respected management gurus such as Gary Hamel, Peter Senge and John Hagel have abandoned it, as have a growing number of corporations intent on leading in the innovation economy. As MIT's Yaneer Bar-Yam claims[89], society is now far too complex for our hierarchical model of representative democracy to work.

> "It is absurd to believe that the concentration of power in one or a few individuals at the top of a hierarchical representative democracy will be able to make optimal decisions on a vast array of connected and complex issues that will certainly have sweeping and unintended ramifications on other parts of human civilization."

Nevertheless, governments today, despite facing even more complex operating environments than private companies, remain rigidly wedded to the hierarchical leadership model of organization, one that predates universal education, let alone computers and the Internet.

According to Morris Rosenberg[90], a well-respected former Canadian Deputy Minister, governments were designed for a time when issues had clear boundaries and good solutions had clear, unambiguous pathways. That worked pretty well, he suggests, before the advent of globalization, the digital revolution, and the explosion of diversity brought about by Internet connectivity. Today's issues are much more interconnected and they are a lot more complex. In this new environment, politicians, he said, are reluctant to tackle complex issues precisely because their outcomes lack certainty; they are constantly evolving; and they require collaboration with others to succeed. In essence, politicians can no longer bank on the political benefits accruing to them from their involvement on these issues.

In an environment where knowledge, resources and power are widely distributed, any attempt to concentrate learning, innovation and adaptive capacity in one place, such as the CEO, the Minister, or Director, is far too limiting. It's like trying to command the weather. You might be able to influence some portion of a complex social system, but it is just as likely that your actions will trigger changes in unpredictable ways, often creating other problems, or unintended consequences. Couple this with the slow response times of bureaucracies, and what you get is a recipe for poor government performance that is *perpetually out of sync* with its environment.

Such is the fate of our current structures and institutions of government that were designed for less complex and turbulent times. They can no longer cope because, like their leaders, they are out of their depth. Many of government's basic operating norms are outmoded, despite a lingering belief to the contrary that is actively encouraged by governments and political science academics that were weaned under the old model. These now contestable norms include[91]:

1. Government is the ultimate authority for divining social needs and setting social rules;

Chapter 2

2. Government knows best because it has the largest storehouse of knowledge and expertise;

3. Government has all the resources needed to solve social problems;

4. Government has all the authority and coercive power needed to affect solutions;

5. Government has ethical and moral purposes that transcend those of its citizens[92] giving it special insight into the "public interest";

6. Government can affect collective trade-offs by bringing representatives of various interests to one place whereupon they can engage in elite accommodation;

7. Government is the only actor that can be trusted to deliver public goods and services—services like education, health care, public infrastructure, steering the economy, and the provision of social supports;

8. Government is the only social body that can keep you safe;

9. Government is obligated to reinforce traditions of leadership and followership to ensure stability; and

10. Government changes slowly, which is for the betterment of all.

These norms were underscored by a very linear model of public policy (**Figure 2**).

Figure 2: A Linear Model of Public Policy

Percieved Need and Concept → Development → Consultation (llimited) → Disemination & Implementation → Impact Assessment

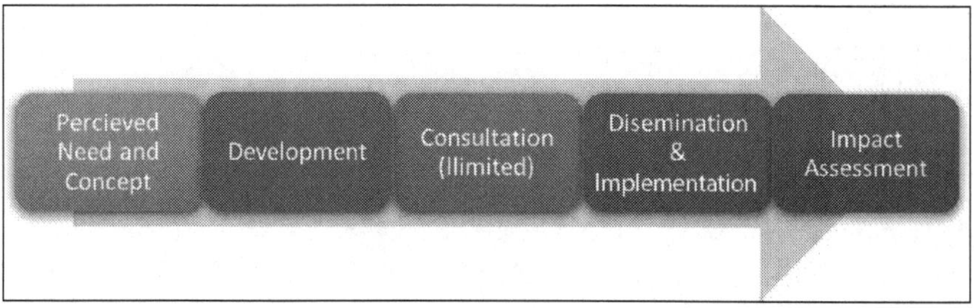

Yet, in the current environment, governments no longer have all the knowledge, resources or power to resolve issues of importance to their citizens on their own. It is for this reason the rhetoric surrounding collaboration and partnership has become so commonplace in the public sector. However, as Nik Nanos has lamented in *Policy Options*,[93] "increasingly, fewer Canadians have confidence that our leaders can address the concerns that matter most to them," precisely because they require that governments must work with others.

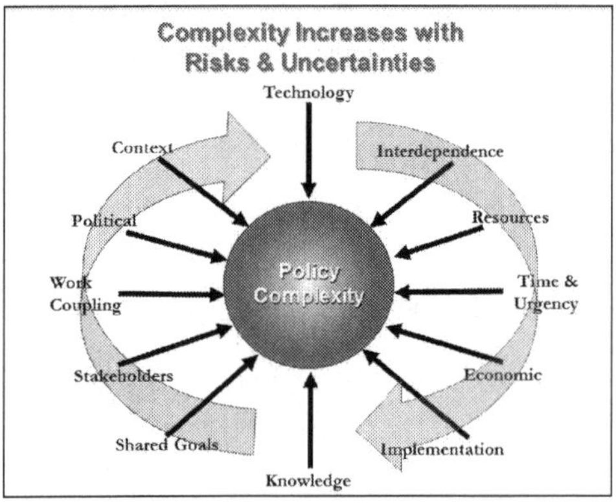

The problems that matter most to citizens are complex and "wicked"[94]; they exist within ecosystems of causes and effects; they are constantly evolving over time; and whatever the desired ends might be, those goals tend to change even as the potential means to those ends may emerge. As a result, the solutions to problems require cooperation among numerous stakeholders to permit the contributions of many different minds, many different kinds of resources, and many different types of power. Unfortunately, the public sector was not designed for collaboration, but for the exercise of control.

Figure 3: Non-Linear Policy Model

Therefore, instead of a straightforward, linear process of policy development, what we have is an increasingly unpredictable, uncertain and non-linear process due to these multiple contributions (**Figure 3**). But while it may be obvious that governments cannot achieve their goals on their own, it is much less clear to those in government *how* they must work with others in order to achieve their collaborative policies and program goals.

This lack of recognition for the need to develop collaborative skills and frameworks has created an odd cognitive dissonance within many government organizations—believing, on the one hand, that they must behave in a certain traditional way, and knowing that if they do they will likely be ineffectual, or on the other hand, being willing to embrace the promise of collaboration and better results, yet still fearing a more collaborative approach, not only because of its unfamiliarity, but also because it tends to turn traditional, paternalistic government practice on its head.

Against this backdrop of cognitive dissonance, there are shifts in public sector behaviour that reflect real pragmatism and not just theory and speculation. On the margins, we can see a lot of experimentation to achieve results. These experiments illustrate a shift to more participatory, small "g" governance regimes where coordination is achieved through a variety of relational mechanisms that permit governments to work in concert with various stakeholder groups.

We can also see a general collective frustration with governments that is manifesting itself in the growing legitimacy of populist movements that are superficially bent on "draining the swamp" of established political and bureaucratic elites. We can also see this change expressed in lower voter participation; in expressions of blatant disregard for government, such as the growing underground economy; in the public's use of social media to coordinate amongst themselves; and in their active pursuit of new technologies that may provide alternatives to government.

Sadly, we also see governments, fearful of their loss of control, becoming even more leader-centric and willing to ignore decades of democratic practice in "neo-patrimonial" tendencies; willing to renege on their agent-citizen contract, setting themselves apart from the citizens they are meant to serve; and willing to answer only to the interests of a few select voices, rather than finding ways to include all the voices of society in a collective conversation.

These multiple and competing influences are reshaping our sense of what democracy is and can be. In some modern democracies, for instance, we see attempts to:

- diminish or gloss over the inconvenient diversity and complexity that so troubles hierarchies. If diversity exists, then pretend it doesn't, or vilify it as a way of rallying groups who might identify with your frustrations with government, à la Trump[95], or the "Leave" campaign that destined the UK to exit the European Union;

- fight a war against the encroachments of globalism and internationalism, that have generally raised (although not always uniformly) the quality of human experience to levels never before seen in human history, even as they have confronted us with increasing diversity in terms of languages, ethnicities, religions, philosophies, organizational models, perspectives, and levels of prosperity. Today, for instance, there are more than 300 million people who live outside their country of origin. This diversity has increased the potential for conflict, and for many "it is undermining a liberal global economic system that has taken 70 years to build."[96]

For some, the response to all this diversity is to create more walls (literally and figuratively), to impose social uniformity by restricting the free movement of people, to ghettoize identifiable groups, to weed out unbelievers and different thinkers, to punish those who are different for whatever shortcomings and injuries—both real and imagined—that one might experience.

- emphasize security measures over cooperation to lessen insecurities about diversity. After two decades of coming together, many countries are now focusing on the challenges of interdependence and the risks that that interdependence exposes them to. "Yet", as Nikolas Gvosdev writes, "over the coming years . . . an increasing number of the issues in world politics will revolve around whether countries put their trust in international cooperation for profit, versus taking unilateral national action for security."[97] It presents a very base choice—profit or security—but it is also one which international institutions are not capable of dealing with, despite its baseness;

- reduce the impacts of uber-connectivity by attempting to control the flow of information by creating artificial barriers, including the cultivation of asymmetric privacy—privacy for government and transparency for all others—in the name of "national security";

- reassert forcefully and repeatedly the myth that someone must be in charge; and

- revert to pre-modern forms of governance (i.e. leader-centric) because of fears that things are now "out of control" and the mistaken, populist belief that only some fictional "white knight" can save us.

Taken to extremes, these attempts to reassert some element of control may well engender a resurgence of the old, strongman-style of governments that were based on fear and fealty to a leader that were commonplace over 200 years ago. I suspect that whether we end up transforming or retrenching, the change in current governance practice is not likely to happen quietly.

While this growing complexity may drive an evolution in government, for now public perception nevertheless seems to be that government is becoming more unethical, more incompetent or both. As a result, the public is less inclined to follow existing leaders and parties while retrenching and becoming more tribal and less willing to reach out to others. This behaviour erodes further the ability of governments to act as a legitimate brokers, arbitrators and guiding forces in a diverse society. And it holds potentially huge dangers for government, as Bo Rothstein once described, because the "failure to establish universal and trustworthy political institutions" undermines not only the social capital of society, but also the willing compliance of citizens that is dependent on that social capital.[98]

Given the growing social complexity, the current situation is more likely a matter of the maladaptation of previous models of government, rather than individual failure (although there certainly are some big individual failures). However, this maladaptation should not be something to fear in and of itself. If history teaches us anything, it is that *in the long run* (although not always in the short run) humans can respond quite well to this type of challenge. We have created ever more complex environments around ourselves, and then invented more and more sophisticated mechanisms to coordinate ourselves within them.[99] We have repeated this cycle again and again over the span of human existence, constructing in the process increasingly more sophisticated human civilizations.

The concern should not be in our human capacity to respond to the challenge. Rather, the concern should centre on whether we can shake ourselves awake to apply our capacity. We seem to exist in a semi-comatose state

Re-Imagining Government - Part 1

induced by our public entitlements and our carefree willingness to abdicate our portion of our shared ownership in our collective enterprise.

Even though the stakes are high today—existential, even—I believe our capacity to reimagine ourselves is greater. Indeed, the future has already begun to unfold: we just don't know enough yet to determine which version of it will ultimately win out.

But if we want to be certain that we aren't blindsided by a future that we don't want, we must begin to seriously imagine the kind of government we need, in order to create the future that we do want.

Chapter 3
Government Ill-Suited for Tomorrow's Challenges[100]

"The world has reached a critical turning point . . . reboot all the old models, approaches and structures or risk institutional paralysis or even collapse."

—Tapscott and Williams[101]

Democratic governance seems in decline everywhere. Autocracy is on the rise. But wasn't Churchill right when he said, "democracy is the worst form of government -- except for all the others"? So why is democracy getting such a bad rap today?

The simple answer is that governments are not meeting people's expectations. The value of government is no longer clear in many of the basic functions that governments are meant to serve. That said, there are also many bigger issues which seem completely over the heads of governments everywhere.

It's a truism to say that the Internet has connected us like never before. What is less obvious is that it has also given us the means to tap the creativity of the entire human population—if only we could orchestrate how. Yet, that very same process of making connections has exposed each of us to a whole new world of differences—in terms of language and ethnicity certainly, but also in terms of understanding, perspectives, values, beliefs and assumptions—creating a profound basis for social friction.

It therefore provokes the question: "How can we mitigate the Internet's divisive effect, while simultaneously taking advantage of all these differences to work together innovatively to create a better world?" This is a fundamental governance question. How we inevitably answer it, will nevertheless transform our currently constructed governing institutions—possibly in ways that make them unrecognizable by today's standards.

That said, for as long as we have known them, and whether we always liked it or not, governments have been continuously transforming. This should not be surprising. Unlike the static structures of government—like the Parliament Building, or the Capitol Building, or the Supreme Court Building, or City Hall which are generally used to represent government—governments themselves are actually *process structures* that undergo constant transformation due to the ebb and flow of the people and ideas that move through them.

Governments are more like rivers than buildings. You can stand in one place and watch the "river," but the river itself, the water, is constantly changing. The river you see today is not the same river you saw yesterday, nor will it be the same one tomorrow. Every drop of water will have been replaced. Similarly, governments are shaped: by the flow of people, both elected and non-elected; by the conversations within and without of them; and by their interactions with the social artifacts that are created by those conversations—the laws, the economy, the infrastructure, the culture, and the collective well-being.

Those conversations show what is really important to people, what people feel needs to be attended to, what is seen by them to be possible—and also what they feel is not, what they believe should be treasured, and how we should all be together. You don't change a government by destroying a building; you change it by changing the collective conversation that underpins it.

But while change may be normal and natural for a government, the degree of change required in governments today is unlike anything that has come before. It isn't likely to be simple or incremental. This is because many of the original rationales for structuring our governmental institutions have either disappeared or been greatly diminished. The Internet alone has, for instance, prompted such a large-scale societal transformation in how we move information and conduct our conversations, that today, if we were to start from scratch, our conversations would likely produce entirely new structures of governance and government. Nevertheless, if the Internet is making the old models of government obsolete, what is emerging to take their place?

The current structures of Western governments are a legacy, or a lingering shadow, of feudal systems long forgotten in the public mind. Despite the superficial nod to democracy, the meme that still dominates governments today is that "the only conversation that matters, happens among a handful of people working in a few guarded places." Leaders are everything. Followers are nothing.

Yet in today's world, the new Internet-based meme says that "conversations should be open to all and can take place anywhere, anytime." They may be initiated by any single person, anywhere in the world, and they can ultimately snowball to include hundreds of thousands, millions or even billions of people. Those who may have once been pigeonholed as followers, now don't need anyone's leave to change things in society, and social cooperation needs no top-down direction—it can be self-catalyzing and self-generating.

In the past, the important conversations happened as a product of elite accommodation, with citizens always deferring to the wisdom of "expert" leaders. Today, however, leaders don't matter much in an Internet world. Today, "you are what you share."[102] This reality is giving rise to an increasingly democratic character in public conversation, one that is peer-to-peer and citizen-to-citizen, and it is often happening within self-organizing networks of collective intelligence.

As **Figure 4** depicts, today those peer-to-peer conversations are being influenced by a wide array of complex, dynamic and interdependent issues, as well as forces that are being generated by new technologies and the Internet, which together have the capacity to alter, not only the structure and activities of our governments, but also the fundamental legitimacy of governments as mechanisms for social coordination. These pressures are creating impetus for change on existing government structures, but they are also creating great stress on them when they do not adapt well.

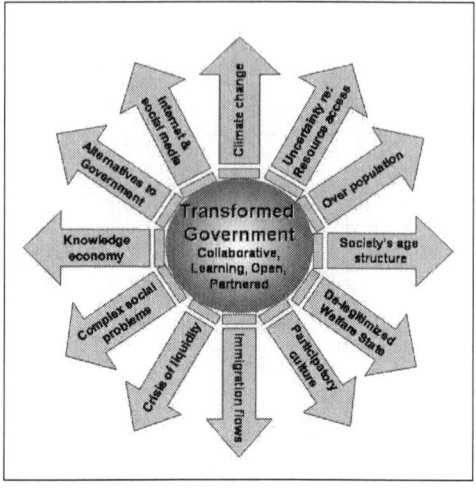

Figure 4: Government is being transformed

Despite recurrent budgetary challenges and continued calls for less government, governments remain the primary authority to resolve many of the socio-economic problems that afflict citizens. However, those problems are increasingly so complex and chronic that they do not easily avail themselves to simple black-and-white solutions. These "wicked problems"[103] include such issues as: climate change, human migration, the escalating income gap, perpetual economic growth, access to basic resources, and over-population.

What all these issues have in common, however, is that they demand greater coordination and collaboration among *all* of society's actors—something that traditional governments were never designed for.

Chapter 3

Issues in Pursuit of Collaborators

International cooperation to limit the effects of climate change

The recent international agreement on climate change in Paris in January 2016 notwithstanding, we have already topped the safe climate change limit set by climatologists of 400 ppm of CO_2 in the atmosphere, and catastrophic global warming seems pretty much inevitable[104]. So far, cooperation has meant lowering the bar on climate emissions to a level where no one will feel any pain, and weakening enforcement protocols so that they can be considered largely meaningless.

Yet despite the early ratification of the agreement by the world's two largest emitters—the US and China—Donald Trump's ascension to the US presidency has complicated global cooperation as he has walked away from the agreement to make the USA the only country in the world not to participate[105]. Nevertheless, his behaviour seems only to have strengthened the resolve of the rest of the world to find a cooperative solution—even if it is without the US.

But while serious global cooperation on climate change remains somewhat limited and tenuous, it may yet lead to broad governmental cooperation to help to mitigate some of the more dire consequences of climate change. Says Nick Mabey, CEO of E3G, "Climate change is unique . . . it has no hard-security solutions. In fact, the *only* solution is cooperation."[106] However, the international community has little experience with sustained cooperation. Beyond its predisposition for win-lose diplomacy, it has neither the frameworks nor the skill sets to affect or sustain cooperation between countries over long periods of time.

Increasing human migration flows

Due to multiple sources of instability—regional strife and conflicts, such as the Syrian civil war; the effects of climate change; a shrinking amount of livable, arable land; and growing income inequities—the flows of human migration are increasing and they are expected to grow further. During times of scarcity, migration is often the only hope for survival. Yet historically speaking, it has also been a profound cause of inter-group conflict. For instance, Hungary's Prime Minister Viktor Orban has begun referring to Syrian refugees as "Muslim invaders."

The very volume of such migrations may well move otherwise compassionate governments beyond the point of trying to balance helping migrants and protecting the interests of their citizens, to a point where they have to choose between their own continued existence and outright conquest [107].

The current European experience is a case in point. Once open to embracing hundreds of thousands of refugees fleeing from war torn Syria, many Europeans are now wanting to stem the tide and close their gates to protect themselves from being overwhelmed. This fear is already evident among many European leaders today as they try to cope with the exodus of refugees from the Middle East and North Africa, and most especially Syria. As the impacts of climate change proliferate, we can expect the current situation to become exacerbated further. According to former US national security advisor Leon Fuerth*, "Governments with resources will be forced to engage in long, nightmarish episodes of triage: deciding what and who can be salvaged from engulfment by a disordered environment."[108]

---

* Leon Fuerth is co-author along with John Podesta and former CIA Director, James Woolsey, of "The Age of Consequences: The Foreign Policy & National Security Implications of Global Climate Change."

Chapter 3

An escalating income gap

While there is clear evidence of an overall reduction in global poverty*, there is also evidence of a growing income gap *between* First and Third World countries[109] (excluding China and India), as well as *within* the countries that are home to 71% of the world's population. Canada's richest 1%, for instance, took almost a third of all income gains between 1997 and 2007[110], according to a 2010 study (**Figure 5**).

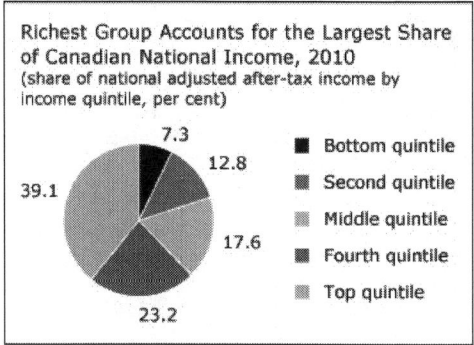

Figure 5: Source: *How Canada Performs*, Conference Board of Canada, Ottawa, January 2013

Forbes recently reported[111] that *eight people* (not 8,000 or 800 but 8 single people) have as much wealth as half the world's population. What's worrisome about this is that large income gaps like this have always proven to be socially destabilizing.

This raises, not only the issue of what constitutes a fair distribution of wealth, but also the issue of the costs that are often offloaded onto society by individuals and organizations in pursuit of their wealth: costs such as pollution, climate change, economic instability, health and safety—costs that tend to be disproportionately born by those who can least afford them.

---

* According to World Bank estimates, 21% of people in the developing world lived at or below the extreme poverty level of $1.25 a day, down from 43% in 1990 and 52% in 1981. Accessed at: http://www.worldbank.org/en/topic/poverty/overview. In addition, the proportion of Canadians living on low income fell to its lowest level (8.8%) since StatsCan began tracking low income in 1965 and when it was 25%. Source: COYNE, Andrew. "Fewer people sit below the poverty line now than ever before. Why are we not talking about it?", *National Post*, 22 July 2013

Perpetual economic growth as the basis of the global economic order

The widespread assumption that annual economic growth rates of 3% or more are somehow sustainable in the long run is proving to be economically untenable in the context of current realities—although significant denial remains. Tim Jackson, former Sustainable Development Commissioner in the UK, describes the current economic growth framework as a *Ponzi Scheme*. He suggests that politicians know this and that they are all too terrified that it will be exposed as such, so if they want to retain power, they must continue to support it.[112]

No biological system can continue to grow indefinitely—and that includes a human economy. However, the idea of "limitless growth" is now such an integral part of our way of looking at the world, everyone just takes it for granted without questioning its veracity, or its consequences. Even now, a growing number of national central banks are employing negative interest rates (i.e. you pay them to hold your money, as a mechanism to jump-start the anemic growth within their economies).

Says columnist and Pulitzer Prize–winning author Thomas Friedman, "What if [the crisis of 2008] is telling us that the whole growth model we created over the last 50 years is simply unsustainable economically and ecologically, and that 2008 was when we hit the wall—when Mother Nature and the market both said: "No more."[113]

It's a view that Wolfgang Streeck takes up in his recent book, *How Will Capitalism End*? He says capitalism is its own worst enemy and it is slowly, systematically destroying itself. "The end of capitalism," he writes[114], "can be imagined as a death from a thousand cuts . . . No effective opposition being left, and no practicable successor model waiting in the wings of history, capitalism's accumulation of defects, alongside its accumulation of capital, may be seen . . . as an entirely endogenous dynamic of self-destruction." Naturally, it begs the question, "What then will replace capitalism?" The scary answer, according to Streeck, is "Nothing."

While the alternative to "limitless growth," "prosperity without growth," has gained a beachhead with some policy makers, most notably in Britain, it should be recognized that all of our economic and policy fundamentals are geared around the assumption of continued growth. Lending and interest rates, investment, resource development, social supports, healthcare—they all assume that we can borrow for today and repay it with interest out of tomorrow's expected growth returns. Yet if growth doesn't materialize, or doesn't materialize fast enough, what occurs is that indebtedness increases until lenders or borrowers, or both, go out of business.

"The failure to take the dilemma of growth seriously may be the single biggest threat to sustainability that we face,"[115] says Tim Jackson. Without growth, borrowing for today looks increasingly like stealing from future generations. How long are future generations likely to tolerate that and we are subjected to intergenerational "wars"?

Renovating the foundations of our global economic system will be a daunting task, one that will necessitate significant cooperation and a cultural transformation among all of the world's business and policy elites. Yet as daunting as that task may seem, it may be much less daunting than dealing with a sustained collapse of the world economic order due to over-inflated or stalled growth in a period of crisis and chaos.

Access to basic resources

Access to food, water, clean air, land, energy, and minerals is becoming increasingly problematic, even in wealthy nations like the US and China. The demands of a growing human population are pushing up against the large, but ultimately finite, capacity of the planet. For instance, "When talking about what the greatest threats are that we face with climate change," says meteorologist Jeff Masters,[116] "I would put right at the top drought and water availability." For instance, Cape Town, South Africa, now estimates[117] it will run out of water by early 2018. We are nearing the point where many governments will begin aggressively (possibly even violently) competing for access to these increasingly scarce commodities from a purely survival perspective.

However, when it comes to supplying these basics of survival, scarcity is not the only problem. Social coordination is at least as big a problem. For instance, Amartya Sen, in his book *Development as Freedom*[118] pointed to the 1974 Bangladeshi famine during which time food production was ironically quite high. He points to the failure of governance, rather than a food shortage, as the reason. Also, as Venezuela's downward spiral of social and economic misery continues to play out, it is easy to see that a better predictor of quality of life is not the abundance or absence of resources, but the level of social coordination and democratic freedom that is enjoyed by the population.

Not having regular access to a new car may inspire some discontent or envy— but not having secure access to food, water or land will drive people into purely self-preservation mode with all the potential for global strife that that entails. "The pain will be unequally shared," says Gwynne Dyer commenting on the resource challenges of climate change, "at least in the early phases of the crisis, and it is this business of winners and losers that poses the greatest threat to global order."[119]

Over-population

Overpopulation continues to be one of the world's greatest problems, as well as being one of the greatest taboo topics in public policy. Given our current usage patterns for food, water, air, land, energy, and minerals, and the current trend in population growth, the planet is unlikely to be able sustain further population growth beyond 2050. Some, like physicist Stephen Hawking, have suggested that, "By the year 2600, the world's population would be standing shoulder to shoulder, and the electricity consumption would make the Earth glow red-hot."*

Serious decisions are therefore looming as to whether we limit population growth (and the attendant decisions of who gets to live and reproduce, and who gets to die), or change radically how we use existing resources. That such decisions are arising just as technology is on the cusp of significantly extending the span of human life is going to add even more pressure. These decisions will fundamentally tax the moral and ethical capacity of

---

* SAVVA, Anna. 2018. "Five ways Stephen Hawking has predicted the end of the world," The Mirror, 1 January. Accessed at: https://www.mirror.co.uk/science/stephen-hawking-predicted-five-ways-11766792

all governments, as well as their ability to work together. Will the more populous, stronger countries push aside smaller, weaker ones in an age-old Darwinian contest? It is an issue that will be further complicated by the growing segment of the population, particularly in developed countries, who may be perceived as less productive due to their age but who tend to control a higher proportion of wealth.

The UN Food and Agriculture Organization estimates that by 2050 a supportable peak human population of nine billion will be reached, provided the necessary investments in infrastructure, trade, anti-poverty and food security policies are in place. And while the sun provides us with all the clean energy we could ever need and at costs that are now lower than fossil fuels[120], we have yet to develop the willingness to effectively harness it and make it generally available. We even have key national leaders promising to bring back the good ol' days of coal and fossil fuels.

We need to recognize, says optimist Erle Ellis, that "our planet's human-carrying capacity emerges from the capabilities of our social systems and our technologies more than from any environmental limits."[121] In other words, it is from the conversations we have amongst ourselves as to what is possible and doable that really determine the planet's carrying capacity.

But even if we discount the hubris contained in Ellis' implied belief that "technology will save us," if we cannot expand our capacity to work together and be more socially innovative, then within the constraints of current attitudes and governing institutions, we will most likely be faced with the choice of limiting human population growth by force.

And, if our response to climate change is any indication, then we are a long, long way from creating any consensus on the conditions for a sustainable population of nine billion, let alone entertain open-ended population levels where everyone in the world tries to experience the same quality of life as your average North American or European does today.

Public sector liquidity

Should governments wake up one day with fresh insights into resolving the previous long-standing issues, their financial capacity to do so might be severely impeded, given the growing epidemic of government liquidity. The "canary in the coal mine" here was first observed within the Eurozone in late 2009, instigated by Greece's sovereign debt crisis. Greece's problems had a cascade effect weakening the financial stability of the other PIIGS countries (Portugal, Italy, Ireland and Spain) and the EU in general. With the Brexit decision in June 2016, this uncertainty is being magnified further. The reality is that if there is another financial meltdown like the one in 2008, the world's major countries do not have the cash reserves to deal with it.

Liquidity concerns have led to a questioning of the fundamental agreements upon which the European Union was founded, turning what in other circumstances may have been initially regarded as a simple recessionary downturn within a single country, into an existential concern for all Europeans. Despite "Band-Aid" solutions to keep several governments afloat, the question remains as to whether governments should be allowed to perennially spend more than they take in as revenue—even if this is a politically popular strategy. Ireland, Greece and Portugal have debt to income levels of over 300%, meaning that they spend three times their annual revenues.

Italy's ongoing financial crisis, for instance, has had the country teetering on the edge of bankruptcy for several years now[122]. In essence, Italy can't compete with Germany and other countries in the EU, and its economy is slowly dying. "Hence, an Italian sovereign default of some variety is now a near certainty," writes Charles Gave[123]. In the meantime, as of this writing, Italy's attempts to salvage its banking crisis may well push its public debt to 133% of GDP[124].

But liquidity is not simply a European problem. In North America we have the recent bankruptcy of Detroit, formerly America's fourth largest city, and US debt to income levels of 560%[125]. And while California's gross debt in the form of bonds is 7.6 % of its economy[126] and is considered huge by American standards, it pales by comparison to the gross debt of Canada's provinces of Ontario at 46% or Quebec's at 55% of GDP[127].

This public sector liquidity challenge boils down to two challenges:

1) *bureaucratic innovation*—how to do the same with less or, in other words, how to do the business of government differently so as to consume fewer resources. But this challenge is further complicated by,

2) the *"entitlement epidemic"*[128]—the growing size of state transfers to citizens, a growing political dependency on such transfers, and the growth of a culture of entitlement that encourages ever more transfers—often in direct response to social coordination failures by governments.

In the absence of effective measures to address social coordination, governments by and large have proven all too willing to use redistribution as a means of mitigating these failures[129].

As a result, the demand for public goods and services by citizens in Western countries has continued to grow, even as the public's willingness to pay for those public services continues to decline. Thus, democratically elected governments are frequently bowing to public pressure to increase transfers to citizens in the short term, even if they may contribute to the lack of overall sustainability and indebtedness of government in the long term.

Alternatives to government

As mentioned earlier, there are a growing number of alternatives to government for social coordination, mediated either by the Internet or by social interaction. People and organizations are finding ways to cooperate amongst themselves without the direction, or even the involvement, of government.

These might take the form of community-based collaborations, or more geographically dispersed communities of practice, or the development of online applications that serve the public interest, or the complete disintermediation of the role of government—in such areas as education, health care, transportation, or the economy, for instance. Social coordination is not only finding new avenues for expression, but it is also generating ways that governments are finding impotent to control.

In essence, "if we, citizens, can do it ourselves, then why do we need government?" One might expect that this realization would put significant pressure on governments to try and transform themselves to avoid the popular perception of their irrelevance. However, the required transformation is seen as disruptive, painful and contentious because of the deep cultural and organizational biases that the people within governments hold, such as the notions that "someone must always be in charge" or the "the State knows best."

Unfortunately, the price of not adapting may not only be anti-elitist populism, or lost opportunities for governments to positively redefine their role in society[130], but the huge costs of underutilizing our collective capacities for innovation and the production of social welfare at just the time when they are most needed. As worrisome is the wasted energy and force that will inevitably be required to buttress our aging public institutions against the never-ending onslaught of change that is occurring outside their walls.

Working together

Although all the above issues have all been reported by the media, they are quickly ignored in our collective conversations in the media and certainly by the governing classes. According to Higham and Paquet, "these warning signals are occluded nationally, and there appears to be no pressure from the citizenry, and no taste among the governing circles to even acknowledge the need for significant repairs"[131] to the governing apparatus. And while government leaders may be aware of these challenges, most, as evidenced by the 2015 federal election in Canada, are willing to sidestep them, either for ideological reasons, or because there is little short-term political capital to be gained from an issue you can't control.

Yet "all these challenges have two things in common," says Ian Johnson, Secretary General of the Club of Rome. "First, they are all anthropogenic, caused by us humans." [This is actually quite a hopeful comment because if we are part of the problem, then we can and should be part of the solution.] "Second, to a broad approximation, these challenges are all *shared problems*, and, as an old English saying goes, a problem shared is a problem halved. Shared problems must be addressed through shared solutions. This requires all of us changing our values, and understanding the commonality of humanity's challenges on earth, and, *they require new forms of governance*: especially of the commons—whether local, national or global."[132]

The overriding observation among these policy concerns is that they are far too big for any single government or organization to handle alone. The need for cooperation is paramount, but the observed capacity of governments to cooperate remains quite limited[133] given the well-entrenched "command-and-control" cultures that permeate both government organizations and the governance culture at large. As the former US Surgeon General, Jocelyn Elders, once wryly observed, for many both in and out of government, collaboration continues to be seen "as an un-natural act between non-consenting adults."[134] Collaboration is often put aside as too time-consuming, too unreliable, too unaccountable, or as a solution of last resort. Not surprisingly, collaborative experience is not valued, not shared and certainly not taught.

Chapter 4
The Digital Era Will Profoundly Alter the Landscape of Governance and Government

In the last chapter we learned that governments everywhere are not only coming up short when considering the usual array of issues and problems, but they are also just overwhelmed by many issues that affect humanity as a whole. So much so, that even speaking about these issues is avoided because there is no gain in doing so because governments have no real answers to bring forward.

Yet many still naively adhere to the belief in humanity's ability to create new technologies that will ultimately overcome the current weaknesses of governments and human beings. And as inspiring as many of these new and emerging technologies appear to be, they often bring their own dangers. That is because they are inevitably designed and used by people who suffer from that ultimate of human failings – not being perfect. No one has all the knowledge, all the resources or all the power to ensure that mistakes aren't made.

Given the billions of human beings connected through the Internet and the emergence of a "global village" infrastructure, to be consistent with Ashby's *Law of Requisite Variety*[135], governments will be increasingly pressured to come up with more sophisticated mechanisms for social coordination that meet or exceed the growing complexity of our increasingly diverse and interconnected world.

On the one hand, such mechanisms must help to moderate the potential for conflict through some form of trust building, moral contracting and the reduction of "free-riding" but, on the other, they will need to foster improved information sharing, learning and collaboration to encourage further innovation and an increased production of social welfare.

As Frederickson and Matkin have observed[136] both of these mechanisms can already be found among policy makers who cooperate online "because information technology is indifferent to borders and sovereignty," [making the Internet] "an ideal policy arena for inter-jurisdictional cooperation." Since the Internet removes connectivity barriers, it increases the shared awareness of problem scope and complexity. Thus, when driven by a better awareness of both problem pain and potential benefits, officials from different jurisdictions "appear to 'learn' to trust and cooperate with officials from other jurisdictions with whom they can collaborate [online]."

Frederickson and Matkin have also noted that "asymmetries in cooperation tend to matter less if there are enough cooperators, and if the overall [perceived] benefits are significant." Their suggestion is that despite the added potential for conflict when more people are connected, the Internet provides a space where the dynamics of cooperation can play themselves out more effectively.

Practically speaking, however, while some social coordination challenges will naturally be met by the application of new technologies (like wikis or social media or the Internet of Things), or by new participatory behaviours among citizens (such as the trends towards "open source" development or participatory democracy), in all likelihood, governments will remain the primary source of social coordination in the near term.

Nevertheless, the demand by the public for demonstrable results will require that governments adapt and cooperate in ways that are not just incremental but truly transformative. If they don't, they risk a further erosion of their already low levels of public legitimacy—possibly even a complete surrender of their role as main provider of social coordination to a growing array of alternatives.

All combined, the forces described earlier in Chapters Two and Three are likely to alter not only our basic assumptions about what we as citizens want from our governments, but how we engage with each other, and, by extension, how we will ultimately relate to our governments—as subjects or as partners. "What is required," say Higham and Paquet, "is a revolution of the mind, a different perspective, and refurbished governance.[137]" If such a shift in collective consciousness can take place, then the changed conversations that will ensue will no doubt fundamentally alter both our expectations of our governments as well as the structures and processes by which governments can then fulfill that changed role.

Still, notwithstanding the very significant nature of the issues in the previous chapters, the Internet remains *the* most pervasive challenge to the established order—both directly and indirectly. Not only is it enabling people of all sorts to connect, but through those connections it is changing our values, our behaviours, and our sense of possibility.

The increased connectivity and access to information brought about by the Internet is giving rise to entirely new and different ways in which people and organizations can communicate, organize and ultimately work together. Thus, the Internet may offer the brightest ray of hope for raising the level of human cooperation to the levels needed to help resolve the previously mentioned global challenges.

That said, the Internet also presents some of its own unique, new challenges—challenges that are often intimately intertwined with its potential benefits. Consequently, dealing with the Internet is a bit Janus-like: the Internet presents opportunities to become more innovative and collaborative encouraging progress on well-known, collective issues, but on the other hand, it raises novel, unfamiliar issues and presents entirely new and unfamiliar risks which until now have not been on the government's radar—particularly when it comes to governments adapting to the deep cultural shifts that are emerging.

Re-Imagining Government - Part 1

The following are eight different, although related, ways in which the Internet and its associated communications technologies are seriously tilting the playing field upon which governments have operated for the last two centuries.

Creating more knowledge

It is said that innovation amounts to seeing old things in new ways. By connecting billions of people around the globe, the Internet has offered billions of new ways of looking at old knowledge and old ideas. Not surprisingly, there has been an explosion of new knowledge. Knowledge today is growing at a phenomenal, exponential rate, currently doubling about every 73 days[138]. To put this in a different way, in 73 days from today we will have added as much new knowledge as has been generated in all of human history prior to today.

This incredible rate of knowledge growth puts huge stress on governments, because their established role as "public expert," demands that they must try to keep up current with all this new knowledge. However, governments have been structured to adapt only very slowly to change, to avoid the possibility of being caught up in momentary radicalism. As a result of this institutional resistance to change, the rate of government adaptation to new knowledge keeps falling further and further behind.

Therefore, all governments, despite their resources, are finding themselves increasingly in the dark with respect to almost any issue. This problem posed by knowledge growth is exacerbated further by an unequal diffusion of knowledge. Some knowledge will be held by experts who can be brought into government, but critical pieces of knowledge are now held only by people outside of government. In this environment, neither the so-called "in-house experts" of governments, nor individual citizens, are likely to have anything close to comprehensive knowledge.

Additionally, to deal with this massive knowledge overload, some governments have sought temporary security from this tsunami of uncertainty and growing ignorance by fleeing from it entirely and taking the position

Chapter 4

that more knowledge is instead unhelpful—at least as far as trying to arrive at quick decisions*.

In place of objective knowledge, governments are increasingly relying on instinctive perspectives that are "self-evident"—at least to them. While this is undeniably a way of arriving at decisions sooner, it is fraught with danger, as "quick" decisions are not necessarily "good" decisions. For over 200 years, democratic governments have tried to use objective knowledge to limit the arbitrariness of State power, yet in today's environment of "too much information," governments are being encouraged to once again resort to governance by fiat and subjectivity[139]. One can easily see this displayed in US President Trump's propensity to skip daily intelligence briefings because he's "already a smart man."[140]

Furthermore, too much information in the hands of ordinary citizens tends to seriously limit the knowledge hegemony that governments have long claimed for themselves. In today's knowledge climate, the odds are that the person or persons who know an issue best do not work for government, and moreover they probably have no interest in doing so. The result is, not only does the State not know best, but sometimes it doesn't even have a clue.

For instance, one of the only people to go to jail for actions related to the 2008–2009 financial meltdown was a Russian-born, former software coder for Goldman Sachs named Serge Aleynikov.** He was charged and convicted for market manipulation and the theft of proprietary code from Goldman. The actual "market manipulation" was the result of computerizing Goldman's shoddy trading processes which ultimately fueled a significant amount of the financial crisis.

However, the alleged theft of "proprietary software" was in fact related to "open source" code that was freely available on the Internet under General Public License, and which Aleynikov had used to develop his programs for Goldman. For its part, Goldman knew this and tried to illegally appropriate

---

* In government, arriving at a decision is usually considered much more important than the implementability or outcomes of a decision, because of the longer time frames associated with those outcomes.

** The details of Aleynikov's work with Goldman and his subsequent legal tribulations can be found in LEWIS, Michael. 2014. *Flash Boys*, W.W. Norton Co., New York, NY.

this open source code for itself simply by adding its own logos to the material documenting the code.

Unfortunately for Aleynikov, neither his high-speed computer trading program nor its "open source" code elements were understood by the FBI, the judge, the DA or the jury and so Aleynikov was convicted and imprisoned basically on the say so of Goldman Sachs. However, after spending over a year in jail, his case was immediately overturned on appeal, on the grounds that the laws he stood accused of breaking did not actually apply. According to Michael Lewis, Goldman was using Aleynikov to deflect its own misdeeds, and the US justice system simply took their word for it because the technical details were so far above their understanding.

In today's world, the only thing that might come close to comprehensive knowledge on most issues is a collective pooling of stakeholder knowledge, including that of government. In the past, such thoughts would have been totally impractical, which is why we adopted our "representative" style of democracy. Today, however, such capabilities have become a trivial matter because of the Internet.

Therefore, given that we are all connected and we can share our knowledge with anyone, there now exists a new societal foundation to challenge the knowledge dominion of governments. This is further underscored by the inability of governments to reorganize themselves around processes of collective learning, rather than around their traditional focus of avoiding waste—which almost everyone agrees they do badly anyway.

"Institutions must be redesigned from the ground up," says Deloitte's John Hagel[141], "to address a totally different rationale. Instead of pursuing *scalable efficiency*, institutions must learn how to pursue *scalable, peer learning.*" The current lack of focus on collective learning, leads to a typical experience in government where different parties advocate their differing views, while being deaf to the views of others.

This is reminiscent of the old story of the blind men and the elephant, where individuals with only partial knowledge try to lay claim to "truth" from their point of view, while completely missing the big picture and with practical consequences for society that can be either foolhardy or even tragic.

Chapter 4

Interestingly, a version of this story can be found in almost every culture. In it, four blind men are led into a room with an elephant (they never seem to explain why the elephant is in the room, but no matter). One blind man feels the trunk and thinks it's a snake, another feels the leg and thinks it's a tree, another feels the side and thinks it's a wall, and the fourth feels the curly tail and thinks it's a pig. The question is, who's right?

When I ask this of my students they all laugh, because it's an elephant, right? They're all wrong, they say. But from the perspective of the blind men who have only partial knowledge, they are all right—at least partially. A better question to ask, I tell my students, is "What can be a snake, a tree, a wall, and a pig all at the same time?" This is fundamentally the challenge of policy making with incomplete knowledge. To answer this question, you have to pool your knowledge and then take a creative leap.

The ongoing growth of knowledge will continue to erode the traditional charade in government that "knowledgeable experts" can govern on behalf of a less knowledgeable citizenry. For the most part, any gap in knowledge between experts and non-experts today can be closed as easily as clicking a mouse—putting those both in and out of government more or less on equal footing. We have created an entire citizenry comprised of partial experts. Yet, if those citizens can also create and participate in online knowledge sharing fora, then in all likelihood they may be better informed and more knowledgeable than state actors trying to act independently.

Finally, at a minimum, the rapid advancement and volume of knowledge creation is already generating unsustainable costs for government, in terms of both human and financial costs, just in order to keep up.

Democratizing knowledge

As more knowledge is being created, the Internet has also become the quintessential tool for its global dissemination. Knowledge, which was once poorly channeled through books and academic journals, now flows freely through the "creative commons", blogs, and YouTube videos. YouTube, for instance, has more than a billion visitors *each month*, watching over 6 billion hours of video—that is almost an hour for every person on Earth, up 50% in just one year between 2013 and 2014.

And now, even those staid academic journals may soon be online—for free. In what European science chief Carlos Moedas called a "life-changing" move[142], EU member states in May of 2016 agreed on an ambitious new open-access (OA) target that would make all scientific papers freely available by 2020, in order to stimulate global science and innovation.

Total strangers find can find new knowledge online, comment on it, modify it, accept it or dismiss it. All 3.5 billion Internet users can, and often do, have an opinion (albeit not always an informed one). Some might simply advocate or argue unproductively amongst themselves about who's right or wrong, but others might contribute stigmergically* to the advancement of knowledge by building on what others have contributed before.

In this context, there appears to be a phase transition taking place in the democratization of knowledge—the likes of which has never been seen before, except possibly with the advent of the printing press. It is a shift that is putting *all knowledge*—together with the computing power that goes along with it—into the hands of everyone on the planet**. This is a tremendous opportunity for inciting greater innovation, which, as the EU Competitiveness Council has recognized, depends on those different perspectives coming together.

But it also has its darker side.

---

* Stigmergy is a form of communication that results from information being passed between people by way of modifying some shared environment, like a website, where participants modify their environment and others will subsequently accept, modify or reject those contributions.

** In a recent development, a not-for-profit, global broadcast organization, **Outernet,** has begun operating in order to provide free access to web content through geostationary and Low Earth Orbit satellites, made freely available to all parts of the world. Its goals are to provide information without censorship for educational and emergency purposes, including: news, civic information, commodity prices, weather, construction plans for open source farm machinery and other information; they will be providing access to "courseware," including textbooks, videos, and software; and they will be available also when access to regular Internet connection is unavailable.

Chapter 4

Bill Joy, one of Silicon Valley's iconic early developers and a co-founder of Sun Microsystems, once wrote in *Wired*[143] that such democratization also risks putting all that knowledge, and the power to use it, into the hands of a small number of very disturbed people who might be intent on causing harm to others simply because they can.

This democratization of knowledge, coupled with newer and ever better technologies and computing power, may sometime in the future, result in, not just a terrorist incident, but a global calamity. Joy argued, for instance, that if democratized genome knowledge allowed someone to introduce into humanity an entirely new viral pathogen for which humans had no antibodies[144], or enable a new generation of hacker to propagate "nanobots" that could be pre-programmed to infect and destroy the very technology that we have become so dependent on, then the results would be no less than catastrophic.

As it turns out this can't be ignored as a neo-Luddite reaction of Joy's*, or some futuristic 'Terminator-type" science fiction, but even as far back as 2011 Symantec identified that these types of cyber-attacks are becoming frequent and more problematic. "The findings ... are somewhat alarming, given attacks like Nitro and Duqu that have targeted critical infrastructure providers ... We think that targeted attacks against critical infrastructure providers in the form of Stuxnet, Nitro and Duqu will continue. These latest attacks are likely *just the beginning* of more targeted attacks directed at critical infrastructure."[145] For instance, the US Department of Homeland Security recently revealed[146] that ISIS hackers were attempting to bring down the US energy grid, and, of course, there is the incident of Russian hackers targeting the Democratic National Convention in 2016 and the "WannaCry" ransomware worm of 2017.

Therefore, given the impossibility of preventing the creation of disturbed human beings, it would seem that the only two sensible options at the moment are:

---

* Although the absurdity of calling someone like Joy a "Luddite" is completely lost on some people.

95

1. limit the level of democratization of knowledge, knowing full well that this would also limit the creativity and innovation of human society; or

2. find new ways of limiting the destructive potential of disturbed individuals, something that currently seems equally unlikely.

Neither of these options is very practical or desirable, but more important, neither consideration is being addressed in any serious way in public conversation. With no obvious solution, we are naively proceeding as if the problem doesn't exist, and that there are no risks to the unrestricted dissemination of knowledge and the power to use it.

Heretofore, governments have been designed to detect and respond to large societal-level threats through standing armies, large investments in technology and foreign policy. However, as the experience of the "Parliament Hill shooter" in Ottawa in 2014 or the 'Boston Marathon Bombers" in 2013 or lone wolf attackers in the UK, France and Germany illustrate, today's scariest threats can come from a complete inability to predict or detect the actions of single individuals. How do you protect against a threat you can't see, or may not even know is there?

Knowledge is a double-edged sword. The very thing which is fostering the most connected and creative period in human history, the Internet, may also at the same time be the thing that is creating humanity's biggest menace.

The question of how much democratization of knowledge is a good thing is a big one, and one that cannot and should not be taken lightly, or acted upon by any one government alone because of the possible consequences of penalizing all levels of social creativity, productivity and competitiveness. Different governments will have different opinions, but the solution, like the one on climate change, must be cooperative and global.

Chapter 4

Legal constraints on sharing

Knowledge is like money. The more it circulates, the more social value it creates. The corollary of this is that if you want to maximize the amount of social value, then you need to maximize the rate at which knowledge circulates. The truth of this is immediately evident in the Internet-based "open source" model which, when compared to the value creation that results from top-down organizational models, consistently wins hands down. According to technology guru Don Tapscott, "We are seeing how the new age of networked intelligence renders conventional approaches to value creation insufficient, and in some cases, completely inappropriate."[147]

However, in the past, knowledge was regarded as an asset, in the same way as inventory, plant, equipment, and financial capital were. But unlike these other assets, knowledge is not relinquished when it is exchanged and every new idea is built upon someone else's work. Nevertheless, we have created well-established, institutional and jurisdictional barriers to the free circulation of knowledge. Intellectual property (IP) laws, for instance, were established long ago to limit the flow of knowledge in order for its "creators," and their institutional promoters, to capture greater "rents" from its use.

The Internet and information technologies have, however, assured that new ideas and new technologies are often shared regardless of IP laws, and frequently within a time window that is little more than six months. So while IP laws nowadays do not present a complete barrier to the transmission of knowledge, they do slow down the *open sharing* of knowledge. Knowledge sharing by stealth and re-engineering continues unabated.

Simultaneously, the jurisdictional barriers to the open sharing of knowledge when coupled with the Internet's culture of anonymity have created whole new opportunities for crime and espionage. Through a range of sophisticated viruses, Trojans and other tools, hackers can work at safe distances, hiding behind jurisdictional barriers, with little fear of being either caught or punished.

Thus the Internet is putting pressure to reform established IP regimes to enable added knowledge sharing to maximize innovation and socio-economic welfare, but also to diminish the harmful effects of cybercrime. In the current global system of knowledge development and exchange there are both winners (individuals and some artists) and losers (media and recording industry), so some interests will be resistant to change while others will embrace it. Reforming this system will need a cooperative global effort that works towards a shared goal that at this time is not well defined.

Increasing transparency

Unlike the pre-Internet era, today's organizations and leaders have much less control over information than they once had. When records were paper, the physical limitations of moving large quantities of paper naturally constrained the ability to share documented evidence. Today, however, electronic data somehow, someway always leaks out—through disgruntled employees, altruistic do-gooders, hackers, and human error. It leaks out by accident (as happened when a disk containing 1/3 of the UK's tax files was lost on a subway because the briefcase in which it was stored was forgotten by a luckless public servant), or by deficient organizational security protocols, or by intent. Two of the most obvious illustrations of the latter are the public disclosures through Wikileaks of top-secret US government files, and the ongoing revelations of Edward Snowden about NSA's cyber-spying program, PRISM.

In addition, government leaders are now prone to having their personal lives disclosed almost in real time on Twitter and other social media, much like celebrity movie stars have had to endure for years. For instance, there is the sad case of the former US congressman and New York mayoral candidate Anthony Weiner, and the case of Toronto's former, now (in)famous Mayor, Rob Ford. Simple off-the-cuff remarks that may, in the past, have gone unreported are now instantly published with worldwide Twitter and social media coverage. The more sensational the better. In addition, the accuracy of these reports is rarely questioned, even by established media who would rather publish a tawdry story on the front page, knowing that if a retraction is necessary it will come on page 20.

"I sometimes wonder if (the ugliness of modern politics) is really new," says Alison Loat, co-founder of Canada's Samara Research. "Perhaps things are

Chapter 4

just more visible now that there's more social media, and a faster news cycle. Everyone's warts are out there for all to see. That probably accounts as much for what's happening, as politicians behaving worse than in the past."[148]

Despite there being less secrecy and less privacy, the anonymity that exists throughout much of the Internet still permits many people to wreak great harm. For instance, cybercrime cost Canadians $3.09 billion in 2012[149], affecting 42% of online Canadian adults at an average cost of $383 per individual, up 127% from the previous year. According to the FBI, the estimated conviction rate for cybercrime in the US is only 2%, which means that jail time obviously presents little or no deterrent for crimes that could potentially offer millions or hundreds of millions of dollars in payback.

In this context, governments are simultaneously challenged with strengthening individual privacy at the risk of causing public harm from cyber-criminals and terrorists; OR, weakening individual privacy at the risk of causing individual harm à la "Big Brother" effects from over-reaching governments and corporations. Once again, there is no obvious good answer.

In the end, governments seem to be caught fighting a rearguard action to become less transparent even as the Internet and the public is compelling them to be ever more connected, transparent and "user friendly" and, therefore, ever more vulnerable.

Creating more opportunities for self-organization and collaboration

Over the Internet, social coordination and collaboration need not depend on the establishment and maintenance of relationships as they do in an offline world. This occurs stigmergically.[150] Over the Internet, cooperation happens all the time as a result of individuals generating and leaving behind texts, blogs, pictures or videos for others to find. Collaboration occurs when people find this material and then react to it—like flocking birds—accepting it, modifying it or negating it. When large numbers of people react in this way, a collaborative product, or mass behaviour, can emerge, sometimes spontaneously, and often in unpredictable ways. Thus, a single contribution can be amplified multiple times into a collective but concrete output, such as those that regularly occur in the process of open-source software development, or as happened more specifically with the anti-SOPA protest of 2012*.

How does one incite such mass collaboration? Unlike small group collaboration, it does not require the building of trusted relationships as a prerequisite. While a few basic rules are usually helpful, *action comes first*. Collaborators then react to the initial actions of others—accepting them, modifying them or rejecting them. However, for stigmergic collaboration to be truly effective, it requires access to a large number of people who may *potentially* participate—even if only a relative few actually do. This is the fundamental premise of "open source" as illustrated by the Linux operating system or with Wikipedia. In reacting to someone else's actions, complete strangers can thus collaborate without ever having to invest in a relationship.[151]

This phenomenon of stigmergic collaboration is what underpins the experience of mass collaboration over the Internet and which has given rise to geographically dispersed communities of practice, collaborative decision making involving tens of thousands or millions of people, a broad sharing of knowledge and resources, and new forms of "collaborative consumption" and "macrowikinomics"[152].

Yet for governments, the opportunity for people to connect, share, learn and work together over the Internet, without the intervening power of government to coordinate them all, also creates a significant new challenge to retaining their legitimacy. For if I don't actually need government to fix things, or provide new resources, or make new connections to allow me to be successful, or to underscore social trust and cooperation within my community, or even to provide an education for my kids, then what *real value* does government provide? And on the flip side, if my experience with government is such that it can no longer ensure that I have quality health care, or a safe and secure community, or that I or my kids will have jobs, or that someone will be there in my time of need, tell me again, what is government good for?

---

* In response to the authoritarian provisions of the US Stop Online Piracy Act, or SOPA, many online providers and information sources went offline, most notably Wikipedia, on 18 January 2012 in the largest protest in human history.

Lastly, when people see that the issues that are important to them are complicated further by the absence of collaborative cultures and skills on the part of public sector organizations, then it's likely that government will be viewed more as an obstacle than as a help. If people can interact with their neighbours, or with total strangers over the Internet more easily than with government and collaboratively respond to shared issues and opportunities, then the standing of government as a positive influence in society will decline.

Facilitating greater access to more resources

One of the principal, universally recognized, benefits of government, relates to its near monopoly status for raising revenues via taxation for the provision of public goods and services* from across society. Nowadays, however, crowdsourcing mechanisms that are available on such online sites as *Indiegogo*, *Crowdfunder* and *Crowdrise* are creating new avenues for raising funds for all manner of social purposes (see **Figure 6**). These new approaches to fundraising also provide the added benefit of ensuring that there is enough public support, *before* the funding is ever collected or provided, and that it can be provided in increments to permit experimentation and accountability. Newer tools, like *OpenCollective*[153], also permit supporters and groups to not only raise funds, but also manage them transparently and collectively.

While still largely in their early stages, these online tools are offering clear alternatives to the centralized modes of taxation and decision-making that have characterized government funding of public projects. These new tools operate on the principle that if people want something bad enough, they will contribute the resources to it—if they have the means to do so—instead of the current model of coercing money from citizens and letting centralized decision makers decide how that money will be spent.

While the crowdfunding option presents an obvious collective action problem where some may shirk their collective responsibility versus

---

* This is not to diminish the role of the not-for-profit sector; it's just that the scale and coercive power of the state is currently so much greater.

Figure 6: Leading Public Crowd Sourcing Sites

1. Indiegogo
Indiegogo approves donation-based fundraising campaigns for almost anything—music, hobbyists, personal finance needs, charities and whatever else you could think of (except investment).

2. Crowdfunder
Crowdfunder is the crowdfunding platform for businesses, with a growing social network of investors, tech startups, small businesses, and social enterprises (financially sustainable/profitable businesses with social impact goals). Crowdfunder offers a blend of donation-based and investment crowdfunding from individuals and angel investors. The company has localized crowdfunding and investment to help develop entrepreneurial ecosystems.

3. Crowdrise
Crowdrise is a place for donation-based funding for causes and charity. They attract a community of do-gooders and fund all kinds of inspiring causes and needs. A unique points system on Crowdrise helps track and reveal how much charitable impact members and organizations are making.

4. Somolend
Somolend is a site for lending for small businesses in the US, providing debt-based investment funding to qualified businesses with existing operations and revenue. Somolend has partnered with banks to provide loans, as well as helping small business owners bring their friends and family into the effort. With their Midwest roots, a strong founder who was a leading participant in the JOBS Act legislation, and their focus on the local small business market, Somolend has begun expanding into multiple cities and markets in the US.

5. Invested.in
You might want to create your own crowdfunding community to support donation-based fundraising for a specific group or niche in the market. Invested.in is a Venice, CA, based company that is a top name "white label" software provider, giving you the tools to get started and grow your own.

Source: Barnett, Chance, "Top 10 Crowdfunding Sites For Fundraising", *Forbes*, 8 May 2013.

standardized collection through taxation, this is no less problematic than the well documented risks surrounding centralized decision makers who may have personal interests that may conflict with those from whom they demand taxes.

The existence of these open access funding alternatives may well herald a significant shift of resources from government to the not-for-profit sector, as the principle source of community socio-economic development and support.

Furthermore, it is not only the acquisition of financial capital for public goods and services that the Internet helps to facilitate, but it is also the access to in-kind, intangible and reputational capital that online collaborators can bring to bear as well. On a site like *Mumsnet.org*, for instance, visitors (mainly parents) can swap advice about children, education, work, lifestyles, food, and just about anything parents want to talk about. It is a forum for parents to help parents, and it's also the biggest network for parents in the UK, generating over 9 million visits each month.

Sometimes the Internet can also provide an alternative to the direct hiring of public servants. Instead of hiring experts in-house, for instance, governments can access interested expert volunteers in much the way as open-source software. The *Peer to Patent* initiative, for instance, of the US Patent and Trademark Office, invites the public to participate in the patent examination process. It aims to improve the quality of issued patents by enabling the public to supply the USPTO with information (which it may not have) that may be relevant to assessing the claims of pending patent applications.

The existence of the *Peer to Patent* program represents a clear recognition that comprehensive knowledge cannot be held within a small government group—no matter how expert. For members of the public service this does not bode well. As Richard Susskind argues in his book *Replacing the Professionals* [154], many high-end professional jobs have become so standardized that they are open to replacement by software or robotics, including those of lawyers, accountants, doctors and public servants. While this may seem attractive to budget conscious senior managers, it may also set the stage for serious confrontation between management and public service unions, but it may also encourage a greater utilization of volunteer experts.

The availability of alternative funding and resources creates additional challenges for government, not only weakening its control over particular issue spaces (it may become less able to use its control of purse strings to keep stakeholders in line), but it also adds to the already large coordination and response challenges it needs to keep abreast of things in order to stay aligned with all the initiatives occurring outside of government. Now instead of having to keep track of a limited number of public agencies working on some issue, it must also actively search, often globally, for not-for-profit and business organizations that may have critical new knowledge or resources.

For some agencies, like the USPTO, there is the added challenge of remaining relevant and credible in the eyes of those outsiders who may potentially contribute to the government's work, or else they may lose their voluntary participation. As a consequence, some governments, therefore, are beginning to pay much more serious attention to their own reputations.

Creating more communities

One of the more interesting transformations produced by the Internet has been our re-conceptualization of what we mean by community. "Communities" are no longer defined simply by geographic proximity, but by shared interests and common practices. The processes of connecting and sharing that once animated communities, were severely constrained by proximity and the need for personal interaction. Therefore, within any given geographic space, those forming some interest-based community would likely share only a few of the most commonly held interests—language, ethnicity, religion, family and history. Communities of practice were similarly generalized in forms of work type (unions) or interests (associations).

With the advent of the Internet, however, one can now reach out to anyone around the world who might share your specific interest or work. Thus while you may be the only person in your geographic community with a particular interest, there may well be thousands or millions of people worldwide who do as well. Connecting such geographically dispersed people into networks and communities of sharing has been one of the greatest benefits of the Internet. It has resulted in an exponential proliferation of communities, of every description, and a concurrent development of scale that has given once marginal associations both a strong voice and significant influence.

Yet, as Barbara Hubbard once observed,[155] with ever more specialized communities, there has also been more opportunities for inter-community conflict. Unfortunately, most systems of government were designed to manage only a few conflicts at a time among a small number of communities. In Canada, for instance, these conflicts might have appeared between French-English, Protestant-Catholic, east-west, rural-urban, rich-poor, industrial-agricultural, native-born-immigrant, aboriginal-non-aboriginal—and they were managed largely through processes of elite accommodation and negotiation.

Today, not only are there so many more types of communities, but many of those who previously may have allied themselves with one of the major groupings, may now see their identities and allegiances spreading across a host of much smaller groups—possibly neighbourhood associations, hobby groups or organizational subgroups, or shifting from one group to another depending on the issue.

This has important political ramifications. According to Daniel Kahneman[156], voters tend to vote, not on issues, but for people they perceive to be "like them." Therefore, among political researchers and pollsters, trying to understand how people self-identify is a major preoccupation. However, the growing heterogeneity of the citizenry is making this task increasingly complex. As a result, we see a proliferation of politicians who are pitching their promises, not to how people actually are with all their multifaceted allegiances, but as more simplified caricatures of the population, pictures which may resonate among a few but antagonize many. The old post-war notion that elected officials worked for the whole population, and not just a small subset thereof, has been cast aside in favour of political language and policy making that need only appeal to 20-25% of actual voters to ensure a "majority" government.

In addition, the fragmentation of communities is also eroding our sense of *shared identity* and values, as fewer people see themselves in, or depicted in, national conversations that tend to centre on the old group depictions. Sure, we've added visible minorities and the LGBT community, and we are adding the Indigenous and immigrant communities, but we are doing poorly when it comes to those who refuse to be pigeonholed by geography or a single physical characteristic.

The collective "we" is no longer reserved for this or that characteristic, but for a litany of characteristics—physical, psychological, historical, and ideological—characteristics that are also evolving over time. As our notions of shared identity and values have become "fuzzier," they have further encouraged trends towards citizen disengagement[157] and cynicism. Without an appreciation of "Who speaks for me?", the likelihood is that people won't engage at all.

Framing this in Internet terms, since many of the new groupings and communities are forming online, addressing the "disengagement challenge" would seem to revolve around how to reconnect the increasing number of online identities and communities into a loose network, and infusing it with an emergent, rather than static, sense of identity and shared purpose. It's a phenomenon that tends to occur more in the creation of movements than in organizations or political parties[158].

Still, as much as the Internet has connected people to new interest-based communities, it has also disconnected many citizens from their basic, tribal allegiances to family, religious, racial or regional groups. In essence, the sheer volume of different perspectives today decreases the likelihood of voting being, as it once was, a negotiation among politicians and "tribal chieftains." It has also eliminated the fiction that governments can somehow "divine" common values so as to be able to set policy in the common interest[159]. It's a pluralistic world, with no shared values, and with only the possibility that we can discover some common purpose that can act as a guide for collective coordination.

The ready availability of online information permits individual voters to choose a candidate on their own terms, often sending political parties scrambling at election time to come up with the right mix of messages (sometimes contradictory) to attract extremely diverse audiences and avoid an unpredictable result. It's no wonder that some parties favour proportional representation, which often takes the direct choice of elected representative away from voters, replacing it with a party choice. Nevertheless, with so

Chapter 4

many different communities, it gets harder and harder to identify what motivates a majority of them, except in the basest of terms, leading many parties to simply forgo the old tradeoffs and govern only for whatever slice of the electorate that can ultimately give them a plurality, instead of the old practice of trying to govern for all.

Increasing the self-sufficiency of citizens

In many, many small ways, citizens themselves have begun to assume the activities and functions that have long been associated with governments. For instance, the move to make information collected by governments available to the public, in so called *open data* initiatives is, on the one hand, co-opting citizens to reduce the costs of providing effective government services. However, it is also transforming citizens from being passive consumers of government services into participants and co-creators of their own governance.

This active participation by citizens in processes meant to address things that affect them directly, or that they are just passionate about, lends credence to the idea that today's citizens are just as engaged in their democracy as previous generations—maybe even more so. It's just that the trend is towards more of a "do-it-yourself" version of governance, rather than towards the old system of parties and elections.

These days, it is commonplace that people forget that the agency agreement that is the cornerstone of democratic government is not between a citizen and a party, but between one citizen and another citizen who is elected to work on their behalf. But our elected representatives have long been considered "nobodies"[160] by the reigning governments of the day, so long that the media and the citizenry have just come to accept it. In the shadow of this ignorance, many of today's engaged citizens are more likely to say "no thanks" to parties claiming to represent them and to embrace their democratic ownership more directly. They try and make a difference themselves, rather than be passive consumers of governance.

In fact, today's democratic governments are typically quite challenged to recognize democracy as a mechanism for facilitating the shared ownership of their citizens. For democratic governments everywhere, despite the representative rhetoric of political parties or their voting system preferences (first-past-the-post, proportional representation, ranked ballots, etc.), when they speak of democracy, it is not as an agency relationship; it is as a means of exerting control over citizens. Ideally, they receive a majority mandate for a temporary, four-year dictatorship in which no one can successfully challenge their authority, and where there is no real pressure to accept the advice of anyone.

Former Canadian Prime Minister, John Turner, was once quoted as saying "Democracy doesn't happen by accident. In this country we are taking it for granted. We're not paying attention . . . One of the reasons is that the role of the member of Parliament isn't what it used to be."[161]

Government overwhelmed

Today's governments have neither the capacity for much needed collaboration on critical issues nor the capacity to grasp the rapidly advancing issues surrounding the growth of technology. It's not that governments don't recognize the need for collaboration, but that the antiquated top-down paradigm guiding the actors in government constrains them from focusing on the frameworks, skills and mechanisms needed to make collaboration work.

Similarly, it's not that government doesn't recognize the need to invest in new technologies, but that the use of these technologies fundamentally alters the relationship between governments and their citizens; it introduces demands for entirely new ways of social learning, collaboration and affecting democracy; it abolishes the monopoly of governments on social coordination by providing alternatives; it creates altogether new challenges; and it seriously undermines the legitimacy of traditional hierarchically-organized government organizations*.

---

* Sometimes these two infirmities get combined, as they were with Canada's previous efforts to create a *Secure Channel* platform for citizens to interact with all levels of government, and more recently with the federal *Phoenix Payroll System* that created problems with some 82,000 federal employees who were underpaid, overpaid, or not being paid at all.

Consequently, when the systems and organizational design of government no longer align with the needs of society, it is inevitable that people become dissatisfied with both their government and their elected leaders. Unfortunately, they reflexively presume replacing existing leaders with new ones will be enough to fix the problem. But this is only because leaders have forever been telling them that they're in charge, and they're in control. The reality is that just changing leaders is unlikely to produce the change citizens desire, because it is the system of governance itself that is faulty.

As Donald Savoie has warned,[162] "our political institutions and government bureaucracies face becoming increasingly irrelevant, unless action is taken . . . Unless [they] are able to perform at a higher level, more and more activities will be hived off to the private and voluntary sectors, even those matters that only government can handle, because no one else has the mandate or capacity to take them on . . . [Government] may well be left without the resources to make a difference."

This state of perpetual dissatisfaction then becomes fertile ground for the populists who are willing to promise anything (no matter how irrational), blame anyone (no matter how injurious), or do anything (no matter how ruinous) to secure their control of a population. When they prevail, a government is likely to drift from a democracy to some authoritarian form of oligarchy or dictatorship. For instance:

> "Trump is a product of the crisis of democratic politics, not the cause of it. But he's not the solution, either. [He] shows that principle, conviction, vision—the components of a thriving democracy—are more needed than ever."[163]

To avoid such undemocratic outcomes, the solution cannot simply be swapping out one leader for another, but it must involve a redesign of the system of government, so that governments can learn more effectively and become better coordinators of society's collective intelligence and capacity for change.

This suggestion that governments are out of step with modern realities is not a fanciful indictment by someone unfamiliar with the workings of government. It comes from none other than Canada's Clerk of the Privy

Council, Michael Wernick. In an interview published in the *Ottawa Citizen*[164] on the occasion of the presentation of the *Twenty-Third Annual Report to the Prime Minister on the Public Service of Canada*[165], he suggested that the federal public service was in much need of repair.

Not surprisingly, he described a public service that was *unproductive* ("loads of rules, bureaucracy and process that isn't productive"), that was *lacking in agility* (structures and processes that make it so difficult to "move dollars, people and information around, within and across departments"), that was somewhat *learning impaired* (hobbled by structures that make it too slow, rigid and risk-averse), and that was *worn out* ("we are too slow and not very nimble," and a public service workplace that is old, outdated and tired).

In his assessment, this problem did not rest with public servants *per se*, but with the many structures, processes and cultures of government that are no longer properly aligned to the realities of the day. Wernick identified two principal challenges for government: the escalating pace of change, including technological change, and the complexity of the issues being wrestled with.

In his view, the actions of governing are no longer solely in hands of government, and governance had become widely distributed in society among many institutions, organizations, and actors. This has led to governments not having all the knowledge, resources or power they need to realize their intents. Consequently, a significant amount of the leverage, time and resources that are required to make a difference, must be found external to government, and over which government has little or no control. "All the important issues facing Canada," Wernick said, "are multifaceted and require collaboration, and we have to get better working across silos internally. One of the real challenges ... is [the need for] a lot more space to collaborate and work with people outside the public service".

Yet despite his clarity on the nature of the problem, neither Wernick nor other senior leaders in the Canadian government, have ventured to question why the existing structures, processes and cultures of government were created in the first place, or whether the original rationales from over 150 years ago, still apply. Without such "back-to-basics" reflections, and with the passage of time, one can expect conventional political science wisdom and organizational inertia will eventually set in, immunizing yet again the

Chapter 4

bureaucrats, their political masters, as well as the governing arrangements, from any need for significant change.

Indeed, Wernick already seems to have "discovered" the culprits of the current maladaptation: mental stress and mental illness among the existing federal public servants, on the one hand, and an inability to entice youthful new leaders more successfully into the public service, on the other. Consequently, he has put dealing with them among his top priorities[166]—hinting that, in his view, these are the only sources of the government's misalignments.

Such a narrow focus on mental illness and HR is difficult to understand in the light of the significant list of systemic flaws and failures that are mentioned in the body of Wernick's report. However, this focus will not significantly challenge or imperil the status quo in any way. In terms of the old government paradigm—driven by leadership, management, and the optics of decision-making—these are doable, uncontroversial fixes.

In a recent book[167], *Intelligent Governance*, which I co-authored with awarding-winning author and economist, Gilles Paquet, we made the case that much more fundamental repairs are required if the Canadian public service, and governments, generally, want to retain their social licence in the long term. And those repairs must begin with a revamping of the paradigm that guides both the structures and processes of governments. It is this governmental paradigm that determines which processes are appropriate, and then which tools and structures would be needed to support them.

The next chapter explores what happens when the evolution of society outpaces its governing institutions and its tools of governance, and society fails to address this need for government reinvention.

111

Chapter 5
The Paradox of Populism and the Erosion of Democracy

When traditional democratic governments are repeatedly overwhelmed and technology creates as many problems as it solves, how are people to respond when they see their lot in life declining or at least not meeting their expectations? For an increasing number of people, the uncertainties of democracy may be set aside if some aspiring 'white knight' comes along with any plausible tale of how certainty can be re-established, how 'bad' people can be made to pay for the current malaise, and everything can be returned to the 'golden days'. Yes, I'm referring to the plague of populists that are popping up everywhere.

These days, it seems like we are never very far from discussions about populists, populism and various anti-establishment movements. Several Western democracies, including the US and the Philippines, and several autocratic regimes, like Venezuela and Russia, are clearly being driven by these appeals to populism. And many more countries, like the UK, Italy, France and the Netherlands, seem to be flirting with it.

On the one hand, some people celebrate the rise of populism as a great rebirth of democracy, while others decry it as a downward slide into authoritarianism —fascism, even. But how can one concept generate such polar opposite views?

What is equally strange is that the person at the centre of these populist movements, the "man of the people," is usually a member of the country's social elite, that same "elite" that the populists say they are targeting, and frequently a member of a political dynasty. Even stranger is that once in power, this "man of the people" commonly sets about dismantling the democratic institutions initially set up to protect the people from the centralization of power, while simultaneously making the political environment more favourable to the very elites he was supposed to take down.

For instance, the Trump administration's tax 'reform' bill introduced a tax plan that focussed on cutting business tax rates from a rarely paid 35% to 15%, while adding a "pass-through" provision that would allow wealthy individuals to pay the lowered corporate rate*. The plan would also eliminate the alternative minimum tax, or AMT, that was established to ensure that the very wealthy are not able to use legal loopholes to avoid paying taxes altogether. Far from being "a man of the people," populist leaders like Trump tend to manipulate the system, not only to the benefit their *über* rich peers, but, as one analyst has pointed out[168], to benefit themselves personally, often in flagrant defiance of conflict of interest rules.

Ultimately, what should be even more concerning is the tendency for populist leaders to centralize power in themselves, as the only person capable of divining and responding to the interests of the "common people." Says populist Nigel Farage of the UK Independence Party, "Real power in the modern day resides ever more 'massively' in *personalities*, not formal titles. What keeps it alive is the *charisma* of those who possess it, their ability to rally the masses and to make deals and connections *as expediency dictates*."[169]

In other words, governing power must rest with commanding individuals—and not with democratic institutions, like the judiciary or elected representatives, or with distributed bodies, like the citizenry. Unlike the traditions of democracies for the last century, for the populists, the institutions of government exist to represent a leader, not the body politic. While the populists tend to present democracy in only the thinnest of veils, their actions more accurately reflect autocracy, pure and simple. Yet significant

---

* US President Trump is said to have used roughly 500 such "pass-through" arrangements in his income tax.

numbers of voters in ostensibly democratic countries support these populist options. The question is why?

What do we mean by populism?

Theoretically, populism is a democratic doctrine that claims average people are being exploited by a privileged "elite," and it professes to correct this social imbalance by taking power away from those "elites" and empowering someone to champion the "little man" against the corrupted influences of established politicians in the pocket of the rich and powerful.

Despite this "Robin Hood" veneer, populism is nevertheless a doctrine that has repeatedly proven to be driven by envy and a willingness to seek violence against those perceived as being different. It tends to be guided by a less-than-critical belief in a charismatic leader, who is thought to be alone in his understanding of the problems faced by the common masses, and who it is believed can act decisively to make things better for them, by utilizing his "special" knowledge and moral authority, against the "self-serving" elites.

Notwithstanding its democratic veil, populism has historically tended towards authoritarianism and autocracy. Not that it can't remain democratic, it's just that it rarely is. For it to be truly democratic, it would need to empower citizens, both as individual and collective owners of their democracy, instead of consistently encouraging the abdication of their ownership rights as citizens in favour of the "great man."

In the same spirit, it would obviously also need to foster the use of effective tools for collective learning and collaboration in order to permit citizens to work better together, instead of participating in some form of mob action. Yet more commonly, populism expresses itself in herd mentalities or in the forceful rule of demagogic leaders.

Populism has repeatedly surfaced when the mainstream governing institutions begin to be perceived as failing the interests of everyday citizens. Populism plays heavily on people's fear of change, of difference, or of "the other," while often exacerbating those very fears through the promotion of intimidation or violence against "the others."

Interestingly, these "others" often gain social prominence when societies have been relatively successful in dealing with both their internal conflicts and their capacity for social innovation. Consequently, people inevitably find themselves reaching out and connecting to other communities, other peoples, and other areas of the world in ways that are initially meant to enhance social wellbeing further. The very success of a society encourages social diversity, but at some point that added diversity begins to challenge the very institutions that contributed to society's success in the first place.

For instance, economic prosperity attracts migrants and new talent. Restricting this can cause economic stagnation but immigration nevertheless adds to competition in the labour market, which may mean I lose my job. If educational and training supports are not properly designed to help me adapt, I may find my quality of life declining. As a result, I may blame either immigrants (caused by economic success) or elites (caused by bureaucratic maladaptation). In the end, the added complexity causes some citizens to lose confidence in their social institutions, and to retreat into the arms of demagogues and autocrats who make promises of returning to some sort of fanciful good ol' days.

It is here, with its frequent association with snake-oil demagogues, that populism seems to generate the most hostility. In response to legitimate citizen concerns about increasing diversity and uncertainty, these self-promoted "saviours" invariably promise a return to certainty and predictability by exploiting the prejudices and ignorance of citizens, while simultaneously shutting down rational conversations and fora for social cooperation.

A frequent key goal of these demagogues is to overturn established norms of political and social behaviour—customs that have been built up over long periods of time in order to reduce the internal conflicts in society—often in the guise of attacking the "elites," while freeing themselves from any civil constraint on their own actions.

In the past, populist political parties fed on public perceptions that wealth was unequally distributed due to cronyism, nepotism, insider trading, or group affiliations, and that the masses needed to take back what was rightfully theirs. Today, however, "the electoral success of these [populist] parties . . . can be attributed mainly to their ideological and issue appeals to traditional values," write Inglehart and Norris[170]. "The rise of populist parties reflects, above all, a reaction against a wide range of rapid, cultural changes that seem to be eroding the basic values and customs of Western societies … The net result is that Western societies face more unpredictable contests, anti-establishment populist challenges to the legitimacy of liberal democracy, and potential disruptions to long-established patterns of [political] party competition." This rise is illustrated in **Figure 7**.

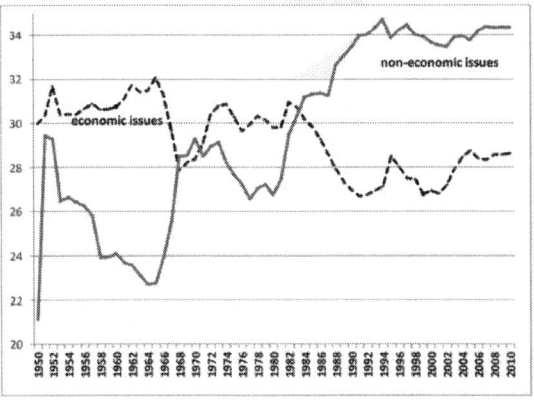

Notes: Scores on the vertical axis are calculated by counting the number of economic issues, and non-economic issues mentioned in each party's electoral manifesto for the most recent election, weighted by each party's share of the vote in that election, giving equal weight to each country.

Source: Party Manifestos data from Austria, Belgium, Canada, Denmark, France, Germany, Ireland, Italy, Netherlands, Norway, Sweden, Switzerland and United States, in Zakharov (2013).

Figure 7: Rising salience of non-economic issues in the party manifestos of thirteen Western Democracies 1950-2010

Thus, populism begins with a dissatisfaction with the status quo, a feeling that the game is somehow rigged against you despite your best efforts, and a sense that some group is manipulating the system for their own benefit. According to researchers using the European Social Survey data from 2002 to 2014, the growth in populism is associated with the growth of four key cultural values: authoritarianism, mistrust of global national governance, anti-immigrant sentiment, and right-wing ideological self-placement[171]. Richard Florida concurs, saying that populism is not, as it once was, about economics. "It is about racism, sexism, homophobia, and cultural backwardness. It is revenge—not of the economically insecure, but of the cultural left-behinds."[172]

Without a clear countervailing notion, people tend to fear the uncertainty associated with these kinds of changes. But rather than increase the public's capacity to adapt to change—say, through education, public dialogue, or improved public services—populism reinforces their lack of adaptive capacity and encourages their dependence on con men masquerading as "saviours" to make things right.

The role of the "great leader" is as someone skilled in reinforcing people's fears and capturing their imaginations about who's to blame and why. The "great leader" claims a special status because no one knows things quite like he does (according to him), and because he's so special, he can deliver on promises to turn things around for the masses one way or another. In the end, it doesn't matter whether what he says is true or not. It's enough that what he says aligns with people's fears and is sufficiently plausible that people can easily imagine that he could make the desired difference if what he says were true.

It is at this point that people uncritically abdicate their ownership of their communities and their nation, and surrender it to someone who can spin a good tale—regardless of its veracity. The well-established cultural narrative that "someone must be in charge," together with a fear of the unknown, conspire to rob people of their basic rights of citizenship. "Claiming to speak for 'the people,'" says Ken Roth of Human Rights Watch, "they treat [human and citizen] rights as an impediment to their conception of the majority will, a needless obstacle to defending the nation from perceived threats and evils."[173]

Once citizens accept to move down this path, the next step of populism is to identify the "enemy of the people"—the group on whose shoulders all the perceived shortcomings, slights, disappointments, and offences in life can be blamed. This form of populism reinforces the deep psychological conviction that all the inadequacies in my life are not my fault. They are the fault of these "others." To get my life back I must change them—not myself. It's a view that fosters envy, incites anger, and ends in vengeance. And it's a vengeance that those who feel somehow slighted can now rightfully and legitimately participate in due to the egging on of the "great leader," as Trump frequently did in his campaign speeches.

Chapter 5

If all that matters are the declared interests of the majority, the thinking seems to go, why not embrace the autocrat who shows no qualms about asserting his "majoritarian" vision—no matter how self-serving it may be—and subjugating all those who disagree? Doesn't democracy say majority rules?

Illustrations

Although there are many populist and would-be populist leaders worldwide, four currently stand out—either because of the degree of their national excesses, or their potential to destabilize large regions of the world—President Donald Trump of the USA, President Recep Erdoğan of Turkey, President Rodrigo Duterte of the Philippines, and President Vladimir Putin of Russia.

Donald Trump (the Needy Narcissist)

The last decade has not been good for many Americans. First there was the crash of the financial sector leading to the Great Recession, then the non recovery, then the hollowing out of the US manufacturing sector, and the recurring stories of corruption in both business and political elites. Americans were also confronted with growing numbers of "others"—immigrants (both legal and illegal), Muslims, non-Europeans, terrorists—who challenged their values and their sense of identity.

In response, Americans have increasingly embraced authoritarianism[174] in their outlook as a mechanism to deal with their fears and uncertainties. "The extreme nature of authoritarians' fears, and their desire to challenge threats with force, would [ultimately] lead them toward a candidate whose temperament was totally unlike anything seen in American politics—and whose policies went far beyond the acceptable norms. A candidate like Donald Trump."[175]

Trump was originally a realtor, promoter and reality TV star, and as the wild card in the 2016 US presidential election, he ran on an anti-elite platform typified by his "drain the swamp" language. He stereotyped migrants as threats, vilified refugees, dismissed multiple allegations of sexual assault, attacked the legitimacy of the judiciary, made disparaging remarks towards the disabled, categorized journalists as "enemies of the people," pledged to roll back women's rights, derided neighbours and allies, and cozied up to traditional US rivals. But it was his apparent willingness to address people's fears with force that allowed him to tap into a growing authoritarian mindset that spanned voters from all parties.

For instance, he painted all refugees as security risks even though few refugees are allowed to enter the US in comparison to other Western nations and those who are, are subjected to a much more extensive vetting process than those entering the US for business, education, or tourism. Trump promised to stop illegal immigration from Mexico by building a great wall, creating a great metaphor for how he will make Americans safe. He even toyed with reintroducing "enhanced interrogation techniques" (torture) like waterboarding, and practices of spying on US citizens, "if that's what people want," to demonstrate his willingness to get tough on threats.

Since becoming President in 2017, he has repeatedly presumed to be the privileged interpreter of what Americans desire, regardless of existing treaties or laws that were enacted to protect the rights and interests of all Americans, both at home and abroad. Twice he has tried to stop all travel into the US by people from several Muslim countries only to be rebuffed by the US justice system.

Yet for all of his apparent nativism and xenophobia, Trump appears to be a man without an agenda or ideology. He has no allegiance to his past promises, to his supporters, to historical allegiances, or to particular values. Says David Frum, former Republican speech writer for President George W. Bush, "Trump has scant interest in congressional Republicans' ideas, does not share their ideology, and cares little for their fate. He can—and would—break faith with them in an instant to further his own interests."[176]

He is a man without content, says David Auerbach, a mirror, willing to be whatever people want him to be at the moment as long as that inspires their adulation. "Trump's profound and sweeping ignorance of all things outside himself serves his narcissism; knowledge would only put constraints on his ability to be what people want him to be and what people will love him for"[177]. He is thus really just an attention-generating machine, devoid of any

Chapter 5

authentic political ideas, with no motive other than to dominate, and with no clear plan of action, other than the spectacle of himself. There is only "the Donald" as Americans came to know him on reality TV.

Trump's tendency to be self-serving is already evident, in his roll back of taxes for the rich, his disregard of conflict of interest rules, his commitment to ending Obamacare, his granting of ethics waivers for top White House staff, and his compromising financial ties to Russian banks. However, the more obvious challenge presented by Trump is his inherent unpredictability as the "most powerful man on the planet" and his willingness to turn his back on anyone, whenever it's convenient.

Not coincidentally, long-time and close US allies like the UK, Germany, France and Canada, after a year of Trump's unpredictable behaviour, have publicly recognized the risk of the trusting too much in such a volatile, unreliable person and are creating increasing distance between themselves and the US administration[178]. Whatever else Trump may be accomplishing, he is creating a nation alone.

Recep Tayyip Erdoğan (the Paternalistic Nationalist)

Turkey is a country that seems beset by problems. It exists on the edge of a Middle East that is perpetually in turmoil. It currently lives in the shadow of the Syrian civil war, with millions of refugees who have flooded across its borders. Various jihadists, anti-Syrian militias, and Kurdish militants are waging war from its territory either against Syria or against the Turkish government. Its citizens are divided between secular, religious and nationalist groups, and its population is ethnically divided between a majority of Turks and significant populations of Kurds, Alevis, Greeks, Armenians and Jews—not to mention three million Syrian refugees. This diversity is the context for Recep Erdoğan, President of Turkey.

When Erdoğan first came to power as Prime Minister in 2003, initially he did a lot of good. He fostered economic growth, he engaged in peace talks with the Kurdish PKK, he strengthened civil liberties, he tackled government corruption and he strengthened ties with the European Union. He also gave a voice to religious conservatives, who had been silenced under the previous military or quasi-military regimes for decades. Despite this, Turkey's economy, once a pillar of strength in the region, began to grow more slowly, plagued by cronyism, poor management, and a collapse of the tourist industry brought on by instability in the Middle East.

Against this challenging background, Erdoğan has shown increasing intolerance of his critics, and the very diverse voices that comprise Turkey's population. In February 2014, for instance, audio recordings appeared on YouTube[179] and were widely discussed in Turkish social media in which Erdoğan appeared to be part of the corruption that he had pledged to eliminate. He was heard instructing his son how to conceal very large amounts of money. In response to the ensuing public fallout, Turkey's Parliament, dominated by Erdoğan's party, quickly passed a bill that allowed the government to block all Internet sites and gain data access to all Internet traffic in the country. On March 20, Erdoğan promised to "rip out the roots" of Twitter[180].

Later, in the summer of 2016, elements of the Turkish army attempted a coup —ostensibly organised by supporters of Fethullah Gulen, a widely popular Turkish cleric, who was once a staunch ally of Erdoğan against the Turkish military, but who was now based in the US.

According to Erdoğan, supporters of Gulen had penetrated the Turkish bureaucracy, judiciary and the army in the tens of thousands and they were trying to destabilize the country. The coup failed mainly because Erdoğan took to the Internet to rally support, and rob the coup of popular support. While this response to the coup was cloaked in the guise of protecting Turkish democracy, Erdoğan took advantage of it to crush all opposition voices, whether or not they were those of the Gulenists.

Since the coup attempt, Erdoğan has governed Turkey under a state of emergency that has amounted to a blatant abuse of presidential power. His government has arrested over 50,000 people[181] and another 120,000 public servants[182] have been fired from their jobs—including teachers, journalists, police, judges, military, and politicians—only a fraction of whom were likely to have been involved in the coup.

In addition, some 1200 schools, 54 hospitals, 15 universities, and 195 media outlets have also been closed. Anyone, or any organization, that

Chapter 5

Erdoğan could imagine as a threat, has become vulnerable and subject to arrest, including:

- ordinary Turks who may have gone to Gulenist schools;
- people who simply saved their money in a Gulenist bank;
- Kurdish sympathizers; and even
- children who may have mocked Erdoğan on social media.

Under the cover of cleansing the Gulenists from government, Erdoğan has used popular support against the coup to restart the war with the Kurdish PKK, beginning with the firing of 12,000 Kurdish teachers, 24 Kurdish mayors and the arrest of the co-chairs of the Peoples' Democratic Party. In January 2018, Erdoğan decided to invade Syria to cleanse it of Kurdish forces who had been battling ISIS but who now posed a potential threat to Turkey since ISIS had been defeated.

Increasingly, Erdoğan's government is being compared to the phoney "democracies" of nationalists such as Viktor Orban of Hungary and Nicolas Maduro of Venezuela. In their model, elections are winner-take-all contests, with any democratic traditions or rules that may have governed the behaviour of elected winners in the past being deemed as obstacles to an elected government. In this anything-goes climate, the winning party also gains the right to subvert future elections and democratic institutions in their favour, including the manipulation of judiciary and the press to achieve their leaders' goals.

For instance, on 16 April 2017, 51.3% of Turks voted in a referendum to abandon their system of parliamentary democracy in favour of an executive presidency led by Erdoğan for whom there will be only minimal checks on his power from Turkey's Parliament. In effect, the populist backlash against the military has fashioned a democratically elected autocrat.

Within weeks of this vote, Erdoğan began a new round of arrests and firings. Now, however, with the popular acceptance that the repression of critics was legitimate, and with the independence of the Turkish courts and other democratic checks and balances destroyed, there is nothing in Erdoğan's way to appropriate further power to himself. "He says that only a strong president can galvanise the state, and see off its enemies. Naturally, he is talking about himself."[183] For Erdoğan, the State and he are one.

Rodrigo Duterte (the Saviour / Punisher)

Even among populists, President Rodrigo Duterte of the Philippines stands out, with his open calls for summary executions of suspected drug dealers and users—and even of the human rights activists who defend them.

Rodrigo Duterte, who served for almost 30 years as mayor of a remote provincial capital, Davao City, became President of the Philippines in June of 2016. In his election campaign, he swore that he would kill drug dealers across the nation, sparing nothing in the way of violent imagery. "If by chance that God will place me [*in the presidency*]," he promised, "watch out because the 1,000 [*people executed while he was a mayor*] will become 100,000. You will see the fish in Manila Bay getting fat. That is where I will dump you."[184]

As leader of the left-wing populist party, PDP–Laban, Duterte has praised Adolf Hitler's efficiency in mass murder, bragged about his sexual prowess, pondered why he wasn't the first to assault a raped woman, insulted the Pope for causing traffic delays, and boasted about personally executing three men—to name just a few of his controversial statements. After citing Hitler and the Holocaust, he said he would happily "slaughter" three million drug addicts.

As President, he continues to incite extra judicial killings and vigilante death squads. Duterte's death squads have been killing drug dealers, drug users and anyone who could be painted as such. The death toll in his war on drugs since he took office in June of 2016 had topped more than 2,500 killings by police and 3,600 by vigilantes. International agencies, including Amnesty International, have estimated that by January 2017 more than 7,000 had been killed, with more bodies continuing to pile up.

According to Amnesty, police are now paid "per hit" by their bosses. These under-the-table payments can be as much as $300 for each alleged drug offender they kill[185]. There are stories about *Oplan Tokhang* ("knock and

Chapter 5

plead" in a local dialect), that describe a police practice of arriving at the door of suspected drug users and asking suspects to surrender themselves. Many who did were later found dead. Many who refused were also found dead.[186]

"Human Rights Watch found that the official police reports of these incidents invariably asserted self-defense to justify police killings, contrary to eyewitness accounts that portray the killings as cold-blooded murders of unarmed drug suspects in custody. To bolster their claims, the police routinely planted guns, spent ammunition, and drug packets next to the victims' bodies. No one has been meaningfully investigated, let alone prosecuted, for these killings."[187]

> *"My order is shoot to kill you. I don't care about human rights, you better believe me." —Rodrigo Duterte, 6 August 2016*

But many Filipinos are willing to gloss over the killings as justifiable and Duterte's poll ratings remain high. "The streets are much safer now," many in the capital will tell you. "Here in the Philippines we need a ruler with an iron fist."[188]

That iron fist also falls upon Duterte's critics as well as on drug dealers. One such critic has been Senator Leila de Lima, who was arrested on drug trafficking charges in February 2017. De Lima chaired the Senate Justice and Human Rights committee investigating extrajudicial killings and had vigorously objected to Duterte's crackdown on suspected drug users and dealers. In a stunning allegation in 2017 by the pro-Duterte Speaker of the House, Pantaleon Alvarez, that stretched beyond credulity, the woman who was trying to hunt down corruption and drug crime—de Lima—was actually intimately enmeshed in it. Alvarez called her "the No. 1 drug lord in the whole Philippines."[189]

However, long before any arrests were announced, Duterte had vowed to destroy de Lima. She had spent almost a decade investigating allegations he was the leader of the Davao City death squads while he was mayor. In turn, he has persistently mocked and raged against whatever she said and did, but then she was a Senator and he was a mere Mayor. Now the tables had been turned.

Despite her arrest and jailing, de Lima has professed her innocence and vowed she would not be intimidated by a leader she calls a "serial killer." "I have no connection to the drug world except going after them," she said. "Suddenly, I am the Pablo Escobar of the Philippines? Jesus, where is the proof? They can look and look—they will find nothing."[190] She has seized every opportunity to criticize Duterte. "I will never accept the extrajudicial killings. I will never accept the violations of human rights," she said. "I won't be quiet."

In addition to Senator de Lima's detention, the regional director of Makati City's Bureau of Internal Revenue, the Philippines IRS, was found murdered on the street late last year. Next to him, envelopes of cash totaling more than US $7000 were left untouched, arguing against a simple robbery gone bad. Almost immediately after this apparent assassination, 90 employees of the internal revenue bureau resigned by official count. Unofficial estimates put the number over 300[191].

Around the same time, the Deputy Commissioner for the Bureau of Customs, Arturo "Art" Lachica, was ambushed by a gunman on his way home and died of multiple bullet wounds. Just days before his death, he vowed to eliminate corruption in government by being more transparent in its BOC's operations, but he had also been identified as a defendant in a corruption case[192]. Given that Duterte had also given *carte blanche* to kill corrupt officials, many suspect Lachica was another victim of an extra-judicial execution.

Duterte had warned of impending purges of corrupt officials in both bureaus —customs and tax. Duterte had cautioned that, even if there wasn't enough evidence, employees could be killed on technical grounds. He seemed to say that guilty employees should hope there was enough evidence to try them in court because; if not, they may just end up dead. He added: "If I am not able to present evidence in court, I can't put you in jail. I will kill you, so it's even. It will be hard that way."[193] Put another way, his indifference to evidence and the rule of law may be untenable, but he has also given free rein to people to kill any official they perceive as corrupt.[194]

Says Alexandra Wrage, founder the anti-corruption NGO TRACE, "when a government declares that it is acceptable to kill its citizens without due process or, really, any process, outrage should come easily, but the response in Manila was muted. Everyone agreed that they were experiencing fewer bribe demands by government officials. As with the killing of drug dealers and purported terrorists, there seems to be a vaguely regrettable sense that the killings should be stopped, *but perhaps not quite yet.*"[195]

In late May 2017, ISIS linked rebels began attacking people in Marawi, a mostly Muslim city of 200,000 people on the southern island of Mindanao. Almost immediately, Duterte declared martial law and threatened to expand it nationwide if need be. He has also suspended writ of *habeas corpus* to allow detention of people without lawful authority. However, it was his remarks suggesting that wherever martial law was declared, his soldiers could rape up to three women each and he would "take responsibility" for their actions that have drawn worldwide criticism[196].

Despite knowing about the Philippine President's controversial war on drugs, Trump had a brief phone call with Duterte in April 2017 wherein he commended his bloody war on drugs, according to a transcript obtained by the *Washington Post* and the *Intercept*. Said Trump, "I just wanted to congratulate you because I am hearing of the unbelievable job on the drug problem. Many countries have the problem, we have a problem, but what a great job you are doing and I just wanted to call and tell you that."[197] The US President has clearly bought into Duterte's superhero fantasy of being the "Punisher" of all those not in his favour. When the two met in Manila later in November 2017, Donald Trump hailed his "great relationship" with the Duterte[198].

Vladimir Putin (the Kleptocratic Tyrant)

Putin began his career in 1975 as an intelligence officer with the KGB, but after the fall of the Soviet Union he was appointed by Boris Yeltsin to head the FSB (Federal Security Bureau), the KGB's successor, and also as head of Yeltsin's Security Council. In August 1999 Yeltsin dismissed his prime minister, promoting Putin in his place.

Shortly thereafter, in September 1999, four Russian apartment buildings were blown up, killing 300 people. The Russian government quickly attributed the bombings to Chechen separatists and Putin was put in charge of a new war with Chechnya, gaining overnight fame as the "defender of the nation."

However, as David Satter, an American journalist living in Moscow at the time, writes, "Moscow had been awash with rumours, that a massive provocation was coming. But I became convinced that the bombings were a false-flag attack when a fifth, unexploded bomb was discovered on September 22 in the basement of a building in Ryazan, southeast of Moscow, and local police arrested three persons who turned out to be not Chechens—but agents of the FSB!"[199]

When Yeltsin resigned in December 1999, he appointed Putin as Acting President until official elections could be held. Putin was easily elected in early 2000 and then again in 2004. One of his first acts was to ensure that all charges of corruption against Yeltsin and his family would not be pursued. Similar corruption charges against Putin himself, involving $100 million of fraudulent sales of raw materials going back to when he was a member of the St. Petersburg city government, were thrown out in 2000 due to a "lack of evidence," or the disappearance of key witnesses like Marina Salye.

Due to term limits, Putin was forced to leave the presidency in 2008, but not before securing the presidency for his protégé, Dmitry Medvedev, for whom Putin then served as prime minster until 2012, when he was once again elected as Russia's president.

As President, Putin has presided over one of the world's most corrupt governments. Transparency International has estimated the annual cost of bribery in Russia at roughly $300 billion[200], an amount equal to one third of Russia's GDP, the entire GDP of Denmark, or thirty-seven times the $8 billion Russia spent in 2007 on "national priority projects" such as health care, education, and agriculture[201].

According to Karen Dawisha, a respected scholar of Russian politics at Miami University, the essential character of Putin's system of governance is colossal corruption of which he is a prime beneficiary. Not surprisingly, Putin is now considered the world's richest man with an estimated net worth of $200 billion[202] (more than twice that of Amazon CEO Jeff Bezos or Microsoft founder Bill Gates).

Chapter 5

The practices of Putin's kleptocracy are fairly typical of many criminal organizations, including: taking bribes from companies who seek business permits, accepting kickbacks from inflated no-bid government contracts, privatizing government assets to enrich associates, real estate scams, exporting raw materials purchased at state-subsidized prices and then illegally reselling them at much higher prices, money laundering, accepting "donations" from partners who wish to continue feeding at the government trough, election-fixing,; hidden offshore accounts, protected partnerships with the formal criminal underworld, and intimidation and even elimination of would-be whistle-blowers.[203]

To prosper within this system, Russia's oligarchs must above all else demonstrate absolute loyalty to Putin. The Kremlin's standard defence of Putin's authoritarian rule is that he is no worse than the West's increasingly troubled and corrupt governments or their human rights records[204]. But as several of Russia's billionaires have discovered, the punishment for defiance or exposing corrupt practices is imprisonment—or worse, assassination. Putin seems to be a modern embodiment of John Locke's classic assertion that, "where law ends, tyranny begins."[205] In Russia, Putin is the law.

The list of those assassinated is long, but recently it involved former Russian lawmaker Denis Voronenkov, who was shot dead in broad daylight on the streets of Kiev in March 2017 after fleeing Moscow for the Ukraine. The assassination carried the "obvious signature of Russian special services," according to Ukrainian President Petro Poroshenko. "Voronenkov was a key witness of Russian aggression against Ukraine."

Only a month before his assassination, Voronenkov said in an interview, "Americans should realize that Putin and his guys are convinced that he spins the planet with his feet like a soccer ball. The FSB cyber-forces are quite powerful globally. Now they do not just listen to you (they listened and recorded all my phone calls for eight years). They also attack other states."[206] A favoured strategy for silencing suspected troublemakers, he said, was to charge them with corruption in a system that is rampant with it.

For instance, after the Russian government "stole" the Yukos oil company in 2003 and imprisoned its founder, Mikhail Khodorkovsky, for 10 years, "Putin gave the entire team of General Feoktistov a green light to rob and persecute businessmen," according to Voronenkov. He also claimed that in 2014 the FSB simply took over businesses, jailing thousands of people for false economic crimes. Vornenkov expected a similar fate in jail awaited him. Alas, his prediction proved too optimistic.

Others besides Voronenkov and Khodorkovsky have met similar fates, including: Boris Nemtsov, formerly Deputy Prime Minister under Yeltsin, who was assassinated in 2015 within sight of the Kremlin; Vladimir Yevtushenkov, who was arrested in 2014 on suspicion of money-laundering (although charges were dropped after he gave up his stake in the Bashneft oil company to the state); Boris Berezovsky, a Russian media oligarch, who fled Russia for the UK but was assassinated in 2013; Sergei Magnitsky, a lawyer investigating tax fraud among the oligarchs was killed in 2009; Alexander Litvinenko, a former KGB anti-corruption officer who was poisoned by FSB agents in 2006; Paul Klebnikov, the former Russian editor of *Forbes* assassinated in 2004 for looking too closely into the 1999 bombings; and Sergei Yushenkov, an enigmatic member of Parliament and head of Liberal Russia, in 2003, presumably for being a Putin competitor.

The national press was one of Putin's first institutional victims; it took him only a year to assert control over the Russian media. Journalists, like Anna Politkovskaya, were assassinated. Unfortunately, she was but one of Russia's many famous journalists who were killed in 2006 (in all 82 journalists have been murdered in Russia since 1992, according to the Committee to Protect Journalists[207]). Critical media have been shut down, social media was overwhelmed by an "army" of internet trolls[208], and Russian-sponsored disinformation media were spawned and continue to flourish to this day.[209] Without the media to shine a light on the workings of government, both the electoral system and the judiciary were quietly dismantled.

"One of the autocrat's favourite falsehoods", says former Russian journalist Masha Gessen[210], "is the implied equivalency between civil resistance and insurgency, giving them free rein to violently suppress peaceful protests the world over." Furthermore, since beginning his last term as President, Putin has presided over a Russian economy that has been weakened by falling oil prices, a failure to diversify, and rampant corruption.

Chapter 5

For instance[211], when American businessman Bill Browder and his lawyer, Sergei Magnitsky, uncovered evidence of a huge $230 million corruption scandal and reported it to the Russian authorities, they were accused of tax evasion. Bowder was barred from re-entering Russia but Magnitsky was jailed and ultimately beaten to death in 2009. As it has turned out, Putin was the primary beneficiary of that corruption.

Fearful that popular discontent could once again spill over into the streets of Moscow as it did in 2011, Putin sought to pre-emptively silence his critics, jailing or assassinating opposition leaders and journalists, introducing restrictions on public assemblies and protests, and crippling civil society groups.

In parallel to these local restrictions, the Kremlin has also sought to bolster approval for Putin's autocracy by mobilizing public nationalism: first, in support of Russia's occupation of Crimea, which triggered European Union sanctions and only deepened Russia's economic decline, and then with the 2014 incursion into eastern Ukraine (an "uprising" inspired by Russian special forces), which among other things shot down Malaysian Airlines Flight 17 killing all 283 passengers.

More recently in Syria, Putin has backed Assad's slaughter of his own people, directing Russian bombers to add to the carnage. Each of these efforts has been spun by Russian propagandists as a way to counter the supposed moves of Western governments seeking to isolate and weaken Russia. The view that Russia is simply a victim defending itself is one that resonates widely in Russia.

Lately, Putin has been casting himself as a supporter of conservative Christian movements[212], nationalists, gay rights opponents, and of course anti-immigrant organizations. He's willing to lend support to any political movement—far right or far left, separatist or nationalist—as long as it disrupts the status quo between and within Western nations. Says Ronald Brownstein, "they [the populists] like his strength, what they perceive as defense for strong traditional values, nationalism, and opposition to Islam."[213] But, as Browder claimed before a recent US Senate hearing, "What you need to understand about the Russians is there is no ideology at all . . . Vladimir Putin is in the business of trying to create chaos everywhere."[214]

For instance, former White House senior advisor, Steve Bannon, has portrayed Putin as a champion of both nationalism and conservative cultural values. "One of the reasons [Putin is attractive]," Bannon said, "is that they believe that at least Putin is standing up for traditional institutions, and he's trying to do it in a form of nationalism—and I think that people, particularly in certain countries, want to see the sovereignty for their country, they want to see nationalism for their country."[215] Despite these comments, Bannon was careful to recognize that "Putin and his cronies [are] a kleptocracy, that they are really an imperialist power that wants to expand."

Gessen has noted an important similarity between Putin and US President Trump. For both men, she says *"Lying is the message.* It's not just that both Putin and Trump lie, it is that they lie in the same way and for the same purpose: blatantly, to assert power over truth itself."[216] For instance, in responding to several ongoing US investigations into Russia's interference in the 2016 US presidential election, and the reported back channel communications with Donald Trump's son-in-law, Putin now claims the hacking of the DNC is the result of American hackers (despite the clear evidence obtained by US intelligence agencies of Russian involvement).

The goal of Putin's statement, says EJ Dionne, is to deflect attention away from Trump and his dealings with the Russians, while providing something plausible for Trump supporters to believe in. Surprisingly, this seems to be working as 32% of Republicans still view Putin favourably[217]. "In the process, Russia is trying to spread fear among American politicians in both parties that if they dare criticize Putin's regime, as Clinton did when she was Secretary of State, they risk being attacked in the same way she was".

"I don't think we should underestimate the degree to which the undermining of the fabric of Western society is a fundamental aim of what Putin is all about," said Ivo Daalder[218], President Obama's former permanent representative to NATO and now president of the Chicago Council on Global Affairs. "We are in a very different time period that has far more to do with the 1920s and 1930s than it does with 2010. We are at a tipping point where the success of these [populist] movements raises fundamental questions about the [viability of the] international order we are living in."

Chapter 5

Pick any defining feature of populism, and you'll find it absurdly reflected in Putin. He is perceived to be *anti-elites*, yet he is ex-KGB with almost absolute power at home. He is the elite of the elites. He regularly presents himself as a *"man of the people,"* although he is also the wealthiest man on the planet due to his consistent plundering of his own citizens. He is viewed as a *strong leader* but his willingness to do anything—murder, assassination, even war— to get whatever he wants belies any sense of morality or duty to his followers. And he shares the populists *belief in the mob*—not the democratic notion of the rule of law, shared ownership, or collective learning across society—but the ability of one group to dominate all others, crushing any criticism or resistance along the way. Functioning democratic institutions are seen as obstacles by Putin precisely because they can protect the rights of all groups, and create a check on centralized power for the good of all. Yet despite these inconsistencies, Putin still seems to command a majority of support in Russia.

And like the populists on either the left and right, Putin desires to walk away from any form of collaboration, both nationally or internationally, seeing it as a personal constraint and producing unaccountable partnerships, trade agreements, and global institutions. Instead he favours the consolidation of power to a central authority (preferably himself). He has expressed commitment to democracy only so far as being elected, but afterward he has shown little regard for the pluralistic nature of society that is characteristic of Western democracies in which negotiation, compromise, learning, and rule of law all matter more than the decisiveness as of the leader.

During his campaign, Trump often repeated stories from Putin's disinformation media and spoke with a great deal of warmth about Mr. Putin. In a town hall meeting with NBC's Matt Lauer, for instance, Trump said[219] that he considers Putin a stronger leader than Barack Obama.

> *"If he says great things about me, I'm going to say great things about him. I've already said, he is really very much of a leader. I mean, you can say, 'Oh, isn't that a terrible thing'—the man has very strong control over a country,"* Trump said. *"Now, it's a very different system, and I don't happen to like the system.*

But certainly, in that system, he's been a leader, far more than our president has been a leader."

The costs of populism

Do these illustrations suggest populism is bad? I guess that depends on whether you feel afraid, whether you feel overwhelmed by change, whether you see the growing diversity in your life as a threat, whether you feel that the existing governing elites are not paying enough attention to your concerns, and whether you feel so disempowered and weak that only a strongman solution can protect you from the big bad world.

If that is how you feel, then populism may well be your thing. But know that it comes with significant costs. And . . . that it is not the only option you have.

Populism tends to undermine basic democratic institutions that have evolved to prevent the concentration of power in the hands of a few. It steals democratic ownership and surrenders it to people who tend to be autocrats and follow authoritarian forms of governing. In the end, it simply swaps out one elite for another, usually a more oppressive one. Populism tends to limit freedom, because the populists fear a pluralistic world and the need to cooperate with others. Therefore, it also tends to discourage social cooperation and increase inter-group conflict. It diminishes the value of human rights and it is willing to take vengeance on those critics who can be painted as "enemies of the people." Lastly, populism encourages simple responses to complex problems.

Immediate costs

Its immediate costs include:

- Reducing our existing problem-solving capacity and creating additional coordination problems—some of which may have already been addressed by established institutions, even if these solutions might be improved upon.

- Heightening inter-group conflicts between those who may form a majority of populism's supporters (but who nevertheless may be a minority of citizens) and the remainder of other citizens. It creates a destructive "us" vs. "them" mentality in the citizenry that invariably spirals negatively in terms of social cooperation.

- Increasing social instability and violence by legitimizing violence against others "not like us." By demonizing and de-humanizing the "others," populist regimes remove the fundamental civil restraints against targeting groups that have evolved in society over time. If these targeted groups then respond in kind in defence of themselves, it is presented as further evidence of the desire of "the others" to undermine society, thus justifying even more violence against them.

- Encouraging general economic decline by retreating from building a more fulfilling future by constraining innovation and entrepreneurship, falling into the fantasies of some bygone, golden era that never existed.

- Increasing economic inequality. In any authoritarian regime, the only "us" that matters are the people immediately connected to the regime. Its friends and family members will benefit immensely from the regime's corrupt practices and nepotism. The regime's supporters on the other hand, will just have to be satisfied with whatever they get, while the regime's critics will be lucky if they aren't jailed or worse. Far from bridging society's inequalities, populist regimes tend to exacerbate them.

Opportunity costs

Equally important for the future well-being of society are the opportunity costs that populism imposes on society. These include:

- Forgoing the opportunity for increased collective problem-solving capacity which would lead to increased prosperity and social well-being. Instead of reducing the costs to society of various complex problems, the "us-them" mentality encourages collective shirking behaviours and the move of problem costs onto "the others" as much as possible. The net social benefit becomes negative.

- Reducing the capacity for social innovation. Innovation occurs when more and different knowledge and experience, coupled with new resources and diverse powers come together to create more than the sum of the parts. Diversity is the key source of social innovation. Populism, almost by definition, works to reduce diversity, thus reducing the capacity for social innovation.

- Forgoing the opportunity to foster greater peace, stability and prosperity. When the diverse elements of a society come together to address an unacceptable status quo, the process of collaboration invites mutual understanding and respect, co-learning, sharing, and common benefit. These in turn increase the likelihood of successful adaptability, stability based on progress, and peace based on mutual interest. By turning their backs on diversity, populists forgo greater peace and stability for some imagined fantasies of the past.

- Populism encourages the avoidance of attending to the evolution of the institutions of governance in accordance with growing social complexity. Instead populism encourages a retreat to modes of governance that were already discarded, in the past to achieve the existing levels of socio-economic success.

- Moving forward on a truly global agenda of human development and possibility. If no one is, or can be, in charge, then the corollary is that everyone is. Therefore, to truly maximize social well-being and the possibilities for human life, all humanity should be involved. We need to develop human collective intelligence. Populism, by contrast, continually restricts social intelligence to small groups and individuals, thus ensuring that the full potential of social well-being is never realized.

It is understandable that people, frustrated by a perceived lack of progress in their lives and by a political elite that is either unable or unwilling to help, will gravitate to populists as a protest move against the "establishment." The populists usually support "cleaning the slate" candidates. But rather than empowering citizens in a broad collective enterprise and supporting their rights as democratic owners, the history of populism suggests that it steals ownership from them and encourages their dependence on demagogues and autocrats who represent a different, narrower elite.

The consistent messages of populist leaders are that "I am your voice," "I have all the answers," "I will take back what is rightfully yours," "I will punish the wicked and destroy all the barriers," "I will return certainty to you and make life like it once was," "Just trust me, I will make life better." Dissatisfied and disillusioned with the ineffectiveness or corruption of the status quo, many citizens can adopt a "what have we got to lose" mentality when faced with a choice between populist and establishment candidates.

Unfortunately, they often do have a lot to lose—first and foremost being the future of their democracy, let alone a sense of shared trust among themselves and their neighbours, and their collective capacity as a community to make a difference.

Whether populism is expressed as some form of a mob action, or as an appeal to some self-proclaimed "white knight," its primary effect is to erode democracy. As we have seen, this is happening today just at the moment when more democracy is what being called for.

It may be that the governance status quo is unacceptable, but the reason for this is generally that the complexity of society has outgrown the systems and institutions that have been put in place to guide it.* Those systems and institutions were not designed to address today's complex evolving problems or to operate on the basis of knowledge, resources and power being so widely distributed. Furthermore, these systems were not designed to promote effective collective learning, but instead relied on a handful of people who needed to be saints to make it work, rather than just being human.

Political leaders are not rewarded for fixing problems but for taking positions, positions which can and do change suddenly and regularly with the winds

---

* According to Reg Alcock, former President of Treasury Board Canada, for instance, the Canadian government's purchasing rules date back to 1841 (26 years before Canada was even formed) because governments are unwilling to trim the old rules, even while they continually add new ones.

of popular angst. Not to be too cynical, but the actual fixing of society's problems now lies completely outside the scope and abilities of our current model of politics. Nevertheless, we should not forget that we have come to this place because our governments have been somewhat successful in the organization of society. That said, what we have changed before, we can change again.

For instance, having been witness to the excesses and evils perpetrated by governments in WWII and in the Cold War, societies enshrined certain inalienable rights for themselves and agreed to a series of human rights treaties internationally in an attempt to deter future abuses. Protecting those rights was understood as a foundation for citizens to live in a free, safe, open and prosperous society. When governments committed to respecting human rights, they served all their people better by avoiding corruption, arbitrariness and the non-cooperation that so often accompanies autocratic rule. Those governments seemed better positioned to listen to their citizens, and to help them address their problems.[220]

While this understanding proved to be true—as evidenced by a historically unparalleled growth in both human population, technological innovation and global prosperity—it has also generated even more diversity, and new opportunities for social conflict. So much so that that the rights-based system is now regarded by some as a shield to hide behind for those in society wishing to do us harm. I submit this is an illustration of how we have outgrown our post-WWII institutions of social coordination. We now have to reimagine the future that we want together and then reinvent how we work together to achieve it, in order to build a better future for our children's tomorrow.

It is apparent that what is ultimately needed is not held by a few politicians (no matter how strong their interest and commitment to the public good is), but it is held in bits and pieces by many people and organizations—from many backgrounds and many places.

Most simply, what is needed is a way to access all that knowledge, all those resources, and all that collective power—to bring it all together and to apply it in ways that continually make our communities better. To do so will require some kind of platform that is open for all to participate in, but

Chapter 5

it will also require a willingness from citizens to contribute their bit out of a shared sense of ownership in a collective purpose and enterprise. Complex problems require complex solutions.

Populism, on the other hand, encourages overly simplistic responses. If climate change is too complex, deny it. If poverty is too chronic, blame the poor. If health care is destined to bankrupt governments, ignore it or cut it back for those in need. If crime seems too scary, slap on mandatory minimums and hide the convicted out of sight. If the economy is on life support, blame anyone and everyone but make sure you and yours are protected at least. If the press becomes too critical, target them as an "enemy of the people." Some well-funded Trump supporters have spoken of recruiting a "troll" army, explicitly modelled on those used by Erdoğan and Putin, to dominate the social-media space, intimidating critics and overwhelming others through a fog of nastiness, threats and misinformation[221].

For populist leaders, if people feel insecure, make them feel more insecure—all the better to increase their reliance on you. Tell them there is a clear and identifiable foe, and then just let people vent their fears on "the others" rather than on you.

In the end, all of these authoritarian strategies have the effect of making people feel less confident of their ability to make a difference, less self-sufficient, and of fostering greater dependence on the "great leader."

At this point in time, society in most developed nations has evolved to a point where democracy can no longer remain as a pseudo-monarchist practice involving only periodic interventions by the citizenry. It needs the collective knowledge, resources and power of all of its citizens in an ongoing way in order to make any serious headway on a host of social issues.

However, instead of fostering collective intelligence, populism fosters collective stupidity, defined as harming oneself by one's own actions, or causing losses to others, while deriving no personal gain or possibly even incurring losses yourself.

Most importantly, populism distracts from the bigger issue of evolving better, more complex public institutions to guide and support even greater degrees of prosperity and human welfare.

Responding to the populists

As Venezuelan economist Andrés Miguel Rondón wrote in the *Washington Post*[222] in January of 2017, the biggest challenge in dealing with populists is in proving that you belong to the same tribe that they do—that you are just like them. "The problem," he says, "is not the message but the messenger. It's not that [a populist's] supporters are too stupid to see right from wrong, it's that you're more valuable to them as an enemy than as a compatriot."

In Venezuela, he said, "it took opposition leaders 10 years to figure out that they needed to actually go to the slums and the countryside. Not for a speech or a rally, but for a game of dominoes or to dance salsa—to show they were Venezuelans, too, that they weren't just dour scolds and could hit a baseball, or tell a joke that landed."

Rondón's advice to anti-populists: show concern, not contempt, for the real wounds experienced by those who brought the populists to power, and by all means, be patient with democracy.

10 responses to populists

Since populism reflects a level of desperation at dealing with a complex social "system" as it is, an obvious alternative way of dealing with it is to make the "system" better by learning how to work more effectively with others—just as many community collaboratives and partnerships have learned to do over time.

In this way, what might at first seem like an insurmountable problem to one person becomes a doable exercise in the context of cooperation among multiple stakeholders. In this way, citizens don't have to relinquish their ownership in society to anyone or surrender their belief that they can make a difference. They can continually re-affirm it through their actions with others.

The following are ten conversations that could be fostered in any community that would have the effect of strengthening that sense of shared ownership, mutual interdependence, trust and cooperation. They are also likely to encourage more effective problem-solving and social innovation.

1. Reduce people's fear of "the other" / of difference, and highlight their commonalities

Ask, what are the things that people have in common—kids, families, parents, communities, desires for safety and security, opportunities for prosperity and well-being, etc.?

Make the work personal. You need to shift from the abstract notion of working with groups or organizations and recognize that you are working with friends, neighbours, concerned citizens—people just like you.

2. Strengthen your collective purpose

Where are the points of your respective dissatisfaction? Are these due to changes in the environment, in collective culture, or to changes in the institutions? What is it that needs to change?

Regardless of past or present, what is the shared possibility that you can all identify for yourselves and for your families? Leave the past in the past. The future is the only thing you can change.

Who needs to be involved in this shift? What can they contribute? What do they need in return?

3. Strengthen individual sense of ownership in collective endeavour

How are people contributing to the status quo by their actions or inactions? This, in reality, is the only thing that people ever have power to change—themselves. Yet no matter how small this personal change may seem, collectively it can amount to a powerful force for transformation.

What tangible and intangible resources do you and your partners have or have access to?

Everybody knows that owners act differently than renters. As a citizen you are a part owner. Remember that owners, just like you, need to care and take responsibility for what they own.

4. Target the ability of people to work together not the elimination of their differences

Differences are not a problem to be overcome. They are an asset to be built upon. Show how the inclusion of differences can create the possibility you desire.

Different perspectives create a more comprehensive understanding of reality. As a result, they help generate more effective responses.

To change the status quo you need people who want and have the power and resources to make change, who have knowledge to contribute, who will be affected by any change, and also those who have the power to stop change. You cannot make a significant impact without all of these contributions. So how will you include them?

5. Make more democracy not less

Neither centralized leadership nor diffuse markets are effective at solving complex problems[223]. Top-down, centralized leadership doesn't entertain different perspectives well and has limited capacity to learn. Markets, on the other hand, tend to homogenize diverse inputs limiting their value. Democracy embraces diversity, manages the conflicts that arise from them, and generates the creative responses that can be sufficiently complex because they are more than the sum of their parts. Therefore, protect democracy and find ways to make it stronger, more inclusive and effective.

6. Minimize the influence of leaders

In situations where complexity dominates and significant uncertainty and unpredictability exist, leadership is antithetical and unproductive. Leaders are the ones with the answers, they are the ones in charge, they have the power to compel others to fall in line, and they have all the resources they need to do the job.

Where issues are complex, just the opposite is true: leaders don't have all the knowledge, the resources or power to achieve their goals. Those elements are distributed among many people and organizations. Gaining access to that distributed knowledge, resources and power will not be the result of compulsion but persuasion and a willingness to cooperate. In general, leaders are not good at this.

7. Foster stewardship

For groups to work together, they need to develop the capacities for coming together, facilitation, the sharing of experiences, the understanding of their mutual dependence, co-learning, collaboration, and trust building. This is the role of stewardship not leadership.

Furthermore, stewardship processes should be created that are not dependent on personalities. Groups should make use of inquiring systems, heuristics, and other social mechanisms to simultaneously foster democratic diversity and to reduce the natural tendency for that diversity to generate unresolvable conflicts and obstructions.

Foster collective learning and experimentation to make progress on complex issues. Answers only tell you what you already know, which is already insufficient when you have decided to deal with complex problems through collaboration. Questions, on the other hand, open the door to new possibilities, especially in the context of a diverse audience. Make time to ask lots of questions.

8. Increase transparency

In any shared endeavour, people need to be confident of their progress together, that it is real, and that they are not being taken advantage of by their partners in the process. This means being open and transparent with both collaborators and the public. This openness also adds the possibility that over time, others can join in and contribute additional knowledge, resources and power that may not have been initially considered, but may be nonetheless essential for your collective success.

9. Showcase instances of social innovation when people work successfully together in collaboration

Don't take all the credit. Be generous and give credit unreservedly to those who are willing to cooperate. If your own contribution is valued, let others speak to it.

Publicly celebrate your steps of progress and use them as validation both of your work and of your commitments to each other.

10. Don't be too willing to discard the democratic institutions that have brought us so far. Think about how to make them better.

Why do we have certain institutions? What gave rise to them? Why did people choose those institutions? Are the current conditions the same? How have they changed? Are there new ways of accomplishing the same things?

Attachment to tradition simply because "we've always done that" is dangerous in that it erodes the legitimacy of the very institutions you may trying to support. While the notion of representative democracy, for instance, may be outdated as originally conceived, a regional or national forum for the discussion of issues and to foster collective learning (as opposed to imposing answers) may not be such a bad thing. Neither the retention or reinvention of governance processes are automatically bad in themselves. Our reimagining process should consider to what end are they to be used, are there better tools and processes that are available to us today, and how will we know if we are successful?

Chapter 6
The Emerging Dimensions of a Government Reimagined[224]

> *"There's good reason to think that democracy is better suited than either hierarchies or markets to solving certain kinds of complex problems. To solve these problems, you need to bring people with many diverse points of view (each of which can capture different facets of the problem) into contact with one another so that they can argue about solutions and determine the better ones."*
>
> —Henry Farrell[225]

Let's summarize what we've learned so far in examining the challenges being faced by governments today.

The problems faced by governments are increasingly complex. They have no simple answers. No one is in control—nor can they be. Instead of selecting from a menu of fully crafted "expert" solutions and trying to implement them regardless of their practicality, there is a need to follow a path of continuous experimentation to constantly get closer to the social possibilities we desire.

The original rationales for representative democracy that gave rise to the current structures of government no longer exist. Citizens are well educated, they have access to almost all knowledge through the Internet, they can connect with each other, and even share resources. Top-down, siloed, hierarchical governments have proven to be far too slow, ineffective and lacking in innovation to deal with modern challenges. The institutions that were structured on this top-down model are quite incapable of dealing with the levels of diversity and complexity that present themselves in modern life. Without transforming those institutions, one must consider reducing the level of diversity and complexity in society. This is a guaranteed recipe for social violence and reduced social well-being. Yet this seems to be the strategy of the populists.

Leaders and leadership have become generally mistrusted, perceived by citizens either as ineffective or unethical or both. There is a growing perception that regardless of which elite leads them, the systems of government are not meeting the needs of the people.

In today's context, there are many pressing social needs that demand that we find ways for multiple parties to work together collaboratively. Leadership is particularly ineffective—antithetical even—when trying to instill cooperation among many diverse people, all of whom have only partial knowledge, resources and power to enact change and who are working together only by choice. However, governments are not good at facilitating cooperation. Their *modus operandi* remains control.

We place leaders in roles to control, when what is required is the capacity to bring people together to facilitate their collective learning and collaboration. Yet democracy—*"rule by the people"*—together with a strong shared commitment to the collective ownership of the nation, region or community, remains the best mechanism to coordinate in complex social environments.

While it has always seemed easy in a democracy to swap leaders in the hope of seeing real change, the more difficult problem today is that our democratic governance system itself is out of sync with the realities of the day and must ultimately change.

Chapter 6

What makes this especially difficult is that governments are generally not designed with the frameworks, tools or skills to be effective collaborators. The old mechanisms of political parties, centralization, elected "representatives," episodic elections and hierarchical government no longer work. Despite the need to tap into more of the knowledge, resources and power that citizens possess, governments are not designed to *"let citizens in."* They are not designed to have citizens as participants in their own co-governance beyond periodic voting. In practice, governments have evolved into forums that have become hyper-partisan and dangerously competitive and that are good at only two things: blaming others and avoiding blame in a politically charged environment.

The unwavering commitment of governments to uncritically tie themselves to this tradition is shackling their capacity to adapt to the complex needs of modern society. Not only does this system stifle social innovation, but it also encourages strongman-type responses to the persistent coordination failures exhibited by existing democratic institutions. Growing numbers of citizens see government as so perpetually ineffective or unethical, so illegitimate that they are willing to embrace change—any change—even when it comes in the form of noxious, old-style, authoritarian governments that bring to mind many of the great social tragedies of the past. "What have we got to lose?" they say.

Fortunately, there are other options that may unfold if government cannot or will not change. For instance, government may just become irrelevant in the minds of citizens in comparison to the many emerging technological solutions —from the blockchain to artificial intelligence. These technologies have the potential to simply replace the need for governments altogether in the provision of social coordination. Yet in doing so, would we ultimately risk losing our "humanness" if we relinquished coordination to some technology or artificial intelligence?

Without a doubt, the differences generated in a creative, prosperous society will continue to grow, resulting in increasing pressures towards social conflict if left unattended to. However, if we can match that new levels of social diversity with similar levels of diversity and complexity in our coordinating mechanisms like government, then there is also the possibility of growing the well-being of society further.

In response to the current and emerging challenges, we must be willing and free to re-imagine and reinvent our systems of government with the tools and capacities that we have on hand today and not simply recycle the old mindsets, tools and capacities from yesteryear.

In analyzing these challenges, I suggest that there are five metanoia, or mental shifts, that will likely prove crucial in transforming government:

- recognizing that no one's in charge;
- moving from systems of leadership and control, to systems of stewardship and shared ownership;
- focusing on scalable learning over scalable efficiency;
- redesigning government around collaboration; and
- generating stewardship from process design.

No one's in charge

In a world where partnership and collaboration are increasingly demanded, the very concept of leadership is now problematic. Our obsession with the need for someone to be in charge presents one of society's biggest obstacles to effective governance and government. Leaders resolutely proclaim to be in charge, when none can be. When what is needed is a capacity to ask questions, our leaders purport to have all the answers. When facilitation among peers is required, leaders compete to command. When power must be shared, leaders instinctively try to impose their power. When distributed governance is the only option, leaders fight for control.

When it is greater cooperation and collaboration that is required, having someone in charge no longer matters—except in a negative sense. On the other hand, the ability to help people discover how to work together does matter—a lot. That role must be more supportive than commanding, more fostering of positive relationships, and more facilitative of effective learning than imposing answers, so that each partner gets what they need in order to continue the process of working together. This, however, is not how leaders work.

Cleveland once defined "leadership" as "bringing people together to make something different happen."[226] Notice the absence of any sense of control in his definition. In fact, leadership is a simple social mechanism to facilitate coordination and cooperation among the elements of a relatively uniform community (**Figure 8**). Communities form in response to the belief that more value can be obtained by working together than can be gained by working separately.

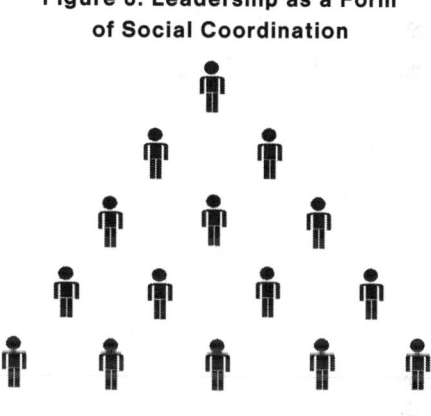

Figure 8: Leadership as a Form of Social Coordination

"In human organizations, coordination occurs because individuals influence each other's' behavior," notes Yaneer Bar-Yam[227], founder and president of MIT's New England Complex Systems Institute. "A control hierarchy is a mechanism designed to enable a single individual to control collective behaviour." The key issue which leadership is meant to solve, governance, is an attempt to coordinate the independent behaviors of many individuals into something more coherent, less conflictual and more productive.

Leadership is, therefore, a social device to help coordinate the productive activities of various community members, while mitigating the potential for conflict that inevitably comes with a variety of members. While leadership is a tool to "bring people together," it is most commonly used to command coordination among them, and to ultimately "lay down the law" should they not cooperate. And, it is so deeply rooted in our culture, that for many people it is just not possible to imagine community members cooperating on their own without a leader directing them. But, as we have seen, it is a cultural element that is already changing.

However, it is important to realize that leaders don't become leaders on their own. Leaders are created by followers[228]—no followers, no leader—and followers choose leaders* on the basis of:

1. their perceived "*ethicalness,*" that is, they are seen to operate for the collective good; and

2. their perceived "*effectiveness,*" that is, they are capable of coordinating various community actors in a value-adding way. The net collective benefit is therefore seen to increase with leadership.

While the notion of leadership has evolved over thousands of years, the concept most consistently associated with it is that leaders are always identified as being the people "in charge." Leaders have always told followers what to do, and followers have, well, just followed.

Yet in recent years, the notion of leadership has become increasingly more nuanced and varied—and a lot more confusing. We've heard about servant leadership, collaborative leadership, bureaucratic leadership, leadership by example, team leadership, democratic leadership, autocratic leadership, narcissistic leadership, facilitative leadership and many other types.

In fact, a quick scan of the *Harvard Business Review* yields over 8,000 leadership articles and over 50 different variations in leadership style (**Figure 9**). According to Barbara Kellerman, the founding director of the Kennedy School's Center for Public Leadership, our obsession with leadership has spawned an entire global industry, accounting for more than $50 billion annually—and that's just in terms of corporate training and development![229]

---

* That choice might be coerced, might stem from accepted tradition or bloodline, or it might be direct voluntary choice. But followers must agree to that choice.

Figure 9: A Plethora of Leadership Styles

Traditional: Leader as Cause		Leader as Catalyst
Functional	**Dysfunctional**	**Stewardship**
Expert leadership	Autocratic leadership	Servant leadership
Hierarchical leadership	Coercive leadership	Facilitative leadership
Bureaucratic leadership	Bully leadership	Team leadership
Authoritative leadership	Narcissistic leadership	Collaborative leadership
Elite leadership	Ideological leadership	Empowering leadership
Visionary leadership	Totalitarian leadership	Collective leadership
Decisive leadership	Pathological leadership	Participatory leadership
Delegative leadership	Despotic leadership	Relational leadership
Consultative leadership	Cult leadership	Emergent leadership
Laissez-faire leadership	Non-leadership follower	Authentic leadership
Transactional leadership		Partner leadership
Task-oriented leadership		Community leadership
Charismatic leadership		Action-oriented leadership
Leadership by example		Transformative leadership
Paternalistic leadership		Level 5 - Quiet - leadership
Romantic leadership		Learning leadership
Coaching leadership		Dialogic leadership
Political leadership		Boundary-
Efficient leadership		spanning leadership
Change-		
oriented leadership		
Goal-oriented leadership		
Executive leadership		
Leader as theorist		
Cross-cultural leadership		
Situational leadership		
Strategic leadership		
Adaptive leadership		
Exchange-style leadership		

So much has been written on the subject of leadership that whole sections of bookstores and libraries are dedicated to it, and, of course, our entire system of public sector governance is predicated upon it. Unfortunately, as the notion of "leadership" has evolved, and as the contexts in which it has been applied have changed and multiplied, the whole idea has become so unwieldy that it is no longer a helpful term to determine what someone actually means when they use it.

Mostly though, what generally falls under the rubric of "leadership" involves taking charge, imposing, managing, dominating, being in control, providing answers, finding fault, persuading, correcting, punishing, rewarding, or inciting fear. Even among charismatic and romanticized leaders, it is the will of the leader that ultimately prevails, albeit readily, over the will of followers.

To wit, over time leadership has traditionally been expressed in terms of the *"leader as cause"*,[230] the *"great man"* theory,[231] the person at the top of the hierarchy, the master chess player directing (or manipulating) a collective game in which others play the role of pawns, inconsequential tools to be used or discarded at the leader's discretion. Leaders are *"in charge,"* because it is believed that everything flows from them.

Unfortunately, this concept is highly patriarchal and, at worst, it has been (and still is) responsible for some of the most unpleasant excesses in both organizations and in human *"civilization."* Nevertheless, over the last forty years, leadership has wormed its way into every discipline, every industry, every government and every not-for-profit institution. Leadership is now widely regarded as the principal path to achievement, influence, wealth and power. Today one cannot gain stature in any career without first being regarded as a *"leader"*—no matter what one's professional or technical expertise might be.

Yet despite our cultural attachment to it, the idea today that one person can be in charge of any kind of complex, human organization is fast falling into disrepute. Despite the immense sums being spent on leadership training, there is no real evidence that it has made much of a difference. "We are no more capable today of making good leaders, or reducing the effects of bad leaders, than we were forty years ago," says Kellerman.[232] "Leadership," says the former Auditor General of Canada, Denis Desautel, "has essentially become a game without a master."[233]

"Large corporations are vast and complex entities with customs and attitudes that are hard for any one leader to change. So why," asks Justin Fox of Time Business, "do we [still] talk as if the CEOs are truly in charge?"[234] Or as economist Tim Harford observes, "I see . . . people who, in the face of an incredibly complicated world, are nevertheless absolutely convinced that they understand the way that the world works."[235] Kellerman is even more blunt about it: "The leadership industry is a fraud."[236]

However, the failure of leadership is not simply because of a failure to produce enough good leaders. On the contrary, says Brooks, it's because the entire "leadership class" is being exposed as ineffective or "fundamentally self-dealing."[237] The incessant "corporate scandals and the recent worldwide financial catastrophes [have shaken] the cult of the heroic CEO to its foundations."[238] The problem with leadership is not simply the presence of bad leaders, implying that all we need do is replace a few bad apples with a few good ones. The bigger problem, especially for government, is the growing perception that leaders generally are incapable of coordinating a complex society, either because they are seen as unethical, or ineffective, or both.

The increasing complexity of society resulting from the growth of knowledge, technology, and connectivity has meant that the interactions among the diverse elements of humanity have far outpaced the ability of any single person, or even a small group of people, to understand or control collective action. "The machinery of government," says Savoie, "has not been adapted to the complexity of today's society and the requirements of the modern economy."[239]

Nevertheless, in our Western system of representative democracy, we still choose to believe (against obvious evidence) that a single person, a leader, can be in charge and make decisions for everyone, while remaining somehow Solomon-like—that is, wise, fair, open and honest. Our systems of government have all been designed around this premise of leadership. But since no one today has all the knowledge, resources or power to effectively problem solve on behalf of all citizens, no one can be considered to be in charge or be an effective leader.

As a result, many in government have simply abdicated their responsibility to solve social problems in favour of taking positions which help them obtain and retain power. Our institutional systems, which were once structured around holding leaders to account for when they were in charge (a reaction to self-serving monarchs and tyrants), now completely fail in this regard. Furthermore, in many instances the role of the leader itself is now so greatly diminished that it is has become not much more than a brand image, a mascot, a celebrity endorsement, a publicity stunt, or a focus of entertainment[240] instead of a rallying point for society.

In the media, for instance, we hear the unrelentingly message that *"specific leaders are the problem."* While this gets public attention, much like a reality TV show, and it sells advertising and party memberships, it is a huge, oversimplification. Furthermore, the constant repetition of this narrative underscores the perception in the public that all leaders, any leader, can't be trusted. "Nearly every pillar of American society has revealed itself to be corrupt, incompetent or both," says *Time* magazine[241]. This is not a strictly a corporate trend, nor has it been solely an American trend, as evidenced by the MP expense scandal that wreaked havoc on the UK Parliament in 2009,[242] or the rejection of those in the UK government that was implied by the popular support for Britain's exit from the EU.

This loss of trust in democratic leaders has become so generalized that a whole generation of young people around the world have "become more cynical about the value of democracy as a political system," according to a recent Harvard study[243]. They are "less hopeful that anything they do might influence public policy, and more willing to express support for authoritarian alternatives." Few things, in my mind, reflect such a striking condemnation of both current leaders and our systems of government as the fact that the future is giving up on them.

Despite its warm and fuzzy international reputation, Canada has not been immune to this trend. In recent years, we have witnessed what at times appeared to be an endless parade of federal, provincial and municipal leaders through the justice system, accused of ethical violations or outright criminal behaviour. Four Senators were accused of financial impropriety, prompting the national news media to claim there is public "contempt for the whole institution."[244] The testimony of a former Canadian prime minister was declared by the presiding judge of the Airbus inquiry "to be not worthy of any credence."[245] The presentations in front of Quebec's Charbonneau Commission were an almost daily circus of naming high-profile public figures*, who had received illegal payments, or who had consorted with mobsters. This included an icon of Quebec municipal government who was later arrested and convicted on "gangsterism" charges—that is, running a criminal organization. Sadly, for many citizens, there seems little distinction between those leaders who have been shown to be unethical or criminal and those leaders who just haven't been caught. Then these same leaders are suddenly "surprised" that citizens would turn to non-establishment populists in a last-ditch effort to see real change.

Nevertheless, as significant as these ethical lapses may be in contributing to the declining status of public leadership, they tell only part of the story. There is also the growing perception that leaders in government are no longer "in control" or "in charge" as evidenced by their ineffectiveness in numerous uncertain and complex policy environments. For instance, while every national leader claims to have power to direct their country's economy, none do. The global economy is so interconnected that events or changes in one area can have a huge influence around the world and there is nothing these national leaders can do about it except possibly mitigate any negative fallout. This frequently demonstrated leadership incapacity is undermining the public's confidence—even among the majority of ethical leaders.

In today's environments—where leadership has become widely distributed and individual leaders lack the full knowledge, resources or authority to accomplish their goals—individual leaders can continually take a beating. They can become easily lost amid a plurality of stakeholders in successful, shared governance approaches, or at the other extreme, because their "take charge" attitudes result in legitimate efforts at cooperation being derailed.

For instance, GE's iconic, "take-charge" leader Jack Welch, who for over a decade has successfully claimed a level of control and credit for change at GE in the 1990s, has been revealed as more of a figurehead than the "great man in charge" of modern myth. In an interview with a *Financial Times* reporter, Welch's successor at GE, Jeffrey Immelt, shared his perception of

---

* Most recently, Quebec's former Deputy Premier, Nathalie Normandeau. *Source:* SHINGLER, Benjamin. 2016. "Nathalie Normandeau, ex-Quebec deputy premier, arrested by UPAC", *CBC News.* 17 March. Accessed at: http://www.cbc.ca/news/canada/montreal/ upac-arrest-nathalie-normandeau-1.3495285

Welch's contribution saying, "anyone could have run GE and done well in the 1990s. *A dog could have run GE.*"[246] Why? Because there were so many good people in the middle of the organization that did the actual job of running and coordinating the company.

Being "in charge" was therefore irrelevant. It was essentially symbolic. Harris Collingwood underscores[247] this point saying, "CEOs can [still] matter, but we all might be better off if they didn't," because their potential to invigorate an organization has been shown to matter much less than their potential to damage it. Jeffrey Pfeffer agrees. "Bad leaders can make a huge negative difference—because they drive [good] people out."[248]

Now almost two decades after Welch was at the helm of GE, the coordination challenge is greater still, meaning that CEOs have even less control over their organization's fate. According to the *Mckinsey Quarterly*, "Leaders . . . are operating in a bewildering, new environment in which little is certain, the tempo is quicker, and the dynamics are more complex. They worry that it is impossible for chief executives to stay on top of all the things they need to know to do their job . . . they feel overwhelmed."[249] When this is true of CEOs in private companies, how much more true is it in the more complex environments of public sector organizations?

In the commonplace realities where knowledge is contested, where power is shared, and where mutual commitments must be continually negotiated, traditional leadership behaviours are hugely constraining. If leaders are not feeling "overwhelmed," they may well try to assert themselves, and then their claims of being "in charge" quickly prove empty and fraudulent.

Just the simple fact of increasing the scale of an organization has the effect of increasing complexity, making it ever more difficult for organizational leaders to assert their control. "Many of these [global] companies," says Dave Gray,[250] "are collapsing under their own weight. As companies grow, they invariably increase in complexity, and as things get more complex they become more difficult to control."

The Economist recently posed this question: "Why the big gap between trust in leaders and the institutions they lead?" Their response: "leaders have been slow to adapt to the requirements of a world in which *top down is no longer*

Chapter 6

the best way to lead, or in many cases even a viable one."[251] In any organization, as size and complexity grow, the coordination challenge increases in accordance with Ashby's Law. At some point, either the mechanisms of coordination, mechanisms like leadership, must radically change, or the organization fails.

According to John Hagel, co-chairman of Deloitte's Center for the Edge, failing is what many organizations are doing these days. There has been an erosion of American business leadership that is part of a long, systemic decline that dates back to the mid-20th century. Since 1965, he says, the return-on-assets for all American firms has eroded by 75%. "The erosion has been sustained and significant. There is absolutely no evidence of it levelling off, and there is certainly no evidence of it turning around."[252] So despite 40 years of extensively training would-be leaders how to be "'in charge," corporate productivity has continued to decline. The implication is that leadership training and productivity are not correlated at all, or that they may be inversely correlated.

This point is underscored by another study,[253] one in which the performance of companies that were run by award-winning, "superstar CEOs," consistently underperformed in their markets after their CEO received an award. Hagel also sees this *malaise* being manifested in the declining survival rate of US corporations, which is down by 80% since 1937 to as little as 15 years. He attributes this decline to the fact that "American business leaders were essentially not prepared to move towards a more open and collaborative business model."[254]

And as MIT's Yaneer Bar-Yam suggests[255], the poor performance of this top down, "I'm in charge" model of organization is not restricted to businesses. The very nature of government organizations—large, diverse and complex— lends itself to bad decision-making and unsatisfactory results. Not surprisingly, the recent Canadian survey[256] by the Institute for Research on Public Policy and Nanos Research, found that only 9.4% of Canadians had confidence in the federal government's ability to solve problems, while double that number—18% of Canadians—had no confidence in the government at all. This is a far, far cry from the 70% confidence levels that the federal government enjoyed in the '60s and '70s. And as bad as this was, confidence levels were even lower for provincial governments.

After digging deeper into these results, what is more interesting according to researchers, is that when Canadians said that they had lost confidence in government, what they were really saying was that, much like Hagel's comment about American business leaders, they doubted Canadian government leaders were willing and able to develop the partnerships needed to solve the complex, transformational issues that mattered most to their citizens.[257]

Not only are leaders generally perceived as unethical and/or ineffective, but the very concept of leadership itself is proving to be ineffective as a tool for social coordination. It relies on the power of romanticized myth: a cult of personality which assumes some people are intrinsically special, different from, and better than their followers, and therefore capable of saving them from all types of uncertainties and threats. Leaders are marketed as "white knights," whose followers choose to believe, often without any supporting facts that they can swoop in and fix everything.

Unfortunately, in today's distributed governance world, these would-be "saviours" often create as many new problems as they promise to fix.

Leadership, not leaders, is the real problem

Hayek once identified that the true challenge of socio-economic issues "is determined precisely by the fact that the knowledge of the circumstances of which we must make use, never exists in concentrated or integrated form, but solely as the dispersed bits of incomplete and frequently contradictory knowledge which all the separate individuals possess."[258]

This again is the rationale for all human communities—to bring together that distributed knowledge to produce more than the sum of the individual parts. Thus, the problems of society are not simply strict allocation problems that leaders may be good at. Instead, they are, according to Hayek, problems of "how to secure the best use of resources known to any of the members of society, for ends whose relative importance only these individuals know.

Chapter 6

Or, to put it briefly, *it is a problem of the utilization of knowledge which is not given to anyone in its totality."*

So there it is: if we can ignore for a moment the obvious problem of unethical and stupid people who can at times parade as leaders, *the fundamental problem with leaders is the notion of leadership itself*—the assumption that people with a very finite capacity to possess knowledge, resources and power are expected to know it all and have it all. The fundamental problem is not that they are "bad," or "overly selfish," or "unintelligent"—it is that they are only human, with only a finite human capacity.

However, instead of admitting this, we accept and encourage a superhero fiction of our leaders that frequently manifests itself as a combination of snake-oil salesmanship in the guise of saints, together with a followership of convenience that steers people into voluntary servitude.

"In our political culture," writes Dan Gardner[259], "a leader who acknowledges uncertainty and encourages experiments is 'indecisive.' A leader who permits dissent is 'weak.' A leader who changes his mind in response to new evidence is a 'flip-flopper.' A 'real leader' is one who centralizes power, is certain of everything, who breaks the knuckles of anyone who disagrees, who never admits to being wrong, and who will deny to his last breath ever having changed his mind about anything. A real leader is a Great Man issuing orders from the top of a pyramid."

Citizens have long accepted this myth of leadership because they've never been comfortable with the uncertainty presented by their own ownership of wicked problems. Historically, they have repeatedly turned for reassurance and comfort to leaders claiming certain knowledge, and who were willing to provide them with simple, black-and-white solutions.

But if citizens began to believe more in themselves, or that their own shared knowledge and networks might do the job as well as or better than any leader in government, then what would that do to the illusion that leader is special? Furthermore, what constitutes good leaders, at least as far Gardner describes them, makes for bad collaborators because they lack the skills, knowledge and practices[260] that would permit them to effectively orchestrate the required social cooperation.

The corollary of "nobody's in charge," is that everyone is. It's an upside-down pyramid where one-time followers facilitate change, and one-time leaders are guided by others. What connects them is not an organizational position, or some mantle of authority, but their shared ownership—a shared sense that they have skin in the game. Ostensibly, in a democracy, each citizen is a part owner of a collective entity that is referred to at different times as a community, a nation, or a state. Each citizen shares his or her ownership with all the other citizens. And if, as the evidence suggests, our agents are no longer up to the task of social coordination, then we as owners must re-assume the mantle of our responsibilities as owners.

This element of ownership is key and it is enacted through choice. This means that while each person may believe in a distinct possibility, they must be willing to identify those possibilities and communicate them across their community. Then, together with their neighbours, they can choose a shared future and to work together to bring it into reality.

Rather than seeing the leader as cause, shared ownership lets us see ourselves as cause, whether through our actions or inactions, or through our contributions or our curtailment of such, or through our knowledge or ignorance. As owners, we accept at least partial responsibility for the status quo. Consequently, as owners we can choose to do things differently. To rephrase an old sixties adage, "If you're not part of the problem, how can you be part of the solution?" That is, if you're not currently contributing to the problem (by commission or omission), how can you realistically expect to have any leverage at all towards making a change? Owners choose. Non-owners let others choose for them.

However, in any complex social structure, given a multiplicity of owners, a way must first be found to articulate that shared ownership. Change is not something that can be accomplished independently. The first step towards cooperation and collaboration begins with the recognition that "I can't do it alone." Yet this recognition is the foundation of any human community, even if we don't reflect on it much. Then if we can articulate the future that we want together, hierarchies can give way to networks of shared ownership, and "leadership" can give way to mechanisms of partnership and stewardship that can help reify that shared ambition.

This naturally raises the question that if no one is truly in charge, how can coordination occur among a diverse group of owners, some of whom may have competing organizational and stakeholder interests? Cleveland reminds us that "any human system that works is working because nearly all of the people involved in it cooperate to make sure that it [does] work."[261] Leadership works when people agree that they are willing to cooperate with it.

Similarly, if people choose to cooperate among themselves, then cooperation will happen—not because of fines, or penalties or other forms of coercion. Traffic lights work because most people are willing to obey them. They obey them, because they believe that if everyone behaves in the same way, then there is less likelihood of their getting into an accident, or finding themselves in conflict with others. That mindset guides their cooperation. The fines are there for the few outliers unwilling to cooperate, or to pose a deterrent for those thinking about not cooperating.

On the face of it then, how do we navigate in this "no one is in charge" world, where no one is there to tell us what to do? If not leadership or hierarchy, what mechanism(s) is needed to generate the requisite social coordination among society's co-owners?

From leadership to stewardship

As our discomfort with leaders and leadership has grown, we have witnessed a mounting body of leadership approaches (recall **Figure 6**) that do not fit the *"leader as cause"* mold. For instance, Lester Salamon observed over a decade and a half ago that complex problems and the need to work with others demanded that leaders develop a new suite of skills, in particular, what he described as *enablement skills*. With them, he suggested, a different kind of coordination mechanism was possible that could bring people together to facilitate their learning and working together, as well as help manage their inevitable conflicts.[262]

Although Salamon still envisioned leadership as the principal mechanism of coordination, he posited that coordination could be achieved, not by someone "taking charge" or through their powers of persuasion or coercion, but rather, by the so-called "leader" acting as a catalyst of collective purpose, of shared commitment and of joint action among groups of owners seeking to cooperate.

Instead of followers acting simply as pawns and tools for the success of *causal leaders*, the work of followers was seen as important in its own right, and the task of *catalytic leaders* was to ensure its success. This necessitated "leaders" moving away from attitudes of control and coercion towards more supportive attitudes like, "how can I help?" This explains the intrinsic appeal of notions like "servant leadership"[263] and "facilitative leadership."[264] Within this notion of *catalytic leadership*, the element of "bringing people together to make something different happen"[265] remains, but the bias towards control and dominance is gone.

Is the current generation of leaders up to the task of catalyzing, empowering, and collaborating? A global study[266] by the Center for Creative Leadership (CCL) suggests not. While 86% of the senior executives they surveyed believed it was "extremely important" for them to work effectively across boundaries in their leadership role (see **Figure 10**), only 7% of these executives believed they were currently "very effective" at doing so.

In another similar survey by the CCL, more than 90% of respondents said that collaboration was vital for their leadership success. However, when asked a follow-up question, "Are the leaders of your organization good at collaboration?" fewer than 50% of the respondents replied that their leaders were good at it. "In a horizontal world," say O'Leary and Vij, "there are many times when collaboration is needed, but often one does not know *how* to do it—and do it well. Collaboration yields immense leadership challenges."[267]

This insightful observation comes as a flood of different stakeholder groups try to institute distributed governance arrangements in order to respond to a host of wicked problems through collaboration and partnership. According to IBM's 2012 Global CEO Study[268], more than two-thirds of the CEOs IBM surveyed planned to partner extensively. For instance, employee empowerment was being combined with increasing openness and transparency to offset the command-and-control style of leadership that has so characterized the modern corporation.

Chapter 6

Figure 10: Boundary Spanning Priorities of Senior Executives

Types of Collaborative Outcomes	Priority
❶ Collaboration across functions	98%
❷ Empowering employees at all levels	97%
❸ Developing cross-organizational learning capabilities	91%
Creating a diverse and inclusive organization	89%
Working in partnership with customers (e.g., deeper more open methods of customer interaction)	86%
Creating higher performing virtual teams	77%
Breaking down glass ceilings (e.g., women in senior management)	76%
Facilitating cross-generational collaboration	76%
Developing an organizational global mindset	73%
Leveraging cross-cultural perspectives	70%
Harnessing cross-sector partnerships	67%
Developing corporate social responsibility (CSR) practices	65%
Integrating merged or acquired organizations	64%
Balancing HQ and regional tensions	59%
Flattening organizational hierarchy	55%
Capitalizing on open source innovation	54%

Survey participants were asked to rate the level of priority they would place on various collaborative outcomes over the following five years. **Source:** Jeffrey Yip, Chris Ernst and Michael Campbell. 2011. *Boundary Spanning Leadership: Mission Critical Perspectives from the Executive Suite.* Center for Creative Leadership.

IBM's study involved a survey of more than 1,700 CEOs from 64 countries and in 18 industries, and it identified the growing use of team-based environments, the promotion of experiential learning techniques and the use of high-value employee networks. "The trend toward greater collaboration extends beyond the corporation to external partnering relationships. Partnering is now at an all-time high."

Once again, this is not just a business trend. "To deal with the complexities of today's world," says Wayne Wouters,[269] Canada's former Clerk of the Privy Council and once its most senior public servant, "we need to work with each other [in government], and we all need to collaborate with citizens, the private sector, academia and civil society to resolve the problems and challenges we face . . . Collaboration, consultation, partnerships—these need to be the hallmarks of the Public Service of Canada in the future."

Wouters' comments resonate strangely with the results of the IRPP–Nanos poll referenced earlier. For even as Wouters repeatedly underscored the importance of collaboration in his later years, the IRPP–Nanos poll suggested that the primary cause of the decline in public confidence in government centred precisely around the perceived inability of government to work effectively with others. Some well-worn issues—natural resources, border protection, safe communities, research and development (R&D), trade and international affairs—continue to command public confidence and, not surprisingly, the attention of governments.

But many other issues—health care, jobs, education, First Nations, the environment, the aging population, social programs, living standards, productivity, and, in particular, the balancing of budgets—command much less confidence.

Not surprisingly, these issues illustrate the more complex type of "wicked" problem described by Rittel.[270] Yet the Canadian public, at least, remains unconvinced that those who say they have all the answers in these areas actually do. The required solutions involve many steps and lots of players, which the public interprets as a significant challenge for government. In essence, if governments have to collaborate, the public has little or no confidence that they will or can.

When no one is, or can be, "in charge," the incessant political cries for better, stronger, more effective and forceful leadership are meaningless. Moreover, traditional command-and-control styles of leadership are quite antithetical to cooperation among those whom may legitimately see themselves as "leaders." With no followers, there are no leaders. Moreover, the prized attributes usually associated with being good leaders—their confidence in their own knowledge and judgement, their "take charge" attitudes, their willingness to whip people into line, their dominance—almost guarantee collaboration fails. Yet few seem to grasp that if no one is willing to follow, leadership is irrelevant. Another mechanism is required when working with a group of peers.

A different mechanism for social coordination

Despite our obsession with leadership, one thing to remember is that while it is *a tool* of social coordination, it is not the only one. And, there is no *a priori* reason to rely on it at all—other than our long standing habit of course.

When leader-driven hierarchies are replaced with networks, a trend which is now becoming commonplace, we can see that coordination does not come from traditional leaders. Instead, it comes from all those in the network, either through the words and actions of *catalytic leaders*, or in the form a few basic rules and norms that act as "guiderails" for the interactions among network participants.

Applying this network protocol to some re-imagined future government, we might see those citizens who had previously abdicated their ownership rights in society reasserting themselves. Those who had previously accepted being a follower, might assume responsibility for both their problems and their solutions, and be willing to work in concert with others to achieve their shared goals. In this way, hierarchies would give way to networks of shared ownership, and "leadership" would give way to coordination among owners— a concept referred to as "stewardship."

While the difference between *leadership* and *stewardship* may seem trivial to some, it is critical to distinguish between the centralization of decision-making and control in the former, and the facilitation of distributed ownership and shared decision-making in the latter. If we really want to encourage a different set of behaviours, then we need to start by using a different language. The continued use of the multiple and nuanced notions of "leadership" (as previously listed in **Figure 9**) is not likely to have much real impact.

What my colleagues and I at the University of Ottawa have found is that the command-and-control notion of leadership is so entrenched, that when, for instance, we use the term *"collaborative* leadership," audiences just don't grasp the nuance. Practically speaking, the *"collaborative"* adjective falls off and audiences default to their familiar notions of *"leader as cause."* In the end, therefore, the use of terms like "collaborative leadership" or "facilitative leadership" or "servant leadership" have proven to be a disservice. These terms simply perpetuate the confusion that the coordinating behaviours between "owners" are no different from those between leaders and followers.

In reality, the dynamic between owners and stewards is dramatically different. The collective benefits that are produced by the interaction of owners are generated by owners themselves—not through the agency or direction of a leader. The steward is simply the facilitator of their collective dialogue and decision-making. It is the peer-to-peer relationship between owners that really makes the difference, rather than a relationship of dependency or control. Says Peter Senge, it "often comes down to how people move from fatalism to an awakened faith that they [themselves] can shape a different future."[271]

Therefore, when our discussions turn to collaboration and partnership, I believe it's time that we stop confusing people and drop the leadership language entirely, and begin referring to the *leader as catalyst* phenomenon in a different way.

I suggest adopting the "stewardship" language. Good stewards are ultimately bridge builders and relationship managers. Their principal task is to help to sustain the commitment that each employee, partner or collaborator may bring to the shared work and to help guide their collective process. These are the "self-effacing insiders" once identified by Jim Collins[272] who put their organizations ahead of themselves and focus on surrounding themselves with good, committed and talented people.

If leaders are created by followers, then by that same measure, stewards are created by owners. According to Peter Block, "stewardship begins with [our] willingness to be accountable for a larger body than ourselves—an organization, a community."[273] In this context, ownership is not about control or property rights, it's about choice. In *choosing* to be an owner, we are *choosing* to be accountable for our own condition. And it is this reality of distributed ownership that sets stewardship apart from leadership—because true owners are unlikely to relinquish their ownership over their condition and hand it over to someone else.

Stewardship may involve one person, or it may involve several, each of whom have a capacity to convene, facilitate and look out for everyone's interest. But among a group of owners, it is unlikely that a single person will be in a position to control or dominate the group. Nevertheless, whoever steps into that stewardship role—even for a moment—may be immensely valued for his/her ability to provide encouragement, inspiration, facilitation, education, or conflict resolution in order to help others to cooperate—not as followers or pawns—but as equals.

One of the simplest and most erudite depictions of this comes from Benjamin Zander, conductor of the Boston Philharmonic Orchestra, who once described a truly powerful steward as being someone who does not appropriate power from others, but "depends for his power on making other people powerful."[274] The more powerful, effective and successful he/she makes others, the more valuable and powerful they themselves become. This is the essence of good stewardship. Moreover, "making others powerful," is not something that can be imposed on them but it is yet another choice—to become powerful—that owners must ultimately make for themselves. As it turns out, fostering that empowerment proves to be one of the central tasks of stewardship.

Moving to a stewardship model isn't as simple as swapping leaders to change organizational direction. Not only are there cultural and institutional barriers that perpetuate the belief that only a centralized, leader-dominated, hierarchical structure can do the job with effectiveness and efficiency,[275] but the people themselves—employees, citizens, stakeholders and potential partners—may have to overcome their own habits of dependence and entitlement.[276] The stewardship process may help, but the principle choice remains squarely with those being empowered.

One thing that is often helpful in this regard is the repeated exposure to situations where a single leader obviously cannot resolve the problem on their own. This tends to change one's psychology because if "I can't do it myself," then maybe, just maybe, "I can do it with others." People may be slow to learn this, but eventually it sinks in. And, if "I can do <u>this</u> with others," then maybe "I can do even more with others" and the willingness to collaborate can begin to snowball.

In my work, this has been a common experience among those who have succeeded at collaboration. Therefore, becoming aware of where others have tried and succeeded is often helpful in reducing the perceived risk of embarking on collaboration. When the collaborative stories of others are widely circulated (such as those in **Part II** of this series) we can become more at ease with the collaborative process.

Still, an awareness of a need to come together with others, learn from them, and be open to the possibility of collaborative change with them may only be enough to bring people to the table. It is not sufficient in itself to overcome all of the partners' potential differences, leadership biases, or cooperation challenges that will be found in practice. Since working collaboratively is invariably an exercise in *contingent cooperation* (see **Reimagining Government Part II**), the cooperation of partners must be continually reinforced, even as the potential for non-cooperation is vigorously resisted. This is not accomplished through altruism or decree, but only through a variety of interrelated, heuristic practices applied as the need requires.

Developing these tools to suit a specific collaborative initiative is an important part of the stewardship process. Applying them is not the task of an "all-knowing" father figure, but rather, it is the responsibility of all those willing to participate authentically in a collaborative process of trial and error.

"I believe," says John Hagel, "that the opportunity for [stewardship] in this regard is to flip the natural psychological reaction that we have to uncertainty. All of us, when confronted with uncertainty, tend to magnify risk and discount reward, and that tends to lead us not to act and to stay on the sidelines, hoping that somehow, somewhere things will clarify and then we can move."[277] The central role of stewardship is, therefore, to increase the collective sense of opportunity in a future that everyone wants to live into, while diminishing the perceptions of individual risk associated with moving towards it via shared ownership, social learning and working together.

Once again, if everyone is in charge, then the coordination burden must also be shared, and shared in ways that do not raise one personality above all the others. One mechanism for accomplishing this is to foster personal relationships between the players. In periods of uncertainty and rapid change, for instance, organizations need to develop relational mechanisms that constantly probe their environments, their employees, their networks of suppliers, customers and stakeholders[278] and be willing to co-create with them through what Lane and Maxfield have referred to as *generative relationships*[279]—"relationships that produce new sources of value that cannot be foreseen in advance."

This requires reliance on processes and practices of engagement rather than on the traditional practices that reinforce the dominance of one personality or leader. Instead of falling into the self-deceptive trap of pursuing ends which seem certain but are not, effective collaboration allows participants to hold fast to the group processes that will eventually allow them to arrive at a desirable destination, even if it is not the one they may have initially had in mind. In this manner, both the practice of stewardship and the work of collaboration are more art than science, replete with multiple techniques and skills that permit unique and innovative solutions to emerge.

In the end, as much as good stewardship may be about fostering ownership, it is also about good collective process that does not limit it to a single personality, or even a specific collection of people. Stewardship is a collective capacity that reflects the status of participants as owners with interlocking obligations to one another, and one that ultimately becomes embedded in the culture, customs and norms of their personal relationships, and through them to the relationships between their respective organizations and the public. Everyone is in charge.

Glimpsing stewardship in action— hints of things to come

Since stewardship begins with the recognition that I can't do everything myself, the "in-control," "in-charge" characteristics of leaders become impractical and inappropriate when you require others to come to your aid. If the organizations or the people you need to partner with are not in your organization's employ, then they are unlikely to be responsive to your top-down commands as the leader of your organization. What's more, it may be (as the following *Goldcorp Challenge* story illustrates), that you have no idea who you need to partner with. Not only does this make working together more problematic, but how do you hope to control a relationship with someone you don't even know exists yet?

This loss of real control should ultimately steer leaders, if they were honest, into surrendering their claims of control, and encourage them to open up to the guidance of others. As horrifying as this may sound to many public-sector leaders, it has real benefits—as the creation of *Brazil's HIV-AIDS Strategy* illustrates. When government leaders in Brazil allowed themselves to be led by others, they unlocked significant engagement, resources, experimentation and innovation from both their citizens and their public and private organizations.

In the process, the previous canonical role of top-down leadership can be transformed into stewardship, as erstwhile leaders begin adopting the characteristics of educators, facilitators, brokers, networkers and knowledge mobilizers. Stakeholders, too, can be transformed from followers to owners, participating in learning forums and communities of practice, not unlike the boards of technology start-ups.

Goldcorp Challenge

Don Tapscott has been a long-time advocate of collaboration, especially mass collaboration. In his best-selling book *Wikinomics*, he tells the story of Goldcorp, a small Toronto-based mining company that in 1999 was struggling to survive; its Red Lake, Ontario, gold deposits had apparently been tapped out, according to the firm's own expert geologists. After hearing a lecture about Linus Torvalds and his open-source approach in the creation of Linux, "[Goldcorp CEO Rob] McEwen had an epiphany . . . If Goldcorp employees couldn't find the Red Lake gold, maybe someone else could. And maybe the key to finding those people was to open up the exploration process in the same way Torvalds 'open sourced' Linux."[280]

Chapter 6

Despite being part of an industry long known for its secrecy and strict regard for proprietary data, McEwen recognized that if he was to succeed, he couldn't do it by himself. He needed help from others. Still, he had no idea who those others might be. So, to get the help he needed, he opened up the firm's data stores to the world's geologists. Even more than that, he broadcast them globally to all and sundry by creating the *Goldcorp Challenge*—a competition offering $575,000 in prize money to winners with the best estimates and methods of extracting gold from Goldcorp's deposits.

In response, he received hundreds of submissions from geologists, physicists, computer scientists and many others from all over the world. "There were capabilities I had never seen before in the industry," said McEwen. The net result of his "open source" approach was eight million new ounces of gold were discovered, taking the firm's net worth from $100 million to over $9 billion.

Tapscott and Williams observed that McEwen's genius was to recognize that the knowledge and expertise he needed lay beyond the boundaries of his firm (i.e. he didn't have all the answers), and that to access that knowledge, he needed to find a way to: a) connect with those people who did have it; and b) engage with them in a way that made them willing participants in Goldcorp's own goals.

Brazil's HIV-AIDS strategy

In 1990, Brazil had one of the world's worst HIV-AIDS infection rates on the planet—double that of even South Africa. At the time, the World Bank had predicted that by 2000, 1.2 million Brazilians would become infected. Given Brazil's generally poor economy and meagre health care infrastructure, the Bank advised the government of Brazil to focus on the prevention of future infections rather than on the costly treatment of those already sick. They thought Brazil could not afford the scale of the retroviral drugs needed, or the sophisticated treatment regimes required to deal with the hundreds of thousands of people who were already infected. In essence, the "experts" told Brazilians that the sick couldn't be saved.

In their groundbreaking 2006 book, *Getting to Maybe*, Brenda Zimmerman, Michael Quinn-Patton and Frances Westley explored what happens when a government like Brazil admits to not having all the answers and is willing to seek the help of its citizens. In Brazil's case, there was no charismatic leader to either inspire or coerce the people into action. Clearly no one had all the answers, but the Brazilian government's great insight was their willingness to admit it. Brazilians were not deterred by the pessimistic views of experts and they chose to be guided by their own shared communitarian values that would not allow any ailing citizen to be written off.

As a consequence, the government went directly to their citizens and asked them to intervene and contribute to possible solutions, promising that they would then spread successful ideas countrywide. In response, people from all walks of life, and from organizations in every sector of Brazilian society began to experiment. Rather than seeing a solution framed by scarcity, as the World Bank had done, Brazilians took on the challenge framed by an awareness of the abundance of what actually existed in their country.

For Brazilians the choice was about "how to deliver help": not about "whom help should be delivered to." With a shortage of nurses, nuns became caregivers for those infected. Holiday celebrations became vehicles for disseminating messages of prevention. Even beer commercials fostered images of protected sex. The government used existing trade relations to produce generic retro virus remedies in country.

"The government's brilliance," say Zimmerman and her colleagues, "was to ask questions about how things really worked across the country and to enhance the [existing] natural patterns, relationships and behaviours."[281] The government chose to share leadership with its citizens, committing to highlight and share local innovative successes broadly—whenever and wherever successful approaches evolved. The role of government changed from being the driving force of change, to being the facilitator of the country's collective intelligence. As a consequence of these stewardship efforts, Brazil's infected HIV population remains, even in 2016, only half of what was predicted for 2000 and its infection rate was reduced by 33%, to a level that is now lower than even the USA.

Chapter 6

When it comes to collaboration, "questions are more important than answers," says Peter Block[282]. Answers can only reiterate what you already know. Questions, on the other hand, are pregnant with possibility. Leadership today is obsessed with the illusion of being able to provide answers. By contrast, stewardship is primarily concerned with asking questions, not only to generate collaborative solutions out of previously independent actions, but also to create a new shared possibility that collaborators will want to live into, one that justifies their working together. Embracing this diversity and facilitating innovation, as the Brazilians did, is a strategic part of the stewardship process because it helps to bias group interactions towards inquiry instead of towards answers.

Governance of technology start-ups

Moreover, when we look at the governance of technology start-ups, we can see how intentionally structuring diversity also provides a powerful catalyst for innovation and a foundation for successful activity, just as it did in Brazil.

In any collaborative business endeavour, a key governance strategy is to ensure a diversity of perspectives in order to avoid "group think" and to foster better real-time accountability. This is a well-established practice in governing technology start-ups. Unlike the boards of directors in more mature, less risky companies, the membership of a start-up board is not decided by the CEO. It is a product of the interests of various stakeholders who secure their right to contribute to decision making in exchange for their contributions to the new enterprise.

A typical start-up board might comprise owner-entrepreneurs, angel investors, key customers, bankers, engineers, and even important suppliers—each there to protect their own interests and to contribute their perspective on every aspect of the new business. The board reflects a quality of co-governance, wherein the parties collaborate to create successful outcomes for a firm which will ultimately benefit all of them.

In this situation, no one perspective ends up dominating, because of the independence of the board members. The board becomes, in effect, a learning forum in which multiple perspectives are brought together and aired for more creative impact. Such boards represent a modern adaptation of the ancient parable of the blind men and the elephant, which essentially depicts decision making under incomplete knowledge and where a comprehensive understanding is obtained only by the sharing of information among all the parties (the blind men).

Stewardship and self-organization

Interestingly, this type of innovation through collective learning, or "order through interaction,"[283] as it is called in the literature, is not only what happens in start-ups or via the Internet — it is the essence of all living systems. It is how self-organization arises from the contributions of multiple parts.

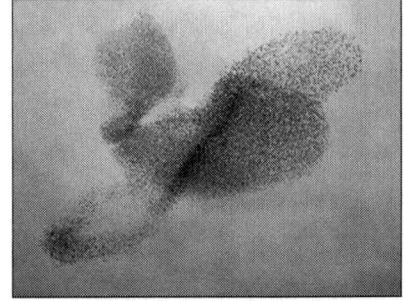

Figure 11: The flocking of starlings is an illustration of self-organization in nature

The Internet, for instance, is a network, and that network connects people, and those people interact in fundamentally self-organizing ways to produce something new. Those same networks generate coordination amongst themselves as the result of each network node responding to changes it perceives around it, in much the same way as flocks of birds (**Figure 11**) or schools of fish do when they move together in what seems to be intricately choreographed patterns. Similarly, as people are connected on the Internet, it becomes possible for them to collaborate—even in large numbers—without anyone being "in charge" or without anyone able to compel others to cooperate. Within such networks, leadership is not a factor. Stigmergy is.

If, as Hamel suggests[284], "bureaucracies have to die" and it is the DNA of managers and the frameworks of leadership that are the problem, what do you replace these leader-driven hierarchies with in order to provide coordination? What do you use instead? The answer lies in the thing that is currently giving leadership such a hard time—networks—and the fact that networks give rise to self-organization.

Chapter 6

For instance, the foundation for the success of open source software is famously captured in *Linus' Law* (after Linus Torvald the originator of Linux) which holds that "given enough eyeballs, all bugs are shallow."[285] But of course, its corollary is also true—fewer eyeballs, means more bugs! If everything must be funneled through a single person, then expect a lot of bugs.

In a world that is increasingly dominated by networks, coordination across the network is the product of lots of nodes and participants, and the process of stewardship becomes increasingly important. Stewardship helps to ensure that data and information flows freely between people and it does so by keeping rules to a minimum, by reducing the potential barriers to knowledge sharing, and by encouraging communities of practice. It is not dependent on certain personal traits embodied in a leader.

Rather, it is primarily based on process design. By this, I mean some collection of acceptable behaviours, inducements to collective learning, various mechanisms, heuristics and affordances (like checklists) that can foster and sustain collaboration, together with the evolution of judgement and connoisseurship, as well as the monitoring of participant actions and performance results. Accountability, which has largely disintegrated under the current practices of leadership, becomes stronger, more immediate, and more transparent under effective stewardship regimes.

The thing to keep in mind is that human communities are also systems—systems where members are constantly acting and reacting to each other in a stigmergic fashion, both in small groups and in very large ones—in essence, we flock.[286] Often this produces quite unpredictable results. In this context, therefore, if we want to inspire cooperation and coherent collective action, then it's very useful to find ways to mitigate contrarian behaviours that are produced by social traps[287] and shirking behaviours* and that undermine cooperation.

---

* These "social traps" undermine collective action through a tendency to exploit cooperation in self-serving ways that end up producing non-rational, collective results.

According to Brian Arthur[288], our entire political economy is based on the assumption of self-organization (markets) and the avoidance of social traps. Simultaneously, it must support a coordinated system of fair exchange, while mitigating the disruptive social impacts of "rational acting" upon which those exchanges are based. Unfortunately, the system cannot always "see" exploitive, unproductive and self-serving behaviours in advance. And leadership has proven to be no deterrent to this type of exploitive behaviour—quite the contrary, as the 2008 financial crisis provided ample evidence of[289].

According to Arthur, one possible solution to this is to develop a collective stewardship capacity to recognize trends and patterns of interaction, "a set of changes that may induce further changes, a set of existing entities creating novel entities." Such a self-organizing capacity must be based on the habits of continuous *inquiry and reflection* that seek to identify possible patterns and propagations of change.

However, identifying those important patterns comes with its own need to explore scenarios, or what Arie de Geus calls "creating memories of the future,"[290] so that we may recognize the relevant patterns if and when they actually emerge in real life in the future. This reinforces the need for stewardship to reflect and ask questions, rather than trying to demonstrate decisiveness based on incomplete knowledge.

In a network environment, to produce the sort of reflective behaviour associated with self-organizing and autocatalytic phenomena described by Arthur, you generally need:

- *dense networks* to effectively propagate (go viral) and stimulate transitions in collective behaviour;

- *rich connectivity* to increase the capacity for more diverse conversations to develop and promote collective learning, suggesting that stewardship design should include network building and improving network communication; and

- *feedback loops,* lots of them, to monitor innovation and change *as it emerges* to encourage a reaction from the network itself. This has given rise to a novel type of assessment, called *developmental evaluation*[291], to continually fine-tune innovation when you cannot predict the ultimate outcome of a single intervention. This type of feedback helps participants focus on their shared governance.

Despite incessant media cries for better, stronger leadership, in a network, coordination is created by network participants themselves. "It is the reality of distributed ownership that sets stewardship apart from leadership."[292] This stewardship in networks becomes a process of learning many things, including:

- who are the collaborators—their strengths, weaknesses, and capacities;
- what are their perspectives and how to translate from one to another;
- how to construct a more comprehensive picture of the problem or issue;
- how the actions or inactions of owners contribute to the problem, thus empowering them to act meaningfully for change;
- what might be possible together;
- how to draw strength and satisfaction from a process of learning together;
- how to become comfortable with uncertainty; and finally
- what works, as well as what doesn't.

In this light, stewardship is a process of "learning while doing," facilitated by cycles of dialogue, learning and unlearning, and group action. By utilizing iterative cycles of trial and error, aided by heuristic strategies that encourage the asking of the right questions at the right time, a system of stewardship can begin to reflect, not only how an issue may be modified through time, but just as important, the co-learning, shared commitment and mutual accountability generated among the collaborators.

Admittedly, more needs to be done to explore and develop both the notions of collaboration and stewardship, but isn't a little uncertainty now with respect to promises and practices of stewardship still better than the obvious certainty of widespread leadership failure?

Re-emphasizing social coordination over redistribution

Lastly, as leadership is giving way to stewardship, a central function of government is being transformed. According to Musgrave,[293] there are three principal functions of government: allocation, stabilization, and redistribution. However, providing coordination among the diverse elements of society has long been government's overarching role. Traditionally, someone with a reasonable grasp of political realities and with a little advice, could coordinate among various groups by allocating knowledge, rules and resources; pulling the appropriate economic levers to ensure stability when markets were heading up or down; and working to promote a sense of social fairness despite the individual vagaries of providence. This contributed to a longstanding public belief that leaders were indeed in charge. They were the "Great Oz" behind the curtain. But such is no longer the case.

The third function, redistribution, is particularly interesting because over the last half century it has evolved from being a simple tool to aid in stabilization to become the central function of government. And, this has occurred in parallel to (one might even say because of), the growing inability of governments to affect social coordination and, as a consequence, the declining public confidence that leaders were actually in charge.

Redistribution entails a transfer of resources from citizens who are supposedly better-off, to those who are supposedly less well-off, through a variety of techniques from taxation and subsidies to the provision of public goods and services. It can also involve transfers from one region or sector to another, according to some negotiated formula. Originally redistribution was used post–World War II as a tool for economic stabilization (e.g. the provision of family allowances to mitigate the decline of military expenditures). However, fuelled by ongoing coordination failures and the philosophy of progressives, by the late 20th century, redistribution had become sanctified as a social goal, desirable in and of itself.

Furthermore, the long decline of productivity originating in 1970s has generated a persistent sense of helplessness and loss of control among government leaders who have been faced with a litany of complex, socio-economic problems. These issues have proved to be increasingly resistant to the top-down, "we're in charge" approaches of Western governments, producing many ill-inspired, ineffective, or perverse interventions.

Early in this period (1971-1995), many still believed that government could ultimately affect good coordination, if only it would adopt more "business-like" practices and management models. These beliefs were then embodied in the notion of "New Public Management" (NPM)[294] and were aimed at improving government efficiency.

For a brief period, NPM became popular in many industrialized countries, but particularly in Australia, the UK and the USA. In Canada, the influence of NPM led to a number of modest reforms (both federally and provincially)[295] that were not very imaginative or forward-looking. Yet despite the more "business-like" rhetoric, these efforts lacked a clear understanding of the frameworks, skills and practices necessary to collaborate effectively across departments, jurisdictions and sectors, in order to enable a more concerted and effective economy.

In the end, the NPM experiment revealed that a reliance on market-based efficiency mechanisms would not, in itself, be enough to solve the tough social problems that demanded more effective social interaction and collective innovation. In addition, the increasingly integrated global economy was producing an array of external forces that began to drive national economies more than the influence of governments, making national stabilization tools increasingly irrelevant. Thus, while governments continued to pursue efficiency in their own realms, their capacity for policy effectiveness and innovation declined due to their inability to foster social coordination within the growing complexity of the public sector universe.

Despite some traumatic government failures during the 1970s and 1980s, there was no real change in the systems or institutional structures of government. This led to a general decline of confidence in government—even among those in government.

Since the mid-nineties, the perception has grown that government is incapable promoting social coordination as a means of proactively solving problems or affecting real socio-economic change. This has shifted the focus of government leaders away from coordination strategies to emphasizing redistribution as a way of mitigating three major challenges:

- *the need to prop up government legitimacy* despite persistent problem-solving failures due to their inability to orchestrate social coordination. Redistribution provided a visible way of retaining some legitimacy by compensating citizens for the problems that governments were unable to solve;

- *the need to satisfy the ideological obsession with "egalitarianism,"* which in most democratic countries has evolved to the status of an absolute right and entitlement; and

- *the need to recycle the government surpluses* from the early 2000s, instead of lowering taxes or reducing government indebtedness in order to appear generous and receive political credit for being so.

The increased focus on after-the-fact redistribution has redirected the attention of both citizens and the media away from demanding that governments reform themselves to produce better coordination. Instead, public attention is now directed towards advocating government to be more generous in redistributing to more and more groups and with ever greater amounts[296]. As a consequence, redistribution has now been elevated to the primary function of government, in order to correct "after-the-fact" all social imbalances generated by increasing social complexity and our outdated institutions of social coordination.

As Paquet and Wilson have argued elsewhere[297], most governments remain unconscious and oblivious to the social rigidities and mental prisons that such "no-fault" perspectives engender. In particular, governments fail to grasp that redistributive property rights, once granted, cannot easily be withdrawn at some later time; or that redistribution—being essentially a process of taking from one person and giving it to another—is inherently conflict-generating and divisive; or that it does nothing to improve collective innovation or performance—quite the opposite, in fact.

In the realm of problem-solving, redistribution is at best palliative, at worst it generates its own unintended negative consequences. One such consequence,

Chapter 6

may be that the "chronic failure fatigue" being experienced by citizens is energizing popular resentment against the role of government and public institutions as a whole, and opening the door to radical alternatives simply because there seems to be "nothing to lose."

Nevertheless, since 2000, redistribution and its handmaiden of egalitarianism have become like social rights—immune to public criticism or challenge. Yet as de Tocqueville showed long ago, the obsession with equality does not subside with progress on equalization, but it becomes "more insatiable as equality becomes greater."[298] Eventually, it's an obsession that turns toxic, becoming a source of widespread envy[299]. In the end, the continuing avoidance by governments of social coordination issues in favour of redistribution will prove to be an unsustainable path.

Now, however, after two decades of redistributive profligacy, there appears to be a rekindled public interest in the coordination game. There is growing interest in the notions of collaboration, empowerment, community-based participation, P3s, and self-governance, as well as other culturally charged processes like networks, self-organization, dialogue, deliberation and inclusion. However, at the level of government, while these cultural shifts are materializing, they are doing so only very slowly[300].

Focusing on scalable learning over scalable efficiency

It's a truism to say that the Internet has connected more people, with more information, than at any time in human history. As of November 2015,[301] for instance, there were almost 3.5 billion people or 46.5% of the world's population who were Internet users (including 33 million, or 92.5%, of Canadians). Of those, almost 1.5 billion people were using Facebook. Each day around the world over 150 billion emails and over 175 million tweets are sent on average. There are 650 million websites. YouTube users watch over 6 billion hours of video per month, and Google makes 1.2 trillion web searches annually. There is almost no part of the planet that now does not have Internet access of one kind or another—including such impoverished and war-ravaged places as South Sudan.

In addition, every day our roughly one trillion connected objects and devices on the planet generate about 2.5 quintillion bytes of data[302]—an amount that is growing so fast that 90% of the data in the world today was created in just the last two years. This data comes from everywhere, including: sensors used to gather climate information, posts to social media sites, digital pictures and videos, purchase transaction records, your cell phone and GPS signals, to name but a few, but soon these data sources will include your fridge, stove, TV, thermostat, chips embedded in your body*, and a host of other electronic devices. The age of the Internet enabled devices, or Internet of Things (IoT), dawns this year, as the number of IoT devices exceeds the number of humans[303], laying a foundation for all electronic devices to talk to each other and to form a basis for electronically generated social coordination.

As discussed earlier, all this burgeoning amount of data is having an explosive impact on the increase of knowledge. For instance, **Figure 12** illustrates the growth of knowledge during the post–World War II period, 1945-2000, in just one staid discipline—geology.

Other disciplines have, not only grown in similar ways, but have experienced knowledge growth that has been even more rapid, frequently giving birth to entirely new disciplines, such as the now commonplace disciplines of computer science, environmental science and systems science. Simultaneously, each discipline has become increasingly more specialized, and the fields of study have become increasingly more narrow. Prior to the 1980s, there were probably fewer than 50 fields of academic study; today, however, Wikipedia lists 1,475 fields[304]—a 3000% increase!

Furthermore, the combination of universal education and the ubiquitous presence of various Internet media have ensured that new ideas are propagated quite broadly and quickly throughout the human population, often to the consternation of the leaders in many countries who would prefer their citizens received a much more selected access. And, as more knowledge circulates, its value increases, not unlike the rule from Economics 101

---

* These may be chips related to the regulation of vital organs or metabolism or chips with personal data such as flight status, as in WARREN, May. 2016. "Swede becomes first person to board a plane with just a wave of his hand", *The Toronto Star*, 31 January

that says that the more money is allowed to circulate, the more the overall value it creates for the economy. The more knowledge circulates, the more innovation is created, and the more value is created for the economy and for citizens as a whole.

Figure 12: Growth of Knowledge in Geology 1945-2000

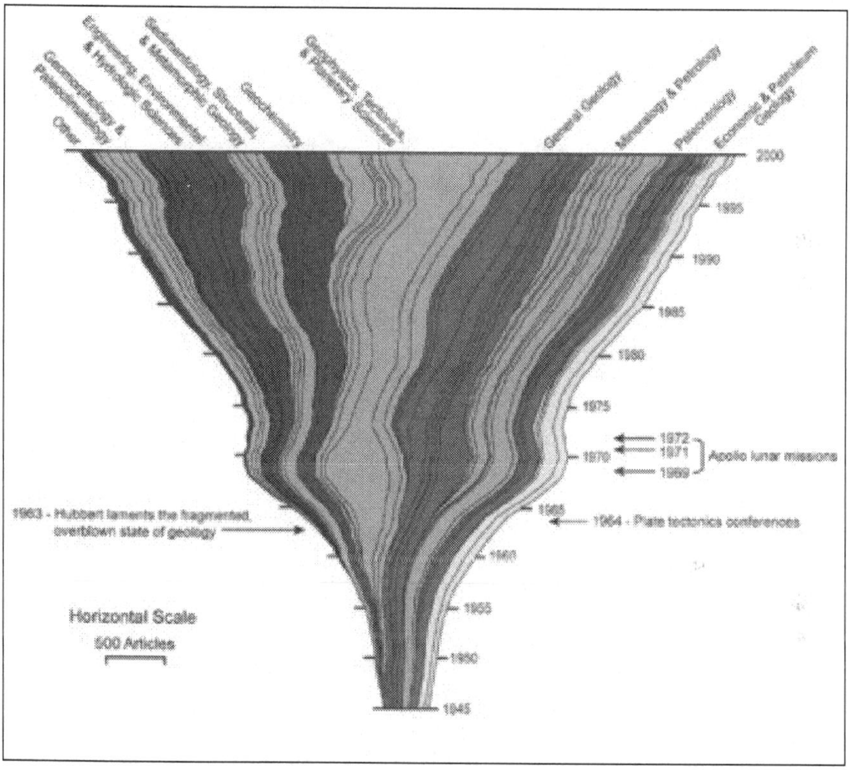

Source: Sarah E. Fratesi and H. L. Vacher, "Scientific Journals as Fossil Traces of Sweeping Change in the Structure and Practice of Modern Geology", *Journal of Research Practice*, Vo. 4 (1), 2008

But, as Clay Shirky cautions, there is a flip side to this coin. "The more ideas that are in circulation, the more ideas any individual can disagree with."[305] Remember in school, when we were all given tests and graded on the quality of our answers. The "right" answer was a scarce and valued thing. Today, however, at the click of a button we can have access to an almost infinite array of "answers." We have more answers than we know what to do with, and the more answers often means the more argument.

As a result, the social challenge today is not in finding answers, but in selecting the "right" answer by asking the "right" questions—something that technology is ill-suited for. Even so, the connectivity provided by the Internet and other social technologies can potentially put more people together to help them articulate important questions, and then help them identify those questions which may generate a broad basis of agreement.

Still, given the current experience on the Internet, it can also give air to so many voices, perspectives, and "truths," it is more like gossip than a real conversation. Today blatant lies and "fake news" can claim equal standing with real facts. Without an accompanying ability for dialogue and learning, there may be little chance of keeping a lid on the chaos arising from so many competing "answers."

From a public policy perspective, this implies an important need to urgently invest in systems of inquiry[306] and collective learning—systems that are open, inclusive, and ongoing—rather than in systems that are designed to simply overwhelm audiences and sell answers. Disagreement, as a natural result of diversity, must become the accepted starting point of any conversation—in fact, an engineered pre-condition—out of which creative questions can then emerge in a broader social context.

Once again, I go back to the parable of four blind men and the elephant. From the perspective of each blind man, they all have good reason to feel confident in their partial experience of reality. All of their experiences are valid—just incomplete. But if the blind men ever hope to understand the whole reality of the elephant, they must find a way to ask that other question: *What can be a snake, a tree, a wall and a pig all at the same time?* To get there, they must learn to share their experiences with each other, to listen carefully, to find ways to trust that each other's experience is valid, and then be able to creatively generate questions that incorporate all of their diverse experiences. The parable illustrates the difficulty in understanding the whole with incomplete knowledge—a difficulty that both citizens and governments the world over constantly struggle with. But it also illustrates the path forward—honest and authentic conversations that lead to creativity.

More data, more answers, more contacts, more voices, more shouting. As data grows exponentially and creates environments in which partial answers

Chapter 6

abound, the capacity to socially construct quality questions will become increasingly precious—probably becoming the basis of a new public good.

Yet, despite the trolls, there are people on the Internet who are already learning to have both online and offline conversations together, ones that encourage greater participation in their communities around the issues that concern them. And while it is true that many of these online conversations may be inundated by people shouting answers or acting uncivilly, there are also people who are not scared away and who are opting to work together to find their common story, develop their combined questions, and implement joint solutions to bring about a shared future. Our communities are becoming places where different people with different knowledge, resources and capacities are becoming bound together by their separate but complementary contributions to their shared perceptions of what constitutes common good.

We are in the midst of realizing what McLuhan once envisioned back in the early days of radio as the "global village,"[307] one which he believed would be brought about by "electronic *inter-dependence*." That is, when an electronic media would supplant the traditional text-based print culture as the medium for cultural exchange.

McLuhan speculated that in this new age, humankind would evolve from individualism and many, small, fragmented tribal groupings into a collective identity, reflective of a single global human tribe. Still, despite the many obvious examples of ongoing fragmentation and conflict, we do seem to be on the verge of ushering a truly "global tribe" into reality[308]. Nevertheless, today we seem to be in a period of transition when the glass is both half empty and half full.

In this regard, good stewardship, either in organizations or in government, boils down to designing for effective collective learning. Hagel underscores this point with his observation that organizations must move from being organized around "scalable efficiencies," to being organized around "scalable learning." He says, "the rationale of scalable efficiency is becoming less and less compelling," because your effectiveness is being determined not by how well you use existing resources, but by how quickly and well you can learn from and adapt to your environment. This requires "scalable learning."

In contrast to the efficiency rationale for organizations put forward by Coase a century ago, Hagel believes that "the reason we have institutions today is because we can learn faster as part of an institution than we can alone, [although] most institutions are not structured or operated to deliver on that rationale."[309] The fact that institutions can bring multiple points of view together in common conversation, gives them a potential leg up over individuals trying to figure what it all means by themselves. That is, of course, if institutions are not suffering from the sclerotic, "I'm in charge" traditions that strangle collective learning by imposing a single view from the top.

Some like Barbara Hubbard[310], have likened the Internet to humanity's great neural net, linking us all together—all eight billion of us—into a single collective organism. At some point, she predicts, "it will simply wake up," Others like Heylighen agree[311]. "This evolution that injects ever more intelligence into the Internet, leads to a near-term shift from World Wide Web to "Global Brain" where the "Global Brain" refers to the distributed online intelligence that is supported by various stigmergic mechanisms.

Heylighen shows how these online mechanisms are functionally identical to the mechanisms used by the human brain. He suggests, for instance, that the process of *quantitative stigmergy,* corresponding to the use of human or software agents searching the web, is nearly identical to the process of strengthening neuronal connections that result in bursts of neuron activation spreading across the brain. On the other hand, *qualitative stigmergy,* exemplified online by a variety of collaborative, "open access" sites where people freely improve upon each other's contributions, closely parallels the process of creating symbolic consciousness in the brain through the use of language and other symbols as agents to collectively develop new knowledge.

Collaboration based on stigmergic communication is described[312] as a form of mass cooperation and distributed action, which is not dependent on the formation of relationships or social negotiation, but results from independent contributions, and reactions to them, by collaborators who may accept those contributions, or who may modify or reject them. While stigmergic collaboration remains at arm's length, it nevertheless has the capacity to continually build on what has come before. The ubiquitous connectivity of the Internet has made such mass collaboration ever more commonplace,

Chapter 6

as witnessed by the "open source" movement, Wikipedia, and many other social media phenomena.

As this "global community" emerges, its dynamics will likely reflect those of other human communities as it enlarges collective welfare through increased specialization and diversity, together with more sophisticated forms of cooperation. We should expect to see extensive experimentation with a variety of global mechanisms to mitigate the potential for social conflict, while diversity-inspired innovation adds further to overall social welfare.

The prevalence of innovation over conflict will be largely determined by the social mechanisms we are able to create to foster information sharing: learning and collaboration, on the one hand, and mechanisms to moderate conflict through trust building, moral contracting and the reduction of free-riding, on the other. Thus, the primary challenge of evolving governments will be to create ever more complex processes of social learning, together with a level of coordination that meets or exceeds the complexity reflected in a globally diverse, yet increasingly interconnected, world.

These new structures of social learning are not likely to look anything like the centralized educational models of universities and colleges. Expect *scalable learning* to become much more distributed individually and driven more like a hacker collective. Yes, I would imagine that universities and colleges will still exist (at least a few will), generating standardized courseware in the form of MOOCs (massively open online courses) and maybe, more hopefully, as local places where people can come together to have rich conversations and learn from each other.

But as the Internet fuels a collective capacity for stigmergic collaboration[313], a growing number of people are likely to respond to social problems in a much more self-sufficient way, as evidenced by the popularity of "open data" initiatives, "hackathons," and citizen-driven applications that are being created for community benefit. *Scalable learning* in this context, becomes another way of describing effective local learning that becomes connected, and networked, and almost instantaneously global.

When we combine the technological tools for cooperation, the multitude of partnerships blossoming on every issue front, and an increasingly "activist" citizenry, it's easy to see that the monopoly on social coordination that was once held by governments has ended.

We are becoming less and less dependent on governments as the sole source and provider of public goods and services. Not surprisingly, the reputation of the civic sector has expanded, both in the provision of social forums where "adult conversations" can take place, but also as the trusted delivery agent of public services[314]. This growing self-sufficiency will soon alter the balance in the relationship between citizens and their governments, which still remains psychologically entrenched in the old paternalistic legacy of "the State knows best."

Unfortunately, due to the pace of knowledge growth and technological change, governments are finding themselves more and more in a situation of learning impairment, unable to tackle complex societal concerns, or to respond to the growing public demand for more transparency and better accountability. Citizens are becoming fed up and increasingly don't believe the promises of their "expert" leaders who plead "just trust us, we are working in your best interests." Says Michael Gove[315], Brexit champion and current UK justice minister, "I think people in this country have had enough of experts."

However, since we already know that leaders are not really in charge any more, this frustration would be better and more realistically directed to the systemic misalignment between how governments are structured, and what governments are being asked to do. It's a tension being generated because:

- the required knowledge is often in the hands of both citizens *and* government, resulting in less deference to government as the expert "in charge";

- citizens do not have the same operational overhead or the high transaction costs of government—they are in effect more nimble in their learning and actions;

- citizens are becoming more cognizant of their own ability to contribute, both individually and in concert with other citizens, to produce the solutions that affect them; and

- there are, as a result of the above, growing demands by citizens to become principal actors in their own self-governance, rather than just acquiescing to a role as entitled consumers of governance.

The legitimacy of elected representatives, the cornerstone of modern Western democracies, is increasingly being questioned in many parts of the world, and in its place the model of *"participatory democracy"* is gaining favour. The former relies on centralized learning while the latter utilizes knowledge that is broadly dispersed across an entire population, creates systems to capture that knowledge, and produces the capacities to learn collectively in order to secure social coordination. It is democracy by its actual owners, the people, rather than by their elected agents.

Despite being in its infancy in North America, *participatory democracy* has shown an upward trend in popularity largely because of the frequently perceived gaps between local needs and the standardized needs that are routinely identified by centralized governments. In fact, the very egalitarian nature of modern governments tends to prohibit them from providing customized solutions in local areas, thus encouraging more bottom-up, participatory approaches independent of government.

For instance, in Porto Alegre, Brazil's tenth largest city, participatory budgeting, or *orçamento participativo*, has operated successfully since the late 1980s. This is a bottom-up budgeting process that allows priorities to emerge from small neighbourhood levels to become citywide concerns, a process that permits citizens to set local, annual budget priorities to which elected officials can then allocate tax resources. In another example, Finland has used crowdsourcing to create new laws[316] and Iceland has drafted a new constitution with public input via Twitter, Facebook and Flickr[317]. The New Zealand government has experimented with a wiki in that most sacrosanct of all areas of government operation—policy development—to permit citizens to participate in rewriting its National Police Act.[318] And participate they did—much more so than the government anticipated or could effectively deal with.

Canada's experimentation with participatory-type democracy has been limited to the use of citizen juries, first in BC and then in Ontario, in order to help find alternatives to Canada's unrepresentative "first-past-the-post"

(FPTP) electoral system. That antiquated system frequently elects parties to majority governments even though they may receive less than 25% of the electorate's votes. Unfortunately, those early experiments ultimately failed, primarily due to the lack of support and public education from established political parties that had large stakes in maintaining the status quo.

Nevertheless, one of the main election promises of the current Liberal Government in Canada was to reform the electoral system before the next election in 2019. The Government struck an all-party committee to explore options with proportional voting being principal among them. After a year the Electoral Reform Committee came back with a recommendation for some form of proportional voting as the answer to FPTP.

Unfortunately for Canadians, that wasn't the recommendation the Government wanted to hear. It disparaged the work of the Committee and suddenly became revisionist, saying that FPTP was what Canadians wanted all along (it did get them elected after all). Still in a stinging critique of the ongoing degeneration of Canada's Parliament, the *Globe and Mail* reflected that, "rather than fret over how to make the House more relevant and the Senate relevant at all, it may be better to explore how new technologies can put citizens, rather than politicians, in charge."[319] Maybe the idea of *participatory democracy* hasn't died entirely in Canada.

But how does one go about putting citizens in charge? Should we, as has been proposed by some groups, just let the people decide in a series of referenda? Or would having so many citizens "in charge" be a recipe for social chaos—as others have suggested?

To frame these questions in another way, the issue of getting large numbers of people to "decide" is a secondary one. What is more important is how to get them to effectively "learn" together. This immediately eliminates referenda as primary tools for *participatory democracy*. Referenda are not learning exercises. Once more, the question arises as to how does one scale up learning and collaboration in environments where there are, not only lots of people, issues and answers, but also issues of great complexity?

The success of putting citizens "in charge" hinges on the distinction between collaborative approaches that involve small groups (i.e. are relationship-dependent), and approaches that involve stigmergic or mass collaboration—(see **Reimagining Government Part II**). Stigmergic collaboration works best when lots of people are actually involved. In fact, it's essential.

On the other hand, the opposite is true for small groups—too many people* means too many relationships to manage. Mass collaboration involving millions can work quite well**—precisely because it doesn't have to involve millions of relationships, only lots of people bringing their knowledge and attention to make things better.

Linus Torvalds, the originator of Linux and the open-source software movement says, "I don't think complexity is the stopper—in fact I would (and do) seriously argue that, especially in the face of complexity, you absolutely have to have an open and collaborative development process, exactly because *it's the only thing that scales*. However, it's not enough to be open and collaborative—it needs to be distributed as well. And by 'distributed,' I mean the massive parallel kind where everybody can replicate the whole thing."[320]

From this perspective, *participatory democracy* can work, if it is open to involving lots and lots of citizens (although, realistically, not everyone would participate on each and every issue) who could then assert their direct ownership in the governance process, learn together and stigmergically collaborate on change. Once again, this is different from proportional voting models. And it implies sidestepping the need for citizens to persuade governments to do this or that on their behalf.

Instead of government by referenda, it suggests the need to create a platform upon which many individuals can contribute and learn from one another. It also means cultivating a new ethic of online citizenship, and maybe even new online behaviours.

One of the positive repercussions of the ease and frequency of creating many, new and diverse communities on the Internet (some of which may be global in reach) is that if we can identify a problem, then in all probability

---

* The effective limit of small group collaboration is about 25 people.

** As the Internet itself attests to, given the tools that support it are all open source.

there are many others in the world who may be similarly challenged and with whom we can connect in order to envisage and implement solutions.

We can then ask ourselves, what might happen, if citizens were to simply cooperate amongst themselves, instead of petitioning or pleading with governments to do things for them? If people could self-organize using the Internet to produce all the collective goods and services they need—maybe in the same way that they can now book flights online instead of working through a travel agent—what then would become of governments, whose role until now has been as the main provider of those public goods and services? Is this the direction of a revitalized, new libertarianism (i.e. where no government is the best form of government)?

Certainly, there is some evidence that suggests when citizens can use Internet-enabled tools to come together and learn, they do cooperate more. As a result, *bring your own solution*, is the new BYOS, and is increasingly the hallmark of social coordination. Here are some interesting examples:

- **OpenParliament.ca**—when the Canadian Parliament wouldn't provide parliamentary data to citizens in an accessible format that was easy to read and track, a *single* Canadian* did;
- **TheyWorkforYou.com,** a UK initiative trying to bridge the democratic disconnect by encouraging greater transparency and public engagement;
- **Loomio.org,** an open source web application for making group decisions that was originally created during the "Occupy Wall Street" period;
- **iCitizen Corp.**, which helps people to stay up to date on issues and legislation, rate and connect with elected officials, as well as participate in issue polls, the results of which are then sent to elected officials;
- **Citizen-attache.github.io,** a citizen hackathon to generate insights and analysis for Canada's international aid community;

---

* That citizen was Michael Muloney, a software engineer from Montreal, who simply got frustrated with the opacity of the Canadian Parliament's online efforts.

- **RandomHacksOfKindness,** an international network of events to build solutions that address challenges faced by non-profits, humanitarian and community organizations by making use of public data from all levels of government;

- **Laboratório Ráquer,** or "Hacker Lab," inside the Brazilian Chamber of Deputies that is open for access and use by any citizen so they can utilize public data in a collaborative fashion for actions that enhance citizenship; and

- **DemocracyOS**—an open-source platform created in Argentina that is both web- and smartphone-enabled, and that can be used for voting and political debate that political parties and governments can download, install, and repurpose in a manner similar to the WordPress blogging software.

Consequently, it is not unreasonable to expect that if citizens continue to actively participate in designing and producing social solutions, and as a result coordinate amongst themselves, they will eventually demand a larger and larger share of societal governance as real partners with government, instead of simply being passive recipients of its largesse.

In that future, what then becomes of politicians and public servants? Would they become disintermediated like travel agents? Alternatively, since MPs and cabinet ministers are already "nobodies" in the current system, would this be an opportunity for their resurrection in some other form?

A little reinvention or re-imagination might seem to be in order—if only to ensure the continued legitimacy of public sector. If self-sufficiency is indeed the trend, then would it not be wise for governments to reinvent themselves along the lines of determining the possible mechanisms for:

1. understanding what citizens want; and
2. helping citizens get what they need?

And if citizen participation becomes more the norm, then how would this behaviour be more formally and productively integrated into our existing democratic institutions, beyond the periodic and half-hearted participation of citizens in elections? Such moves would no doubt involve a radical shift from the paternalistic psychology of "the State knows best" that currently dominates governments, towards a more cooperative attitude like "how can we help?"*

Yet given the preponderance of ethno-centric or tribal-type organizations in most governments, citizens will no doubt have to be clearer and louder in asserting their right to act as principals and owners of their own governance before governments will begin to embrace them as partners to any significant extent. Simultaneously, governments will have to extricate themselves from their learning disabilities and develop more self-reflexive and learning attitudes to understand the net-benefit value they could generate for themselves, by moving into this more generous and facilitative role.

There's no doubt that in each government there are pockets of public servants working hand-in-hand with citizens and businesses to achieve shared goals. Highlighting these experiences and illustrating a *Return on Legitimacy* (ROL) for a government from such efforts would do much to lift the culture of public service out of the clutches of the traditional management paradigm it now suffers under. Government needs to tell and learn from its own success stories. Until then, one can expect the legitimacy gap between elected officials and citizens to continue to widen, coupled with the growing resentment of a dysfunctional and ineffective public sector as a whole.

From examining the behaviours in several new online companies, such as Etsy, Lenddo and Good Eggs, Aaron Hurst suggests a new pattern of organization is emerging. "We are in the early stages of a social evolution," he says, "that is creating a new economy, one based on the creation of purpose for people . . . This is a shift from the era of Walmart and Amazon, which created tremendous profits for a few, but eroded opportunities for the many, including local communities, small businesses and artisans." [321]

The new online marketplaces Hurst explored are putting *purpose over profit,* and have made purpose the driver of innovation and growth in

---

* Indications that such a shift in mindset is already occurring in some Canadian quarters such as in BC's Public Health Services Agency and the Canadian Partnership Against Cancer as discussed in Part II.

their companies. Many of the new social enterprise-type organizations have similar orientations. If this trend continues, and *purpose over profit* motivation becomes a significant driver in our economy, it would clearly put the interests of people at its centre, rather than the interests of CEOs, shareholders, countries, tribes or aristocracy.

If this happens, it's a trend that governments would soon have to emulate just as it did with NPM's mimicry of private management in the '80s and '90s. Maybe more so, given the online nature of the companies Hurst studied and the influence that social media, such as Twitter, Facebook, Instagram and YouTube, had over them as vehicles for individuals to shine and for communities to materialize around their shared purpose.

The experience of Canadian musician Dave Carroll is illustrative[322]. In the spring of 2008, Carroll and his band, Sons of Maxwell, were travelling via United Airlines to Nebraska for a one-week tour. Prior to takeoff, Carroll witnessed his $3500 Taylor guitar was being roughly thrown around by United's baggage handlers in Chicago, severely damaging it. Later, although United Airlines didn't deny the experience took place, it delayed for nine months and tried to deflect responsibility onto someone else, until finally they said they would do nothing to compensate Carroll for his loss. With no money for lawyers to fight United in court, Carroll did the only thing he could do—he wrote a song and then he and his band performed it, posting the video on YouTube.

The video, *United Breaks Guitars*[323], immediately went viral—garnering over a half a million hits within three days, drawing international media attention and seriously tarnishing United's brand. Within four days of the video being posted, United's stock price fell 10%, costing shareholders about $180 million and triggering a call to Carroll from United's Managing Director of Customer Solutions, Rob Bradford, who apologized for United's treatment of Carroll and his guitar. Belatedly, United now offered to provide $3,000 in compensation. Carroll accepted, but the money was given to charity, as Carroll had already received two new guitars from Bob Taylor, the owner of Taylor Guitars, who was appreciative of all the attention.

In the past, if customers were bullied by large organizations like United Airlines, then there really wasn't much they could do, except maybe try and mount a lengthy and costly class action suit. Today the Internet gives users another alternative: *a collective voice*—one which can potentially scale to millions of people worldwide, creating a compelling collective counterweight to experts and organizational power that was once perceived to be almost unassailable.

The current generation of digital natives (i.e. those who grew up with the Internet) are more knowledgeable, more educated and have the greatest access to knowledge in human history, plus they are in the midst of an unprecedented period of exponential knowledge growth.

They are more connected, both locally and globally. They are, not only more willing to collaborate and work with others, but they also see it as natural, unlike previous generations who often considered collaboration *"as an unnatural act."*[324] They are more confident in their own voice, more empowered, more participative, and more willing to jump in to make a difference. To these digital natives, creating a collective voice is pretty much second nature.

And as a consequence, they are less deferential to authority, less trustful of both leaders and government, and less confident in government's ability to solve the problems that matter most to them. They are, according to Gary Hamel,[325] "the most authority-phobic generation in history." They also see the world as their home, humanity as their family, and differences as something to be cherished, not feared. This represents a significant shift in social consciousness, and it correlates well with the emergence of what Laloux has called *evolutionary* organizations[326].

Lastly, among these online natives, whether it be in their virtual acts of secession from the US "paper belt,"[327] or in their participation in *RandomHacksOfKindness*, there appears to be a strong desire to seek and realize some grand purpose, one that can unfold not only their own potential, but that of humanity's as well as. They believe that they can be more, and because they do not have to act alone, they do not have to accept the world as it is. They can pool their knowledge and resources to do more. They are connected to others near and far. There is a consciousness of global connectedness that is, on the one hand, being enabled by the many new technologies and the Internet, but is, at the same time, reshaping how they think of ourselves, what they do, and how they do it.

Chapter 6

Re-designing government around collaboration

"In the new world of business," says Thomas Malone[328], "lots of highly connected individuals will each make their own decisions using information from many other places. In fact, this revolution is now possible because new information technologies make it feasible—on a scale never before imagined—for vastly more people to have the information they need to make well-informed choices."

As a result, he says, "new technologies allow [small organizations] to have the economic benefits of large organizations—like economies of scale and knowledge—without giving up the human benefits of small ones—like freedom, creativity, motivation, and flexibility... This revolution has already begun." Says Malone, "we saw its harbingers in the final decades of the twentieth century in talk about empowering workers, outsourcing almost everything, creating networked or virtual corporations."

Without a doubt, the "work" of the last century and a half has been driven by corporations and the organizations created by them. Corporations arose out of the notions of classical liberalism and *laissez-faire* economics, but also from the need to make efficient use of an increasing number of new technologies. Those technologies—whether they were steam engines, electric motors, telephones, automobiles, computers or the Internet—were applied to processes of mass production. The use of machines required lots of people with standardized skills to feed them with standardized inputs, while other people, consumers, were willing to use their standardized outputs. Work was made routine and human input was essentially exorcized of anything that might make it unique, creative or unpredictable. The primary role of corporate management was to ensure that unpredictability was eliminated from the practice of work.

With all the different activities, skills, processes and knowledge involved, mass production also required systems of mass coordination to oversee product development, the production process, and the marketing and selling of products and services, as well as overseeing the accounting and admin processes and ensuring investors were sufficiently rewarded. Each corporation coordinated all these tasks through a single hierarchical system that pushed strategy, innovation, and decision-making together, based on rules for inter-group behaviour handed down from the top. In the process, corporations structured themselves vertically, with senior leadership always being the body that guided the organization and motivated change.

But equally true is that in the last half century that "work" has been reshaped again with the orchestration of many independent players, whether it was among companies in extensive supply chains, various kinds of partnerships, or multi-stakeholder collaborations. In today's context, the top-down approach has proved to be neither smart nor effective. In today's companies, a concentration of responsibility for organizational responsiveness among senior executives, together with a litany of rules for employee compliance, is fostering both learning impairment and an underutilization of talent.

In such organizations, employees rarely bring 100% of themselves to work, and rarely do they feel sufficient ownership in what they are doing to go out of their way to be innovative. In fact, being innovative more often than not means going against orders from the top. Not surprisingly, several recent surveys by Gallup[329], for instance, have found that very few employees are actually engaged in their work, and even fewer are passionate about it.

"That's got to change," says Gary Hamel[330]. As we've already discussed, employees who've grown up in this Internet culture are used to connecting, sharing, learning, teaching and collaborating as a matter of course. For them, *it is not positional power which commands respect, but the power to help others achieve their goals.* For digital natives, coordination is not something that is imposed by someone at the top, but something that emerges in a climate of openness, generosity and shared purpose. Thus, it is that *co-creative cooperation,* or the ability to work openly together with co-workers or partners, is becoming the new "must have" capacity to ensure organizations retain their creative edge.

Sure enough, "the latest management trend to sweep Silicon Valley," according to Greg Ferenstein[331], "requires CEOs to formally relinquish their authority and grant special protection for every employee to experiment with ideas. It's called *holacracy,* and several big-name tech leaders have jumped on the bandwagon." Holacracy is a governance system where authority and decision-making are distributed throughout the organization in self-organizing teams rather than being centralized at the top of the organization. "Twitter co-founder Evan Williams adopted it for his new blogging platform startup, Medium. The [holacracy] movement started making headlines when Zappos CEO, Tony Hsieh, announced that he would transition his entire Las Vegas company—with a billion dollars of revenue and 1,500 workers—to holacracy by the end of 2014."[332]

Still, even if leadership and bureaucracy are becoming a little shopworn and seen by some as an impediment to progress, don't expect them to go away any time soon. Top-down leaders are still the norm in most organizations. Management schools still teach organizational coordination as if only one option existed—top-down. And both employees and society at large remain strong adherents to the notions of romanticized leadership. It amounts to pathological self-delusion, as economist Tim Harford observed. "I see people who, in the face of an incredibly complicated world, are nevertheless absolutely convinced that they understand the way that the world works."[333] Unfortunately, this is not just the perspective of a few narcissistic leaders, but in the face of uncertainty, it is also the view of most people who prefer the convenience and the illusion of certainty, rather than taking on responsibility for uncertain change themselves.[334]

Becoming a trusted platform for others to work together

Still, despite minimal change amongst Fortune 500 companies, the most vivid example of the growth of distributed authority and decision-making is perhaps the Internet itself. It is the product of a shared set of non-proprietary, technical protocols that permit different types of computers and software to communicate with each other. Anyone can create their own community and exchange ideas, interests, music, photos, videos, research and, as we have seen, much else. "The Internet has become the largest, most robust commons in history," remarks David Boilier[335]. "The great virtue of [this] commons is that it can be a responsive, effective way to manage a resource in the public interest without command-and-control regulation and legalisms [typical of government]."

The Internet commons flourishes because no one owns the Internet (at least not currently), and so its users do not have to get permission from, or make payments to, any sort of intermediary. Anyone can do what they want, say what they want, build what they want on the Internet, and then manage their work however they wish. As Boilier points out, "the cable and telephone companies that provide access to the Internet are not allowed to favour large corporate users with superior service while leaving the rest of us—including upstart competitors and non-market players—with slower, poorer-quality service." This notion that the Internet deals with everyone in the same way is a concept known as "net neutrality."

Boilier elaborates by saying, "net neutrality is a key reason why the Internet has been so phenomenally generative. Because the Internet functions as a commons, it enables anyone to find others, strike up a collaboration and generate useful stuff without first having to pay a premium fee, raise capital, or persuade a corporate gatekeeper that the idea is marketable." As a result, we regularly see new types of value being created, often disrupting well-established industries, which so far have included old mainstays like: software development, publishing, travel, media and journalism, movies and investing, to name a few.

The combination of a global commons that nobody owns and ubiquitous sharing practices, is fundamentally rewriting our cultural understanding of *how we work together*. And, it's creating an entirely new paradigm for organizations, including our notions of how we can achieve social coordination, which, historically speaking, we delegated to governments.

There were indications of this paradigm shift even going back as far as 2001, when Larry Summers and economist Bradford DeLong suggested to the Federal Reserve Bank of Kansas City that as marginal costs approach zero, "the competitive paradigm cannot be fully appropriate"[336] for organizing commercial life, and they admitted that "we do not yet know what the right replacement paradigm will be." However, "now we know," according Jeremy Rifkin.[337] "A new economic paradigm—the collaborative commons—has leapt onto the world stage as a powerful challenger to the capitalist market".

According to Rifkin, a growing number of producer-consumers, or *prosumers* as he refers to them, is not only producing and sharing easily digitized products such as information, software, news and entertainment, but they are also contributing to the production of much more tangible products and services, as well. Some of these include:

- ***transportation*** (e.g. Zipcar, Uber and Vrtucar, which provide access to cars without resorting to car ownership);

- ***car production*** (e.g. Local Motors, which permits end users to co-design and co-build their own cars);

- ***renewable energy*** production (e.g. feed-in tariffs which permit users to contribute to, as well as draw from, the electricity grid);

- ***3-D printing,*** which can copy products or even biologicals almost as easily as a paper document;

- ***accommodation*** (e.g. Couchsurfing and Airbnb, which turn that spare bedroom or couch into a hotel room);

- ***tools*** (e.g. Washington, DC's Union Kitchen, which hosts a 7,300 sq. ft. facility to share kitchenware); and

- ***online education*** (e.g. MIT's OpenCourseWare or MOOCs, which permit both educators and students to contribute to educational resources).

The economic consequences of all this sharing are twofold: firstly, *prosumers* tend to bypass both conventional markets and the need for product ownership; and secondly, products and services can frequently be produced at near-zero marginal cost in the collaborative commons.

In addition, the efforts at co-creation and sharing have social consequences. Not only do they afford the opportunity to give fuller expression to individual interests, but they also provide opportunities to reach out and make a human connection at a time when modern, urban life has become increasingly insular.

Couchsurfing.org, for example, provides not only travel accommodation for its six million members who seek and provide lodging in 100,000 cities worldwide, but it also promotes a relationship that rewards both traveller and provider. For those who welcome couchsurfers, they are not just sharing their homes with strangers (an instinctively scary thought), but they are "sharing with friends they haven't met yet." Says Molly Turner, the director of public policy for Airbnb, "What's really going on here is the urbanization of the world and the re-urbanization of American cities. Either consciously or subconsciously, [people] are realizing that that involves the public realm, the commons, sharing goods and services and infrastructure."[338]

Rifkin agrees. "Hundreds of millions of people are already transferring bits and pieces of their lives from capitalist markets to the emerging global collaborative commons, operating on a ubiquitous 'Internet of things' platform. The great economic paradigm shift has begun."[339]

Badger concurs[340], saying, "we're witnessing a paradigm shift toward sharing in the offline world because of the online technology that enables it . . . The Internet has essentially allowed us to expand the circle of people with whom we share. But even more fundamentally, the open-source culture of the web has taught us *how to share*, and made sharing a default of social interaction."

This is significant because in our modern culture, we have so venerated the qualities of independence, individualism, and self-sufficiency, that the habits and practices of *how to share* have remained woefully underdeveloped. That the Internet is encouraging a reinvigoration of these older human skills is important.

According to former World Bank Director and author Steve Denning[341], "the major changes that the Internet has *already* had on the economy include:

- it has shredded the vertical value chains of the 20th century economy, in the process wreaking havoc on middle men, the markups and the margins;

- it has created a vast new set of horizontal value chains, in which millions of people are creating their own virtual meeting places and marketplaces with their own lateral economies of scale;

- it has created a generation of people who began *preferring access* to ownership, and so have stopped buying things; and

- it has shifted the balance of power in the marketplace from sellers to buyers. Customers have instant reliable information about the choices enabled by globalization, and a capacity to communicate and interact with other customers. Suddenly the customer is in charge. Firms can no longer push average products at customers, in the confident belief that sales and marketing will be able to sell them. They now have to figure out what might delight customers and continuously deliver that."

Yet, all this sharing has also had another consequence, one that might be quite disturbing for some. There are more people, especially more different people, whom you now have to consider. People who can voice a different opinion and who might not agree with you, who may want different things than you do, who may compete for your job, who may live their lives under altogether different conditions or rules, and who may want to experience the same level of prosperity, peace and security that you do.

In the past, these "others" were largely invisible and rarely heard from. Now, however, their faces invade the nightly news and their stories fill the pages of your Twitter feed, if not the daily newspaper. This exposure to so many differences has caused some to recoil and to try to put the techno-genie back in the bottle, pretending that all these differences can be made to go away without consequence. It's a strategy, for instance, that the Trump campaign in the US employed with great short-term success. In essence, people are promised a return to the golden years, where, in hindsight, things always seem better.

But just as companies are beginning to engage potential buyers in ways to encourage their participation in co-defining their needs, in co-designing products and services, in testing prototypes, and in providing feedback, governments must find better ways to not only engage with this growing diversity of voices, but also reconfigure government with new mechanisms for shared governance. Policy development and program strategies are going to have to look a lot more like the creation of self-organizing "movements" around people's shared passions,[342] while the old distinctions between social groups and governments will begin to dissolve, even as they have between producers and consumers.

How can government begin to reflect this greater sharing and co-creation? To some, it would seem that as government evolves, in many ways it must begin to resemble the very nature of the Internet itself—connected, networked, open, inclusive, permissionless, facilitative, collaborative, trusted, learning, innovative and adaptive—becoming in effect a platform for human cooperation[343]. Quite clearly, this does not lend itself to perpetuating a leader-centric model of government, but one that embraces networks of shared ownership and individual choice.

Generating stewardship from process design

As previously mentioned, stewardship is more than just an expression of individual personality. It emerges largely as a collective capacity from the behaviours of group members, and from good group process. However, creating effective stewardship from good process design has the additional value of fostering much needed stability in collaborations and partnerships where individual participants may change regularly. Such processes would involve assembling a group of principles, rules, norms, behaviours, mechanisms and protocols, which together could make up something like an "automatic pilot" capable of steering the participants in ways that generate meaningful ownership, a sense of shared belonging, self-organization, social learning, wayfinding, innovation and resilience.[344]

My colleagues and I at the University of Ottawa have described this type of "automatic pilot" as an *inquiring system*. *Inquiring systems* are collections of group actions that are based on a questioning mindset, and that use heuristics, together with the application of various affordances, in order to facilitate participant interactions that foster better collaboration.

The application of an *inquiring system* in fostering better stewardship has six interconnected but separate tasks to perform:

- *bringing together information* from all the relevant actors to ensure a comprehensive understanding in terms of context, issues, actors and possible responses;

- *framing reconciliation* between the participants' perspectives, by creating a suitable space and process to ensure synthesis emerges between them and collaboration jells;

- *avoiding the rush to decision-making* and action, as haste is instinctively undertaken in order to present an appearance of doing something, anything, rather than spending time on the learning that produces results;

- *generating a mix of moral contracts and incentives* likely to fuel the continuous probing, learning and innovation by the participants, as well as their ongoing contingent cooperation;

- *constructing "fail-safe" and "safe-fail" mechanisms* to ensure resilience, because failure in an environment of complexity and uncertainty should be assumed and not ignored; and

- *constructing "negative capability,"** that is, the conditions that can ensure that the collaboration will be robust enough to survive the inevitable conflicts and struggles that will emerge between the participants.

With this type of stewardship process, an *inquiring system* can then operate as a collective learning system that:

- seeks out anomalies;

- mops up all kinds of relevant information;

- seeks out additional collaborators;

- explores problem definitions;

- reconciles and reframes different perspectives and paradigms in a dialogue among owner-collaborators;

- generates testable prototypes;

---

* In the sense that it was used by John Keats as a rejection of established attitudes and preconceived notions in favour of experimentation and a willingness to co-create a future without being encumbered by the past. John Keats. *Letters of John Keats to His Family and Friends*, ed. Sidney Colvin, Gutenberg eBook #35698, 28 March 2011: 48

- learns quickly from each experiment in the mode of "fail early and fail often"; and

- disseminates both the good and the bad news, thereby allowing the knowing-doing gap among the collaborators to be closed over time.[345]

As a part of this collective learning process, the various relationships that are coordinated by the stewardship process are continually being transformed and renewed in an self-referential, autopoietic* way, as new information is metabolized through the interactions among the participants. As such, an *inquiring system* evolves as a complex process for probing into the state, dynamics and growth of the collaborative "organization," resulting in ongoing mutual adaptation and coordination among the participating partners.

Such an *inquiring system* will not be standardized in all private, public and social spheres of life, nor will it be the same in every issue domain. In fact, the nature of the participants and their animating issues will always constrain the system in unique ways. Nevertheless, whatever the sphere or issue domain, there will be common challenges confronted by the designers of any *inquiring system*, in order to produce the requisite stewardship.

These challenges may be described in terms of the four key phases of collaborative governance. These phases include:[346]

1. **Observational:** Does the situation need changing? Is there anything wrong or unsatisfactory with the status quo?

2. **Investigative:** What is the problem? Who needs to be involved?

3. **Relationship Design:** How can we work together to tackle the problem?

4. **Learning While Doing:** How can we learn together and evaluate our progress?

Within each of these four phases, there may be a multiplicity of subsidiary activities and further deeper questions that are linked to the nature of

---

* Autopoiesis is a property of a system capable of reproducing and maintaining itself a specific issue as well as to the interests of the people and organizations involved. Yet, whatever the differences, an *inquiring system* must, at a minimum, build on the practical rules, values and behaviours that are in good currency among its partners to ensure their voluntary participation.

For instance, with collaborators among the child- and youth-related professions, protective and nurturing behaviours must underlie and be incorporated into any process used to guide a partnership serving children and youth. Otherwise, the attention and interest of the partners, who are steeped in these behaviours, will not be effectively engaged.

The inputs of an *inquiring system* will be drawn from the diverse perspectives and experiences of the various partners and collaborators, just as in the earlier example of the governance of technology start-ups. These inputs can then be compiled and acted upon through cycles of learning and unlearning that accompany the "learning while doing" process of the participants. The outputs of this *inquiring system* will be reflected in both modifications to the issue system by the partners through time, and, just as important, their co-learning, shared commitment and mutual accountability.

This "learning while doing" is best facilitated by heuristic strategies.[*] Heuristic learning allows collaborators to efficiently deal with the uncertainty involved in complex tasks, and, although there is no guarantee that any particular heuristic strategy will work, experience suggests that the desired results come faster using them. In contrast, working with algorithmic strategies may guarantee success—but at a much slower pace.

A good example of the difference between these two strategies might be to imagine you've lost your pen in a big room. An algorithmic strategy would have you pace the room back and forth in a tight grid pattern until you find your pen. You are guaranteed to find it, but if it's a big room, it may take a while. Alternatively, you might imagine what you were previously doing and where you were at particular moments in the past. You may find yourself retracing your steps from one place to another and another across the room

---

[*] David Strauss identifies 64 such heuristics that are regularly used in the practice of collaboration. STRAUS, David. 2002. *How to Make Collaboration Work: Powerful Ways to Build Consensus, Solve Problems and Make Decisions*, San Francisco, CA: Berrett-Koehler.

until you find your pen. At any location there is no guarantee you'll find your pen, but you'll probably find it faster than the grid approach.

Large, easy-to-use repertoires of heuristics become part of the tool boxes that effective stewards endeavour to create. These heuristics can be matched to particular issue domains and partnership features, allowing collaborators to formulate an *inquiring system* that is "ecologically rational" (i.e., well matched with their particular environment). The heuristics they use will be comprised of various combinations of skills, abilities, practices and techniques which are used precisely because they have proven effective in the past.

Another heuristic example is the "tit-for-tat" heuristic that is comprised of the abilities to cooperate, to forget, and to imitate.[347] This heuristic is widely used as a tool for instilling cooperative behaviour. However, it is best suited to situations where the partners are unfamiliar with each other and where trust levels are low. In higher trust environments, the "tit-for-tat" heuristic may prove overly tedious among those already confident in the reliability of their partners.

In most governance regimes, the application of heuristics is often a critical factor in determining collaborative success. Consequently, ensuring that these heuristics are available to and understood by stewards and group facilitators is an important feature of a successful *inquiring system*. Unfortunately, neither heuristics nor the connoisseurship skills associated with them tend to be encouraged or consistently applied in organizations generally.

Organizations simply do not make the effort to build up bodies of collaborative learning around them, and therefore, when they collaborate they must repeatedly develop these tools, incurring new collaborative start-up costs each time. Consequently, there is a need to develop some sort of corporate memory around collaboration that is capable of identifying possible heuristics, affordances, or action possibilities[348] as part of the process.

One commonly used affordance is a checklist. It helps to stimulate an awareness of when to use a particular heuristic(s) and its associated skills and behaviours in order to facilitate more cooperative behaviour.

Chapter 6

Checklists are quick and easy to use; they focus the mind very economically on key issues, and they can help do so at the right time. They do not provide answers or ways to generate answers, but they do ensure that key questions are asked at the appropriate time. They are like doors to a building. They provide access but with no guarantee of finding what one is seeking or even how to find it once inside. Yet in this way, a checklist can help stewards facilitate coordination among their partners in an *inquiring system,* by enabling them to address the right questions at the right time. Then, coupled with additional heuristic strategies to deal with the outcomes of such questions, they can afford support to collaboration and further engagement.

The effectiveness of checklists as facilitators of collaboration has been demonstrated in many areas. Atul Gawande, for instance, has documented* the use of checklists to help guide surgical teams in their collaborative activities in an operating room effectively and efficiently. The use of operating room checklists was itself inspired by the use of the same affordance by aircraft pilots. In practice, checklists also evolve as social learning progresses, and as new experiences and contexts materialize. In the aircraft industry, for instance, manufacturers regularly update their cockpit checklists to reflect recent pilot and aviation industry experiences with the aircraft, together with new regulations. In fact, a publication date is usually stamped on all aircraft checklists to ensure that only the most up-to-date version is being used on a flight.

In summary then, the four phases of collaborative inquiry described earlier can be structured around a checklist of stylized questions that collaborators are likely to confront, and in doing so help launch them into more detailed and issue-specific questions that foster shared ownership and action.

---

* GAWANDE, Atul *The Checklist Manifesto.* New York: Metropolitan Books 2009. The checklist results, when applied to the operating rooms, were phenomenal as revealed by the results of an eight-city pilot study that was carried out: complications dropped by 36%, operating room deaths fell by 47%, infections originating in the operating room dropped by almost half (Gawande p.154). Further, analyses of exit surveys of staff members coming out of surgery also helped uncover the key causal mechanism that explained why the checklist approach had been so successful. As it turned out, the key factor was that the use of checklists caused a significant increase in the level of communication among operating room collaborators.

The table found in **Figure 13** is an example of a checklist that might be used to kick-start a collaborative process by defining a context, identifying who should be included, as well as afford the opportunity to reflect on guiding assumptions, structures, technology, and even the theory of what the "collective enterprise" is all about.

The following questions have been generalized from the experiences of many practitioners that my colleagues and I at the University of Ottawa have observed over the last twenty years.

In the table, each column is the locus for a number of key, "not-to-be-forgotten" questions. These 18 questions provide a good skeletal framework for a budding *system of inquiry*. In effect, they can "jump-start" the overall governance of a collaboration, but they can also be unpacked into more detailed and issue specific questions that can lead to an array of *heuristics* and additional affordances. These tools can then contribute to answering the four overriding questions of collaboration: *Does the situation need changing? What is the problem? How will we work together? How will we learn together and evaluate our progress?*

In the course of trying to answer these questions, stewardship is generated as new information comes forward, or as new circumstances materialize, and the interactions among the partners fuels a cycle of collective learning, shared commitment, innovation, and mutual accountability.

Instead of localizing power, purpose, expertise and accountability in the one called "the leader," a checklist like this can help define a distributed governance process that is inclusive of the participants while preserving the ownership of each. It creates an opportunity for the partners to learn how they will be together; it allows the right questions to evolve at the right time; it affords them time to sort out their shared possibilities, instead of rushing to decisions; and it helps structure feedback mechanisms to monitor their progress together, and to affirm their mutual commitments.

The competencies encouraged by such questions can generate a pattern of co-governance that emerges from their group learning dynamics and their interactions with their context—not from the head of an individual actor. This is what Goffman refers to as *interaction order*—a sort of collective

Figure 13: A Provisional Checklist for an Inquiring System[353]

I Does the situation need changing?	II What is the problem?	III How will we work together?	IV How will we learn together & evaluate our progress?
1. Are there any detectable anomalies?	6. What is the task at hand?	a. *STRUCTURAL DESIGN* 10. What practices of collaboration and social learning can you use to produce short-term success and long-term commitment?	12. What feedback and informational loops do you need to enable social learning?
2. What are the salient features of the issue domain?	7. What are the non-negotiable constraints within the mega-community?		13. What processes of formal and informal collective learning do you have in place?
3. What are the causal mechanisms at play?	8. Who are the stakeholders that must be included and how will you involve them?	b. *CULTURE OF COLLABORATION* 11. What are the conventions and moral contracts that need to be negotiated to maintain a culture of collaboration?	14. How will you gauge ongoing performance and partner contributions objectively?
4. Can this be resolved by a single actor?	9. What are the risks and potential rewards among the various partners, and how will these be aligned?		15. How will you gauge changes in attitudes and behaviours among partners?
5. Who are the key stakeholders?			16. How will you resolve conflicts?
			17. What fail-safe / safe-fail mechanisms are in place?
			18. At what point would you dissolve the collaboration?

intelligence, or "social mind."[349] Both individual and collective competencies obviously interact in any collaboration, but when ignited by an affordance like a checklist, those individual competencies remain somewhat harnessed by the context, affording some "action possibilities" while limiting others.

Whether the collaborative checklist I've described above is itself "perfect," or not, is irrelevant. More important, should collaborators begin using it, even as it is, it would likely help to rein in many of the typical leadership biases towards decision-making and immediate action, in favour of encouraging participants to gain confidence and certainty from a process of stewardship *even if the final outcomes of that process still remain uncertain*. That reduction of uncertainty in itself helps to facilitate collaboration.

Furthermore, the process helps to generate more affordances that will be more tailored to a specific context, that both individuals and groups can learn as being useful. "Affordances are not fixed properties: they are relationships that hold between objects and agents . . . To discover and make use of affordances is one of the important ways"[350] to deal with novel situations.

For example, the scenario affordance involved in creating what de Geus calls "memories of the future"[351] allows people to explore issue terrains that are as yet unmanifested, in order to be able to recognize their patterns should they ever become expressed. Such a tool allows people to overcome the ingrained human tendency to not "see" things in their experience that they have not previously considered. This scenario affordance is a powerful tool for fostering adaptiveness.

Learning to recognize when to use which affordance or heuristic, in what situations and under what conditions, is a key element of social learning. It is also at the core of good stewardship and collaboration design. Over time, participants who engage in such social learning become, in effect, "connoisseurs," whose judgement in a particular context has been cultured by experience.

Furthermore, among successful collaborators, it is often observed that they have a greater willingness to engage in additional collaboration as they have cultured both the associated relationships and the collaborative "connoisseurship" to take on more challenging tasks, with the implication that the real and the perceived costs of future collaboration are significantly reduced.[352]

This then is the last major dimension of a newly imagined government—that it may emerge from good process design, rather than be dependent on the limited capacities and whims of individual leaders.

Conclusion

What this review has led us to is that the design of democratic government that was suitable for the mid- to late 1800s, and served us well up until the latter part of the 1900s, is no longer tenable. Not only is that design obstructing collective solutions to the problems of today, but it is completely out of its depth when it comes to solving the problems of tomorrow.

The idea that we can trust *one* person to be in charge of governing a complex, evolving system like a society is completely unjustifiable today, despite the ongoing, knee-jerk homage paid to it by the leaders of political parties, academic experts, media and the public. The modern reality that elected "representatives" now really only represent their leaders, instead of their constituents, should be seen as an obvious anti-democratic cancer, yet the myth of "representative democracy" continues to persist as a compelling cultural force. Not only is there clear evidence to suggest that leader-driven "democracy" is not effective and a constraint against social innovation, but new technologies exist, and others are emerging, that are providing alternatives to this model of government. These technologies enable network styles of governance that are proving to be both very feasible and more effective. In contrast to 1867, when my home country Canada was created, direct, shared governance by citizens themselves is now practical—making representative-style democracy both unnecessary and undesirable.

Interestingly, however, social coordination among the various elements of society, once the central work of governments in the past, is resurfacing in importance due to a more distributed governance environment. Yet, it is demanding that governments refocus themselves on the practices of collaboration and collective learning in ways that are both scalable and as inclusive as possible of people and perspectives.

Furthermore, if shared democratic ownership is to be promoted and sustained, then the actions and policy-making of governments must adjust to *"let citizens in."* It's no longer enough for everyone to rely on "someone" in government to assume responsibility for solving problems when the required knowledge, resources and power are so widely distributed in society. In many ways, it is foreseeable that future governments may simply become facilitators of the work generated by citizens acting in concert with each other.

In that context, "good government" may well evolve into a capacity for creating effective platforms for citizens to collaborate, and for designing the processes which will encourage and sustain their ongoing cooperation. However, we are far from there.

To get there, we must begin by confronting a number of legacy design challenges that constrain the current system of government: by a series of out-dated or flawed assumptions about how governments should work; by distorted mechanisms that have evolved in ways that were never intended, or that are no longer appropriate; and by defective practices that are counterproductive to effective problem-solving, social innovation, collaboration, fairness and even basic democracy.

These design challenges include:

Bad assumptions

- we live in a simple, certain, predictable, Newtonian world;
- someone must always be in charge;
- someone (the leader) can have all the answers;
- leaders are always ethical and effective and therefore worthy of following;
- there exists a single, homogeneous blend of cultural values, which leaders can divine;

- only governments can provide public goods and services; and

- technical rationality should always prevail (i.e. objective science always leads to good practices that should be imposed on everyone equally).

Distorted mechanisms

- elected representatives that now represent governments to their electors;

- "representative governments" that merely look representative;

- the use of political parties that have usurped the democratic ownership of citizens;

- democratic contests that have devolved from exercises in collective learning to simple personality contests among party leaders;

- a fixation on unattainable scalable efficiencies vs. the production of results;

- an obsession with compliance accountability and finding who's to blame;

- an over-reliance on creating in-house policy expertise, leading to very large, but ineffective public service organizations;

- a belief in a policy-making process that is expert-driven, centralized, focused on the short-term and that automatically assumes "the State always knows best"; and

- the use of top-down control as the preferred tool of governing (because it's simple), leading to an overemphasis on the power of coercion vs. co-learning, shared commitment and the power of helpfulness.

Defective practices

- a reliance on quick decision-making, because it is seen as a sign of good leadership while effective learning and collaboration are ignored;

- an over-reliance on now dysfunctional bodies, such as parliaments, legislatures, and councils, that have become largely ceremonial institutions incapable of collective learning, and that present only an illusion of democracy;

- an emphasis on policy-making practices that focus on the taking of positions and the imposition of answers vs. the asking of questions, listening, and collective problem-solving;

- a reliance on standardization and equal treatment as proxies for fairness and effective policy results;

- the centralization of budgeting and planning, with taxes being collected and brought to the "Centre" for redistribution versus the allocation of resources to respond to local needs;

- the informal acceptance of redistribution as government's primary business because it is a short-term mitigation strategy when governments are otherwise unable to foster social coordination; and

- the widespread acceptance of elected representatives as "nobodies," or at best marginal, in the process of governing.

If we believe that democratic governments—rather than autocrats or technology—should be our principal tool of social coordination, then to be effective, governments must be adapted to fit the context of our modern era, which means we cannot shirk from addressing these design challenges.

For me, however, this task must be postponed to Part II of this series on *Re-Imagining Government* due to be published shortly.

Acknowledgements

In preparing this book there have obviously been many, many people whose ideas and perspectives have enriched it. This book stands on the shoulders of those who have wanted to make this world a better place. I hope that it honours their contributions.

I would like to especially thank Gilles Paquet, professor emeritus at the University of Ottawa, for his many contributions as teacher, mentor, colleague, partner, co-author, editor and publisher. His door was always open and whether it was to seek help in resolving a conflict or trying to co-imagine a different future together, he was always willing to listen.

Also, I would like to thank Ruth Hubbard for all of her editorial contributions and my former colleagues at the University of Ottawa, for their many big and small contributions to my understanding of partnerships and collaboration.

I would also like to thank the team at Tellwell Publishing for their help in getting this finalized and out to people everywhere.

Lastly, I wish to thank my wife, Carolyne, for all her patience with me, especially at those times when the technology wouldn't cooperate.

Endnotes

1. BUMP, Philip and Aaron Blake. 2016. "Donald Trump's dark speech to the Republican National Convention", *Washington Post*, 21 July. Accessed at: https://www.washingtonpost.com/news/the-fix/wp/2016/07/21/full-text-donald-trumps-prepared-remarks-accepting-the-republican-nomination/?tid=a_inl&utm_term=.2092bfe1ab2f

2. PAQUET, Gilles and Christopher Wilson. 2016. "Intelligent governance: an alternative paradigm", *Optimum Online*, Vol. 46, No. 3, September. Prepared for presentation to the 68th IPAC National Annual Conference, 28-29 June 2016, Toronto.

3. PERREAUX, Les and Ingrid Peritz. 2013. "Laval's ex-mayor faces gangsterism charges", *The Globe and Mail*, Montreal, 09 May.

4. COYNE, Andrew. 2015. "The things no party leader will say in Thursday's debate", *The National Post*, Toronto, 16 September.

5. ANTONOPOULOS, Andreas M. 2014. "Andreas M. Antonopoulos Educates Senate of Canada about Bitcoin", Senate Committee on Banking, Trade and Commerce, "Study on the use of digital currency", 11th session, 8 October. Accessed at: https://www.youtube.com/watch?v=xUNGFZDO8mM

6. PAQUET, Gilles and Christopher Wilson. 2016. *Intelligent Governance*, Invenire Books, Ottawa, June

7. KENNEDY, Mark. 2012. "Canada risks losing ties that bind, warns former prime minister Joe Clark", *PostMedia*, 25 November.

8. HUBBARD, Ruth and Gilles Paquet. 2015. "The Canadian Federal Public Service: Tinkering Can No Longer Suffice", *Optimum Online*, Vol. 45, Issue 3, September.

9. GUILFORD, Gywnn. 2016. "Harvard research suggests that an entire global generation has lost faith in democracy", *Quartz,* 30 November. Accessed at: http://qz.com/848031/harvard-research-suggests-that-an-entire-global-generation-has-lost-faith-in-democracy/

10   LALOUX, Fredric. 2014. *Reinventing Organizations*, Nelson Parker, Brussels.

11   DIAMOND, Larry. 2014. *Is Democracy in Decline?*, Remarks to the Club of Madrid Meeting, Florence, Nov 24. Accessed at: http://nextgenerationdemocracy.org/624/

12   Ibid.

13   GREENWOOD, Max. 2016. "Trump's Lies Aren't Lies Because 'There's No Such Thing' As Facts Anymore, His Surrogate Says", *The Huffington Post*, 1 December. Accessed at: http://www.huffingtonpost.com/entry/trump-surrogate-claims-no-facts_us_58408f8ee4b0c68e047fd952?

14   FANG, Marina. 2016. "Paul Ryan On Donald Trump Tweeting Lies: 'Who Cares?'", *The Huffington Post*, 4 December. Accessed at: http://www.huffingtonpost.com/entry/paul-ryan-donald-trump-tweets_us_5844b2f2e4b0c68e04818206?

15   DIAMOND, Larry. 2016. "It Could Happen Here", *The Atlantic*, 19 October. Accessed at: http://www.theatlantic.com/international/archive/2016/10/trump-democracy-election-2016/504617/

16   GREENSLADE, Roy. 2016. "Media outlets dare to call Donald Trump a liar, racist and misogynist", *The Guardian*, 1 February. Accessed at: https://www.theguardian.com/media/greenslade/2016/feb/01/media-outlets-dare-to-call-donald-trump-a-liar-racist-and-misogynist

17   ARNADE, Chris. 2016. "What I learned after 100,000 miles on the road talking to Trump supporters", *The Guardian*, 3 November.

18   ____, *Direction of Country*, Real Clear Politics, 3-28 November 2016. Average confidence = 26.3. Accessed at: http://www.realclearpolitics.com/epolls/other/direction_of_country-902.html

19   MOORE, Michael. 2016. On Twitter, 9 Nov. 8:08 AM

20   THE DATA TEAM, 2017. "Declining trust in government is denting democracy", *The Economist*, 25 January. Accessed at: http://www.economist.com/blogs/graphicdetail/2017/01/daily-chart-20?cid1=cust/ddnew/n/n/n/ 20170125n/owned/n/n/nwl/n/n/n/email

21   NORRIS, Pippa; Alessandro Nai; Holly Ann Garnett; and Max Grömping. 2016. *The Perceptions of Electoral Integrity Index by US State*, The Electoral Integrity Project, Sydney, Australia. Accessed at: https://www.electoralintegrityproject.com/featured-dataset

22   GUILFORD, Gywnn. 2016. "Harvard research suggests that an entire global generation has lost faith in democracy", *Quartz*, 30 November. Accessed at: http://qz.com/848031/harvard-research-suggests-that-an-entire-global-generation-has-lost-faith-in-democracy/

23   WHERRY, Aaron. 2011. "The House of Commons is a sham", *Macleans*, 18 February.

24 COYNE, Andrew. 2012. "Parliament's at the point of no return", *Ottawa Citizen*, 19 October.

25 SIMPSON, Jeffrey. 2001. *The Friendly Dictatorship*, McClelland & Stewart, Toronto.

26 FRIESEN, Joe and Bill Curry. 2012. "Prime Minister Harper unveils grand plan to reshape Canada", *The Globe and Mail*, 26 January.

27 BOUTILIER, Alex. 2016. "Maryam Monsef rejects Commons committee's report on electoral reform", *The Toronto Star*, 1 December. Accessed at: https://www.thestar.com/news/canada/2016/12/01/liberal-mps-recommend-breaking-electoral-reform-promise.html

28 BLATCHFORD, Andy. 2014. "EI rate cut: Ottawa skipped internal study in favour of interest group report", *The Canadian Press*, 20 November. Accessed at: http://www.cbc.ca/m/touch/news/story/1.284166

29 SHEPHARD, Michelle. 2014. "How Canada has abandoned its role as peacekeeper", *The Toronto Star*, 31 October. Accessed at: http://projects.thestar.com/news/world/2014/10/31/ how_canada_has_abandoned_its_role_as_a_peacekeeper.html

30 DEN TANDT, Michael. 2014. "If the Tories really loved the military so much, it wouldn't be systematically underfunded", *National Post*, 13 November.

31 GALLOWAY, Gloria. 2014. "Fine print on Ottawa's $200-million veterans fund: It'll take 50 years to pay", *The Globe and Mail*, 28 November.

32 PAYTON, Laura. 2012. "F-35 fighter jet cost questions date back to 2010", *CBC News*, 12 April.

33 HARRIS, Michael. 2014. *Party of One*, Viking Press, Toronto, pg.120

34 MAY, Kathryn. 2016. "PS needs to pick up pace of reforms: Privy Council Clerk", *The Ottawa Citizen*, 25 March.

35 SAVOIE, Donald J. 2003. *Breaking the Bargain: Public Servants, Ministers, and Parliament*, University of Toronto Press, Toronto.

36 KENNEY, Jason. "Modernization Of House Of Commons Procedure, Government Orders", *House of Commons Hansard #33, 37th Parliament, 1st Session*, March 21st, 2001: 1:20 a.m.

37 MCGREGOR, Janyce. 2012. "Canadians lack confidence governments can solve issues," CBC News, 25 July. Accessed at: http://www.cbc.ca/news/politics/story/2012/07/24/pol-premiers-advancer-nanos-poll-priorities.html.

38 LEVERT, Stéphane. 2013. *Sustainability of the Canadian Health Care System and Impact of the 2014 Revision to the Canada Health Transfer*, the Canadian Institute of Actuaries, September 2013. Accessed at: http://www.cia-ica.ca/docs/default-source/2013/213075e.pdf

39   HILTZIK, Michael. 2017. "All the horrific details of the GOP's new Obamacare repeal bill: A handy guide", *The LA Times*, 4 May. Accessed at: http://www.latimes.com/business/hiltzik/la-fi-hiltzik-obamacare-repeal-20170504-story.html

40   COYNE, Andrew. 2016. "Premiers finally come up with something to negotiate in health-care negotiations", *National Post*, 3 October. Accessed at: http://news.nationalpost.com/full-comment/andrew-coyne-premiers-finally-come-up-with-something-to-negotiate-in-health-care-negotiations

41   CTV News staff. 2016. "Healthcare wait times hit 20 weeks in 2016: report", *CTV News*, 23 November. Accessed at: http://www.ctvnews.ca/health/healthcare-wait-times-hit-20-weeks-in-2016-report-1.3171718

42   According to RBC.com statistics for 2016-2017. Accessed at: http://www.rbc.com/economics/economic-reports/pdf/provincial-forecasts/prov_fiscal.pdf

43   DAVIS, Karen, Kristof Stremikis, David Squires, and Cathy Schoen. 2014. *Mirror, Mirror on The Wall: How the Performance of the U.S. Health Care System Compares Internationally*, The Commonwealth Fund, June 2014. Accessed at: http://www.commonwealthfund.org/publications/fund-reports/2014/jun/mirror-mirror

44   MUNN-VENN, Trefor and Andrew Archibald. 2007. *A Resilient Canada: Governance for National Security and Public Safety*, The Conference Board of Canada, Ottawa, November.

45   _____. 2012. *Press Release: Canada's First Infrastructure Report Card*, The Canadian Society for Civil Engineering, Montreal, 14 September. Accessed at: http://www.canadainfrastructure.ca/downloads/news/Canadas_First_Infrastructure_Report_Card_EN.pdf

46   PATRIQUIN, Martin. 2014. "Cleaning House", *Maclean's*, 29 December. pg: 29

47   TENCER, Daniel. 2016. "Automation Will Cost Canada Up To 7.5 Million Jobs: Report", *The Huffington Post Canada*, 28 November. Accessed at: http://www.huffingtonpost.ca/2016/11/28/automation-canada-job-losses_n_13286168.html

48   BRYNJOLFSSON, Erik and Andrew McAfee. 2011. *Race Against the Machine*, Digital Frontier Press, Lexington, MA

49   STONE, Laura. 2013. "Harper government pulls ad about jobs program that doesn't exist yet", *Global News*, 16 August. Accessed at: http://globalnews.ca/news/785793/harper-government-pulls-ad-about-jobs-program-that-doesnt-exist-yet/

50   WADHWA, Vivek. 2014. "We're heading into a jobless future, no matter what the government does", *The Washington Post*, Washington, DC, 21 July.

51   SAENZ, Aaron. 2011."World's Largest Electronics Manufacturer Foxconn Wants 1 Million More Robots In 3 Years. Bye-bye Human Labor", *Singularity HUB*, 2 August. Accessed at: http://singularityhub.com/2011/08/02/

worlds-largest-electronics-manufacturer-foxconn-wants-1-million-more-robots-in-3-years-bye-bye-human-labor/

52 SCOTT-CLAYTON, Judith. 2018. *The looming student loan default crisis is worse than we thought*, The Brookings Institute, 11 January. Accessed at: https://www.brookings.edu/research/the-looming-student-loan-default-crisis-is-worse-than-we-thought/

53 GRAHAM, Luke. 2017. "Finland experiments with universal basic income scheme", *MSNBC*, 3 January. Accessed at: http://www.cnbc.com/2017/01/03/finland-experiments-universal-basic-income.html

54 NUCCITELLI, Dana. 2013. "Survey finds 97% of climate science papers agree warming is man-made", *The Guardian*, 16 May. Accessed at: http://www.theguardian.com/environment/climate-consensus-97-per-cent/2013/may/16/climate-change-scienceofclimatechange

55 WIK, Richard. 2014. *Many around the world see climate change as a major threat*, Pew Research Centre, 31 March. Accessed at: http://www.pewresearch.org/fact-tank/2014/03/31/many-around-the-world-see-climate-change-as-a-major-threat/

56 DAVENPORT, Coral and Eric Lipton. 2016. "Trump Picks Scott Pruitt, Climate Change Denialist, to Lead E.P.A." *The New York Times*, 7 December. Accessed at: https://www.nytimes.com/2016/12/07/us/politics/scott-pruitt-epa-trump.html?_r=0

57 RANDALL, Tom. 2016. "World Energy Hits a Turning Point: Solar That's Cheaper Than Wind", *Bloomberg News*, 15 December. Accessed at: https://www.bloomberg.com/news/articles/2016-12-15/world-energy-hits-a-turning-point-solar-that-s-cheaper-than-wind

58 ___. 2012. "Kent says Canada 'halfway' to 2020 emissions targets", *CBC News*, 8 August.

59 CHEADLE, Bruce. 2013. "Canada won't come close to meeting emissions target: Environment Canada", *The Canadian Press*, 24 October. Accessed at: http://www.ctvnews.ca/canada/canada-won-t-come-close-to-meeting-emissions-target-environment-canada-1.1511806#fmc=no

60 MAS, S. and C. Cullen. 2016. "Justin Trudeau signs Paris climate treaty at UN, vows to harness renewable energy, *CBC News*, 22 Apr. Accessed at: http://www.cbc.ca/news/politics/paris-agreement-trudeau-sign-1.3547822

61 POMERANTSEV, Peter. 2016. "Vladimir Putin's message to the world: you are just as bad", *Financial Times*, 19 July. Accessed at: https://www.ft.com/content/de025422-4d9b-11e6-8172-e39ecd3b86fc

62 GREENWOOD, Max. 2016. "Trump's Lies Aren't Lies Because 'There's No Such Thing' As Facts Anymore, His Surrogate Says", *The Huffington*

Post, 1 December. Accessed at: http://www.huffingtonpost.com/entry/trump-surrogate-claims-no-facts_us_58408f8ee4b0c68e047fd952?

63 FANG, Marina. 2016. "Paul Ryan On Donald Trump Tweeting Lies: 'Who Cares?', *The Huffington Post*, 4 December. Accessed at: http://www.huffingtonpost.com/entry/paul-ryan-donald-trump-tweets_us_5844b2f2e4b0c68e04818206?

64 GARDNER, Dan. 2010. "What the think-thinkers don't get", *The Ottawa Citizen*, 25 February.

65 Police-reported homicides hit a historic low in 2013, as Canada's murder rate fell by 8% to its lowest level since 1966. Source: ELLIOTT, Josh. 2014. "Canada's homicide rate in 2013 lowest since 1966", *CTVNews.ca*, 1 December.

66 ____, 2008. "National crime rate falls for third straight year", *The Canadian Press*, 17 July. Accessed at: http://www.thestar.com/news/canada/2008/07/17/less_crime_could_hurt_tories.html

67 FUNKE, Alice. 2012. "Harper government's assault on reason, scientists, 'Orwellian' and 'alarming'", *The Hill Times*, 9 October.

68 MARTIN, Don. 2010. "Defending access, if not practising it", *Canwest News Service*, 14 April.

69 NATIONAL FREEDOM OF INFORMATION AUDIT 2014, Newspapers Canada. Accessed at: https://nmc-mic.ca/sites/default/files/FOI2014-FINAL.pdf.

70 MARTIN, Don. 2010. *op.cit*. 14 April.

71 COYNE, Andrew. 2014. "Virtue may be its own reward, but it does little for election chances", *Postmedia News*, 24 November.

72 TRAVERS, James. 2009. "The quiet unravelling of Canadian democracy", *The Toronto Star*, 4 April. Accessed at: http://www.thestar.com/news/insight/2009/04/04/the_quiet_unravelling_of_canadian_democracy.html

73 ____. 2011. "MPs' report finds government in contempt", *CBC News*, 21 March. Accessed at: http://www.cbc.ca/news/politics/mps-report-finds-government-in-contempt-1.1091382

74 HARPER, Tim. 2011. "For Conservatives, contrary positions are treasonous", *The Toronto Star*, 17 November.

75 STOYMENOFF, Alexis. 2012. "Scary time" for Canada", *Vancouver Observer*, 26 January.

76 SMITH, Allan. 2017. "Trump echoes Steve Bannon in raucous nationalist speech to the biggest conservative conference of the year", *Business Insider*, 24 Feb. Accessed at: http://www.businessinsider.com/trump-cpac-speech-echoes-bannon-2017-2/

77 PAQUET, Gilles. 2014. *Unusual Suspects*, Invenire Books, Ottawa, ON pg. 9-10

78   MAY, Elizabeth. 2012. *The most damaging things happening to Canada are the things you cannot see*, 3 December. Accessed at: http://elizabethmaymp.ca/news/blogs/2012/12/03/the-most-damaging-things-happening-to-canada-are-the-things-you-cannot-see/

79   COYNE, Andrew. 2014. "A country outweighed by its provinces", *Postmedia News*, 3 December.

80   ____. 2011. "Conservatives dispense with throne speech debate", *The Canadian Press*, 8 June. Accessed at: http://www.ctvnews.ca/conservatives-dispense-with-throne-speech-debate-1.654647

81   TRAVERS, James. 2010. "Changing Canada, one backward step at a time", *The Toronto Star*, 19 June.

82   POTTER, Andrew. 2014. "Why democracy doesn't need a white knight", *The Ottawa Citizen*, 3 January.

83   Quoted in RADWANSKI, Adam. 2009. "Stephen Harper: anarchist?" *The Globe and Mail*, 13 July. Accessed at: http://www.theglobeandmail.com/news/politics/radwanski/stephen-harper-anarchist/article1216560/

84   Quoted in KOEBLER, Jason. 2016. "Society is Too Complicated to Have a President, Complex Mathematics Suggests", *Motherboard*, 7 November. Accessed at: http://motherboard.vice.com/read/society-is-too-complicated-to-have-a-president-complex-mathematics-suggest

85   Adapted from SLATON, C.D. 1991. "Quantum Theory and Political Theory", in *Quantum Politics*, T.L. Becker, (ed.) Praeger Publishers, New York, N.Y., pg. 41-63

86   SAVOIE, Donald. 2015. *What is Government Good At?*, McGill-Queen's University Press, Kingston, ON, pg. 237

87   TAINTER, Joseph. 1988. *The Collapse of Complex Societies*, Cambridge University Press, New York, NY.

88   STREECK, Wolfgang. 2016. *How Will Capitalism End? Essays on a Failing System*, Verso Books, Brooklyn, NY.

89   Quoted in KOEBLER, Jason. Op.cit. 2016.

90   Quoted in, LENIHAN, Don. 2015. "Five big ideas for Canada, but one is the biggest", *National Newswatch*, 28 February. Accessed at: http://www.nationalnewswatch.com/2015/02/28/five-big-ideas-for-canada-but-one-is-the-biggest/#.VPNTji5UU2z

91   WILSON, Christopher. 2014. "Re-Imagining Government", *Optimum Online*, September; Gilles Paquet. 2014. *Unusual Suspects*, Invenire Books, Ottawa, Canada.

92   HUBBARD, Ruth & Gilles Paquet. 2007. *Gomery's Blinders and Canadian Federalism*, University of Ottawa Press, Ottawa, pg. 100

[93] NANOS, Nik. 2012. "Canadians Rate Highly the Issues Close to their Day-to-Day Lives," *Policy Options*, August.

[94] HORST, Rittel and Melvin Webber.1973. "Dilemmas in a General Theory of Planning," *Policy Sciences*, Vol. 4, Elsevier Scientific Publishing Company, Inc., Amsterdam, pg.155-169,

[95] COHEN, Andrew. 2016. "The Republicans are at war with the 21st century", *The Ottawa Citizen*, 19 July. Accessed at: http://ottawacitizen.com/opinion/columnists/cohen-the-republicans-are-at-war-with-the-21st-century

[96] DEN TANDT, Michael. 2016. "West needs to come to grips with reality and fight ISIL on the ground", *The Ottawa Citizen*, 18 July. Accessed at: http://www.ottawacitizen.com/news/national/ michael+tandt+stop+mass+killings+worldwide+defeat+isil+with/12064848/story.html

[97] GVOSDEV, Nikolas. 2016. "Geo-Economics Moves Front and Center as Connectivity Reshuffles Global Politics", *World Politics Review*, 1 July. Accessed at: http://www.worldpoliticsreview.com/articles/19245/geo-economics-moves-front-and-center-as-connectivity-reshuffles-global-politics

[98] ROTHSTEIN, Bo. 2005. *Social Traps and the Problem of Trust*, Cambridge University Press, Cambridge, UK, pg. 27

[99] WRIGHT, Robert. *NonZero: The Logic of Human Destiny*, Vintage Books, New York, 2002

[100] Based on WILSON, Christopher. 2013. "Internet Will Make Governments Unrecognizable". Originally presented at World Social Science Forum 2013: Social Transformations and the Digital Age, Montreal, QC 13-15 October 2013

[101] TAPSCOTT, Don and Anthony Williams. 2010. *Macrowikinomics*, Penguin, Toronto, p. 10

[102] LEADBEATER, Charles. 2009. *We-think: Mass innovation not mass production*, Profile Books, London, UK

[103] RITTEL, Horst and Melvin Webber. 1973. "Dilemmas in a General Theory of Planning," *Policy Sciences*, vol. 4, p. 155-169.

[104] LOVELOCK, James. 2010. *The Vanishing Face of Gaia: A Final Warning: Enjoy It While You Can*, Penguin Books.

[105] STEFANINI, Sara. 2017. "Syria to ratify the Paris agreement, leaving the US alone", *Politico*, 7 November. Accessed at: https://www.politico.eu/article/syria-to-ratify-the-paris-agreement-leaving-the-us-alone/

[106] MABEY, Nick quoted in DYER, Gywnne. 2008. *Climate Wars*, Vintage Canada, p. 165

[107] DYER, Gwynne. 2008. *Climate Wars*, Vintage Books, Toronto, Canada.

108 FUERTH, Leon, John Podesta and James Woolsey. 2007. *The Age of Consequences: The Foreign Policy & National Security Implications of Global Climate Change*, Centre for Strategic & International Studies, Washington, DC. P. 77.

109 MILANOVIC, Branko. 2005. *Worlds Apart: Measuring International and Global Inequality*, Princeton University Press, Princeton, p.180–81

110 YALNIZYAN, Armine. 2010. *The Rise of Canada's Richest 1%*, Canadian Centre for Policy Alternatives, Ottawa.

111 REUTERS, 2017. "The World's 8 Richest Men Are Now as Wealthy as Half the World's Population", *Forbes,* 16 January. Accessed at: http://fortune.com/2017/01/16/world-richest-men-income-equality/

112 CONFINO, Jo. 2012. "Rio+20: Tim Jackson on how fear led world leaders to betray green economy", *The Guardian*, 25 June. Accessed at: http://www.theguardian.com/sustainable-business/rio-20-tim-jackson-leaders-green-economy

113 FRIEDMAN, Thomas. 2009. "The Inflection Is Near?", *The New York Times*, 7 March.

114 STREECK, Wolfgang. 2016. *How Will Capitalism End? Essays on a Failing System*, Verso Books, Brooklyn, NY.

115 JACKSON, Tim. 2009. *Prosperity without Growth? - The transition to a sustainable economy*, Sustainable Development Commission, London, UK.

116 METCALFE, John. 2013. *The Immediate Climate Threat Is Water Scarcity, Not Rising Sea Levels, Atlantic Cities*, 10 October. Accessed at: http://www.theatlanticcities.com/jobs-and-economy/2013/10/immediate-climate-threat-water-scarcity-not-rising-sea-levels/7192/

117 CASSIM, Zaheer. 2018. "Cape Town could be the first major city in the world to run out of water," USA TODAY 19 January. Accessed at: https://www.usatoday.com/story/news/world/2018/01/19/cape-town-could-first-major-city-run-out-water/1047237001/

118 SEN, Amartya. 2000. *Development as Freedom*, Anchor Books, New York, NY.

119 DYER, Gywnne. *op. cit.* p.58

120 RANDALL, Tom. 2016. "World Energy Hits a Turning Point: Solar That's Cheaper Than Wind", *Bloomberg News*, 15 December. Accessed at: https://www.bloomberg.com/news/articles/2016-12-15/world-energy-hits-a-turning-point-solar-that-s-cheaper-than-wind

121 ELLIS, Erle C. 2013. "Overpopulation Is Not the Problem", *New York Times*, 13 September.

122 WALLACE, Tim and Szu Ping Chan. 2016. "Why Italy's banking crisis will shake the eurozone to its core", The Telegraph, 16 July.

Accessed at: http://www.telegraph.co.uk/business/2016/07/16/why-italys-banking-crisis-will-shake-the-eurozone-to-its-core/

[123] TENCER, Daniel. 2017. "Italy Bankrupt, Internet Down: The Wildest Predictions For 2017" *The Huffington Post Canada*, 3 January. Accessed at: http://www.huffingtonpost.ca/2017/01/03/wildest-predictions-2017_n_13818912.html

[124] EVANS-PRITCHARD, Ambrose. 2017. "Italy's €17bn bank crisis is the fruit of unworkable EU policies", *The Telegraph*, 26 June. Accessed at: http://www.telegraph.co.uk/business/2017/06/26/italys-17bn-bank-crisis-fruit-unworkable-eu-policies/

[125] INMAN, Phillip. 2013. "Eurozone: three countries have debt-to-income ratios of more than 300%", *The Guardian*, 9 June. Accessed at: http://www.theguardian.com/business/2013/jun/09/eurozone-crisis-debt-income-ratios

[126] MURPHY, Robert, P. Milagros Palacios, Sean Speer, and Jason Clemens. 2014. *Comparing the Debt Burdens of Ontario and California: Lessons from the Past and Solutions for the Future*, Fraser Institute, March. Accessed at: https://www.fraserinstitute.org/sites/default/files/comparing-the-debt-burdens-of-ontario-and-california.pdf

[127] ____, 2015. Quebec Ministry of Finance, 31 March. Accessed at: http://www.finances.gouv.qc.ca/en/page.asp?sectn=36&contn=335

[128] EBERSTADT, Nicholas. 2012. *A Nation of Takers – America's Entitlement Epidemic*. Templeton Press, West Conshohocken, PA.

[129] PAQUET, Gilles and Wilson, Christopher. 2016. *Intelligent Governance*, Invenire Press, Ottawa.

[130] TAPSCOTT, Don and Anthony Williams. 2010. *Macrowikinomics*, Penguin, Toronto, p. 279

[131] HIGHAM, Robin and Gilles Paquet. 2013. "Reflections on the Canadian Malaise", *Optimum Online*, Vol. 43, Issue 2, June. and OBERTONE, Laurent. 2013. *La France – orange mécanique*. Editions Ring, Paris.

[132] JOHNSON, Ian. 2013. "The Challenge of Scarcity", *The Ottawa Citizen*, 5 September.

[133] HUBBARD, Ruth and Gilles Paquet. 2010. *The Black Hole of Public Administration*, University of Ottawa Press, Ottawa.

[134] BACKER, Thomas. 2003. *Evaluating Community Collaborations*. Springer Publishing, New York, NY, p.10.

[135] ASHBY, W.R. 1958. "Requisite variety and its implications for the control of complex systems", *Cybernetica (Namur)* vol. 1 (no. 2).

[136] FREDERICKSON, H. George and David Matkin. 2005. *Public Administration and Shared Power: Understanding Governance, Networks, and Partnerships*,

Working Group on Interlocal Services Cooperation. Paper 8. Accessed at: http://digitalcommons.wayne.edu/interlocal_coop/8

[137] HIGHAM, Robin and Gilles Paquet. 2013. "Reflections on the Canadian Malaise", *Optimum Online*, Vol. 43, Issue 2, June.

[138] APPLEBERRY, James. Keynote address, EMU Presidential Inauguration, Eastern Michigan University, 20 October 2000

[139] GREGG, Allan R. 2012. *1984 in 2012 – The Assault on Reason*, speech delivered at the opening of Carleton University's new School of Public Affairs, *Ottawa, 5 September*.

[140] TANI, Maxwell. 2016. "TRUMP: I'm a 'smart person,' don't need intelligence briefings every single day", *Business Insider*, 11 December. Accessed at: http://www.businessinsider.com/donald-trump-intelligence-briefings-skip-2016-12

[141] HAGEL, John. 2009. "A Labor Day Manifesto for a New World", *Edge Perspectives*, 7 September. Accessed at: http://edgeperspectives.typepad.com/edge_perspectives/2009/09/a-labor-day-manifesto-for-a-new-world.html

[142] ENSERINK, Martin. 2016. "European leaders call for 'immediate' open access to all scientific papers by 2020", *Science*, 27 May.

[143] JOY, Bill. 2000. "Why the future doesn't need us", *Wired*, April.

[144] ROSEN, Len. 2013. *Democratizing the Genome with Crowdfunding Assistance*, The World Future Society, 23 August. Accessed at: http://www.wfs.org/blogs/len-rosen/democratizing-genome-crowdfunding-assistance. Rosen suggests there is a clear trend to democratize the knowledge of the human DNA to facilitate more innovative disease responses.

[145] SYMANTEC Corp.2011. *Symantec Survey Finds Global Critical Infrastructure Providers Less Aware and Engaged in Government Programs*, Press Release, Mountain View, CA, 31 October.

[146] BENDER, Jeremy. 2015. "They'd love to do damage: The FBI says ISIS wants to go after one of America's biggest vulnerabilities", *Business Insider*, 19 Oct. Accessed at: http://www.businessinsider.com/isis-and-hacking-us-power-grid-2015-10

[147] TAPSCOTT, Don and Anthony Williams. 2010. *Macrowikinomics*, Penguin, Toronto, p. 25

[148] FOOT, Richard. 2011. "What happened to political integrity and respect for Parliament?", Postmedia News, 22 April. Accessed at: http://www.canada.com/news/What+happened+political+integrity+respect+Parliament/4661218/story.html

[149] HARRIS, Misty. 2013. "Cybercrime cost Canadians nearly $3.1 billion over past year", *Postmedia News*, October 2. Accessed at: http://www.canada.com/technology/Cybercrime+cost+Canadians+nearly+billion+over+past+year/8984034/story.html

[150] ELLIOTT, Mark. 2006. "Stigmergic Collaboration: The Evolution of Group Work" *M/C Journal* vol. 9, Issue 2.

[151] WILSON, Christopher. 2011. "On Collaboration", *Optimum Online*, vol. 41 (1) March.

[152] *Op.cit.* TAPSCOTT & Williams.

[153] About OpenCollective. 2016. Accessed at: https://opencollective.com/about

[154] SUSSKIND, Richard. 2016. "Replacing the Professionals", *CBC Ideas*, 2 September. Accessed at: http://www.cbc.ca/radio/ideas/replacing-the-professionals-richard-susskind-1.3542846

[155] HUBBARD, Barbara. *Conscious Evolution: Awakening the Power of Our Social Potential*, New World Library, Novato, CA, 1998.

[156] BROOKS, David. 2008. "How Voters Think", *New York Times*, 18 January.

[157] HOWE, Paul. 2010. *Citizens Adrift: The Democratic Disengagement of Young Canadians*, UBC Press, Vancouver.

[158] PHILLIPS, Robin, et al. 2010. *Brains on Fire: Igniting powerful, sustainable, word of mouth movements*, Wiley Books, Hoboken, NJ.

[159] PAQUET, Gilles and Christopher Wilson. 2016. *Intelligent Governance*. Invenire Books, Ottawa.

[160] FOOT, Richard. 2009. "Withering of Parliament", *Canwest News Service*, 15 January. Accessed at: http://www.canada.com/news/WITHERING+PARLIAMENT/1160170/story.html

[161] *Ibid.*

[162] SAVOIE, Donald. 2015. "What is Government Good At?", McGill-Queen's University Press, Kingston, ON. p. 280

[163] SLATER, Tom. 2016. "The Donald and the turn against democracy", *Spiked*, 27 October. Accessed at: http://www.spiked-online.com/newsite/article/the-donald-and-the-turn-against-democracy/18921#.WLWv4vLe42w

[164] MAY, Kathryn. 2016. "PS needs to pick up pace of reforms: Privy Council Clerk", *The Ottawa Citizen*, 25 March.

[165] WERNICK, Michael. 2016. *Twenty-Third Annual Report to the Prime Minister on the Public Service of Canada*, Privy Council Office, Ottawa. 31March. Accessed at: http://www.clerk.gc.ca/eng/feature.asp?pageId=431

[166] MAY, Kathryn. 2016. "Mental health set as PS priority" *The Ottawa Citizen*, 4 April.

[167] *Op. cit.* PAQUET and Wilson. 2016.

[168] BAKER, Dean. 2017. "Donald Trump's Big Tax Cut . . . For Himself", *Common Dreams*, 26 April. Accessed at: https://www.commondreams.org/views/2017/04/26/donald-trumps-big-tax-cut-himself

[169] SHUSTER, Simon. 2016. "The Populists", *Time Magazine*. Accessed at: http://time.com/time-person-of-the-year-populism/

[170] INGLEHART, Ronald F. and Pippa Norris. 2016.*Trump, Brexit, and the Rise of Populism: Economic Have-Nots and Cultural Backlash*, Faculty Research Working Paper Series, Harvard Kennedy School, Cambridge, MA

[171] FLORIDA, Richard. 2017. "What Is Really Behind the Populist Surge?", *CityLab*, 21 March. Accessed at: https://www.citylab.com/politics/2017/03/what-is-really-behind-the-populist-surge/519921/?utm_source=nl__link3_032117

[172] *Ibid.*

[173] ROTH, Kenneth. 2017. "The Dangerous Rise of Populism: Global Attacks on Human Rights Values", *Global Report 2017*, Human Rights Watch.

[174] TAUB, Amanda. 2016. "The Rise of American Authoritarianism", *Vox.com,* 1 March. Accessed at: http://www.vox.com/2016/3/1/11127424/trump-authoritarianism

[175] Ibid.

[176] FRUM, David. 2017. "How to Build an Autocracy", *The Atlantic*, March. Accessed at: https://www.theatlantic.com/magazine/archive/2017/03/how-to-build-an-autocracy/513872/

[177] AUERBACH, David. 2016. "Make America Austria Again: How Robert Musil Predicted the Rise of Donald Trump", *Los Angeles Review of Books*, 7 August. Accessed at: https://lareviewofbooks.org/article/robert-musil-predicted-rise-donald-trump/

[178] GILMORE, Scott. 2018. "Donald Trump wanted 'America First.' He got 'America Alone.'" *Macleans*, 12 January. Accessed at: http://www.macleans.ca/politics/worldpolitics/donald-trump-wanted-america-first-he-got-america-alone/

[179] ÇANDAR, Cengiz. 2014. "The Erdogan tapes", *Al Monitor*, 27 February. Translated, Timur Göksel. Accessed at: http://www.al-monitor.com/pulse/originals/2014/02/supporters-deny-taped-conversation-erdogan-son.html#ixzz4hovO7KOP

[180] FRASER, Suzan. 2014. "Turkey Twitter ban: Prime Minister Recep Tayyip Erdogan's threat to 'rip out roots' backfires as users link to 'corruption' recordings", *The Independent*, 22 March. Accessed at: http://www.independent.co.uk/news/world/europe/turkey-twitter-ban-prime-minister-recep-tayyip-erdogans-threat-to-rip-out-roots-backfires-as-users-9209621.html

[181] VONBERG, Judith; Lauren Said-Moorhouse and Kara Fox. 2017. "47,155 arrests: Turkey's post-coup crackdown by the numbers", *CNN*, 15 April. Accessed at: http://www.cnn.com/2017/04/14/europe/turkey-failed-coup-arrests-detained/

[182] PAMUK, Humeyra and Ercan Gurses. 2017. "Turkey fires 3,900 in second post-referendum purge", *Reuters*, 29 April. Accessed at: http://www.reuters.com/article/us-turkey-security-expulsions-idUSKBN17V0MH.

[183] _____. 2017. "Turkey's referendum: Turkey is sliding into dictatorship", *The Economist*, 15 April.

[184] _____. 2017. "License to Kill: Philippine Police Killings in Duterte's 'War on Drugs'", *Human Rights Watch*, 1 March. Accessed at: https://www.hrw.org/report/2017/03/01/license-kill/philippine-police-killings-dutertes-war-drugs

[185] RAGEH, Rawya and Matt Wells. 2017. "Philippines: Duterte must end his "war on drugs"", *Amnesty International*, 2 February. Accessed at: https://www.amnesty.org/en/latest/news/2017/02/philippines-duterte-must-end-war-on-drugs/

[186] MALLARI, Delfin, Jr., Philip Tubeza. 2017. "'Oplan Tokhang' back nationwide", *Philippine Daily Inquirer*, 6 March. Accessed at: http://m.inquirer.net/newsinfo/877688

[187] _____. 2017. "License to Kill: Philippine Police Killings in Duterte's 'War on Drugs'", *Human Rights Watch*, 1 March. Accessed at: https://www.hrw.org/report/2017/03/01/license-kill/ philippine-police-killings-dutertes-war-drugs

[188] LAMB, Kate. 2017. "Thousands dead: the Philippine president, the death squad allegations and a brutal drugs war", *The Guardian*, 2 April. Accessed at: https://www.theguardian.com/world/2017/apr/02/philippines-president-duterte-drugs-war-death-squads

[189] PORCALLA, Delon. 2017. "Alvarez tags Leila as No. 1 drug lord", *The Philippine Star*, 14 March. Accessed at: http://www.philstar.com/headlines/2017/03/14/1680923/alvarez-tags-leila-no.-1-drug-lord

[190] ARSENAULT, Adrienne 2017. "Jailed Philippine senator says she 'won't be quiet' about President Duterte", *CBC News*, 24 March. Accessed at: http://www.cbc.ca/news/world/leila-de-lima-interview-1.4040079

[191] CABUENAS, Jon Viktor. 2017. "300 Bir Employees Resign after Crackdown on Corruption", *GMA News*, 15 February. Accessed at: http://www.gmanetwork.com/news/money/economy/599664/300-bir-employees-resign-after-crackdown-on-corruption/story/

[192] GAVILAN, Jodesz. 2016. "Who is Customs deputy commissioner Art Lachica?" *Rappler*, 19 November. Accessed at: http://www.rappler.com/newsbreak/iq/152812-customs-deputy-commissioner-art-lachica

[193] RANADA, Pia. 2016. "Duterte to corrupt BOC, BIR employees: I'm watching you", *Rappler*, 6 July. Accessed at: http://www.rappler.com/nation/138831-duterte-boc-bir-corruption

[194] ROMERO, Alexis. 2017. "Duterte tells businessmen in Qatar to shoot corrupt customs personnel", *The Philippine Star*, 16 April. Accessed at: http://www.philstar.com/headlines/2017/04/16/1690858/duterte-tells-businessmen-qatar-shoot-corrupt-customs-personnel

195 WRAGE, Alexandra. 2017. "Killing the Corrupt: Duterte's Other Death Squads", *Forbes*, 1 June. Accessed at: https://www.forbes.com/sites/alexandrawrage/2017/06/01/killing-the-corrupt-dutertes-other-death-squads/#3c5b905a5d54

196 STERLING, Joe and Buena Bernal. 2017. "Duterte jokes about rape while rallying troops to fight militants", CNN, 28 May. Accessed at: http://www.cnn.com/2017/05/26/asia/philippines-duterte-speech/

197 WING, Nick. 2017. "Trump Praised Philippines President Duterte for Drug War that Has Killed 9,000 People", *The Huffington Post*, 23 May. Accessed at: http://www.huffingtonpost.com/entry/trump-duterte-drug-war-call_us_5924a046e4b0650cc01fd23c?utm_hp_ref=philippines

198 NAKAMURA, David and Emily Rauhala. 2017. "Trump boasts of 'great relationship' with Philippines' Duterte at first formal meeting", *The Washington Post*, 13 November. Accessed at: https://www.washingtonpost.com/politics/trump-boasts-of-great-relationship-with-philippines-duterte-at-first-formal-meeting/2017/11/13/e6612f14-c813-11e7-b0cf-7689a9f2d84e_story.html?utm_term=.e0bf351350d8

199 SATTER, David. 2017. "The Mystery of Russia's 1999 Apartment Bombings Lingers — the CIA Could Clear It Up", *National Review*, 2 February. Accessed at: http://www.nationalreview.com/article/444493/russia-apartment-bombings-september-1999-vladimir-putin-fsb-cia-

200 _____. 2011. *Russia Business and Investment Services Handbook, Vol. 1*, International Business Publications, Washington DC. Pg 24.

201 MENON, Rajan. 2014. "Putin's Kleptocracy", *The New York Times*, 25 November. Accessed at: https://www.nytimes.com/2014/11/30/books/review/putins-kleptocracy-by-karen-dawisha.html

202 KARAS, Samantha. 2017. "Vladimir Putin Net Worth 2017: Russia's Leader May Be One Of The Richest Men In The World," *International Business Times*, 15 February. Accessed at: http://www.ibtimes.com/vladimir-putin-net-worth-2017-russias-leader-may-be-one-richest-men-world-2492300

203 *Ibid.*

204 *Op. cit*. ROTH, Kenneth. 2017.

205 LOCKE, John. 1689.*The Second Treatise of Civil Government*,

206 NEMTSOVA, Anna. 2017. "Russian Whistleblowers Turn on Putin—But Can They Be Trusted?", *The Daily Beast*, 17 February. Accessed at: http://www.thedailybeast.com/russian-whistleblowers-turn-on-putinbut-can-they-be-trusted

207 COMMITTEE TO PROTECT JOURNALISTS. Accessed at: https://cpj.org/killed/europe/russia/

208　HIGGINS, Andrew. 2016. "Effort to Expose Russia's 'Troll Army' Draws Vicious Retaliation", *New York Times*, 30 May. Accessed at: https://www.nytimes.com/2016/05/31/world/europe/russia-finland-nato-trolls.html?_r=1

209　POLYAKOVA, Alina. 2016. "Russia's Likely to Interfere in French and German Elections Next", *The Huffington Post*, 13 December. Accessed at: http://www.huffingtonpost.com/entry/russias-likely-to-interfere-in-french-and-german-elections-next_us_5845e0afe4b028b32338dfb1

210　GESSEN, Masha. 2016. "Autocracy: Rules for Survival", *The New York Review Daily*, 10 November. Accessed at: http://www2.nybooks.com/daily/s3/nov/10/trump-election-autocracy-rules-for-survival.html

211　YORK, Chris. 2017. "Bill Browder's Senate Judiciary Committee Hearing Could Explain Anthony Scaramucci's Bizarre Behaviour", *Huffington Post*, 31 July. Accessed at: Accessed at: http://www.huffingtonpost.co.uk/entry/bill-browders-senate-judiciary-committee-hearing_uk_597ee55ce4b02a4ebb7675a6?

212　ALTMAN, Alex and Elizabeth Dias. 2017. "Moscow Cozies Up to the Right", *Time*, 10 March. Accessed at: http://time.com/4696424/moscow-right-kremlin-republicans/

213　BROWNSTEIN, Ronald. 2017. "Putin and the Populists", *The Atlantic*, 6 January. Accessed at: https://www.theatlantic.com/international/archive/2017/01/putin-trump-le-pen-hungary-france-populist-bannon/512303/

214　*Op. cit.* YORK, Chris. 2017

215　*Op. cit.* BROWNSTEIN, Ronald. 2017.

216　*Op. cit.* BROWNSTEIN, Ronald. 2017.

217　DIONNE Jr., E.J. 2017. "The right's jarring drift toward Russia", *The Washington Post*, April 2. Accessed at: https://www.washingtonpost.com/opinions/the-rights-jarring-drift-toward-russia/2017/04/02/3dc792ea-1647-11e7-ada0-1489b735b3a3_story.html?utm_term=.610a9a0b5682

218　*Ibid.*

219　BLAKE, Aaron, Amber Phillips and Callum Borchers. 2016. "The first Hillary Clinton vs. Donald Trump showdown of 2016, annotated", *The Washington Post*, 7 September. Accessed at: https://www.washingtonpost.com/news/the-fix/wp/2016/09/07/the-first-hillary-clinton-vs-donald-trump-showdown-of-2016-annotated/?tid=a_inl&utm_term=.4396b3d98c10

220　*Op. cit.* ROTH, Kenneth. 2017.

221　*Op. cit.* FRUM, David. 2017.

222　RONDÓN, Andrés Miguel, "How to let a populist beat you, over and over again", *Washington Post*, 27 January 2017

223 FARRELL, H. and Shalizi, C. "An Outline of Cognitive Democracy", paper presented in *LaPietra Dialogue, Social Media and Political Participation*, New York University, 10-11 May 2013, accessed at: http://www.lapietradialogues.org/area/pubblicazioni/doc000071.pdf

224 WILSON, Christopher. 2013. Based on *Moving from Leadership to Stewardship*, a presentation to the Second Annual Canadian Association of Programs in Public Administration Conference, Ryerson University, Toronto, 27-28th May, 2013

225 FARRELL, Henry. 2013. "How Valve demonstrates democracy in the workplace", *The Washington Post*, . Accessed at: http://www.washingtonpost.com/blogs/monkey-cage/wp/2013/11/21/how-valve-demonstrates-democracy-in-the-workplace/

226 CLEVELAND, Harlan. 2002. *Nobody in Charge*. San Francisco, CA: Jossey-Bass, p. xv.

227 Quoted in KOEBLER, Jason. 2016. "Society is Too Complicated to Have a President, Complex Mathematics Suggests", *Motherboard*, 7 November. Accessed at: http://motherboard.vice.com/read/society-is-too-complicated-to-have-a-president-complex-mathematics-suggest

228 BLOCK, Peter. 1998. "As Goes the Follower; So Goes the Leader," *AQP News for a Change*, American Society for Quality, 2(7): 11-13.

229 KELLERMAN, Barbara. 2012. *The End of Leadership*. New York, NY: HarperCollins, p. 154.

230 BLOCK, Peter. 2008. *Community: The Structure of Belonging*, San Francisco, CA: Berrett-Koehler Publishers, p. 41.

231 BASS, B. M. 1990. *Bass and Stogdill's Handbook of Leadership: A survey of theory and research*. Free Press, New York, NY; JAGO, A.G. 1982. "Leadership: Perspectives in theory and research," *Management Science*, 28(3) p. 315-336.

232 KELLERMAN, Barbara. 2012, *op.cit.*, p. xiv.

233 PAQUET, Gilles. 2001. "Leadership in Turbulent Times: An Interview with Denis Desautels", *Optimum Online*, 31(2) p.2-7.

234 FOX, Justin. 2006. "The Limited (but real) Impact of CEOs," *Time Magazine*, 20 October. Accessed at: http://business.time.com/2006/10/20/the_limited_but_real_impact_of/.

235 HARFORD, Tim. 2011. *Trial, Error and the God Complex*, TED Global, July. Accessed at: http://www.ted.com/talks/tim_harford.html?quote=1003.

236 KELLERMAN Barbara, 2012, *op.cit.*, p. xiv.

237 BROOKS, David. 2011. "Who is James Johnson?" *New York Times*, 17 June. p. A35.

238 COLLINGWOOD, Harris. 2009. "Do CEOs Matter?" *The Atlantic*, June, p. 54-60.

239 SAVOIE, Donald. 2015. *What is Government Good At*, McGill-Queen's University Press, Kingston, ON. p. 270

240 GLAVIN, Terry. 2017. "If Trudeau is the free world's best hope, we're doomed," *The Ottawa Citizen*, 2 August.

241 HAYES, Christopher. 2010. "The Twilight of the Elites," *Time*, March 11.

242 ___. 2009. "MPs' expenses: Full list of MPs investigated by The Telegraph," *The Telegraph*, 8 May. Accessed at: http://www.telegraph.co.uk/news/newstopics/mps-expenses/5297606/MPs-expenses-Full-list-of-MPs-investigated-by-the-Telegraph.html.

243 GUILFORD, Gywnn. 2016. "Harvard research suggests that an entire global generation has lost faith in democracy", *Quartz*, 30 November. Accessed at: http://qz.com/848031/harvard-research-suggests-that-an-entire-global-generation-has-lost-faith-in-democracy/

244 GEDDES, John. 2013. "Canada's Senate: Chamber of Disrepute," *Macleans*, 8 March.

245 COYNE, Andrew. 2010. "The judge isn't buying it. Nor should we," *Macleans*, 4 June.

246 GUERRERA, Francesco. 2009. "A need to reconnect," *Financial Times*, 12 March.

247 COLLINGWOOD, Harris. 2009, *op.cit.*

248 FOX, Justin. 2006, *op.cit.*

249 BARTON, Dominic, Andrew Grant, and Michelle Horn. 2012. "Leading in the 21st century," *McKinsey Quarterly*, **June. A**ccessed at: http://www.mckinsey.com/insights/leading_in_the_21st_century/leading_in_the_21st_century

250 GRAY, Dave. 2011. "The connected company," *Communication Nation*, 8 February. Accessed at: http://communicationnation.blogspot.co.uk/2011/02/connected-company.html.

251 M.B. 2013. "Leaders without followers," *The Economist*, 21 January. Accessed at: http://www.economist.com/blogs/newsbook/2013/01/world-economic-forum-davos.

252 HAGEL, John. 2010. Quoted in "Running Faster, Falling Behind: John Hagel III on How American Business Can Catch Up," *Knowledge@Wharton*, 23 June. Accessed at: http://knowledge.wharton.upenn.edu/ article.cfm?articleid=2523.

253 MALMENDIER, Ulrike and Geoffrey A. Tate. 2005. *Superstar CEOs*. 7th Annual Texas Finance Festival Paper. 2 February.

254 *op.cit.* HAGEL, John. 2010.

255 *op.cit.* KOEBLER, Jason. 2016.

256 LENIHAN, Don and Graham Fox. 2012. "Federalism upside down: Who speaks for Canada now?" *iPolitics*, 7 August. Accessed at: http://www.ipolitics.ca/2012/08/07/lenihan-fox-federalism-upside-down-who-speaks-for-canada-now/.

257 Ibid

258 HAYEK, Friedrich A. 1945. "The Use of Knowledge in Society", *American Economic Review*. Vol. 35, No. 4. Sep., p. 519-30

259 GARDNER, Dan. 2011. "The trouble with 'decisive' leadership", *The Ottawa Citizen*, 20 May.

260 RUBIN, Hank. 2002. *Collaborative Leadership: Developing Effective Partnerships in Communities and Schools*. Thousand Oaks, CA: Corwin Press.

261 CLEVELAND, Harlan. 2002. *Nobody in Charge*. San Francisco, CA: Jossey-Bass, p. 23.

262 SALAMON, Lester. *The tools of government: A guide to the new governance*, Oxford University Press, London, 2002

263 GREENLEAF, Robert K. 1977. *Servant Leadership: A Journey into the Nature of Legitimate Power & Greatness*, Paulist Press, Mahwah, NJ.

264 SCHWARZ, Roger M. 1996. "Becoming a Facilitative Leader", *R&D Innovator*, vol. 5 (8), August. Accessed at: http://www.winstonbrill.com/bril001/html/article_index/articles/201-250/article231_body.html

265 CLEVELAND, Harlan. 2002. *Nobody in Charge,* Jossey-Bass, San Francisco, p. xv

266 YIP, Jeffrey Chris Ernst, and Michael Campbell. 2011. *Boundary Spanning Leadership: Mission Critical Perspectives from the Executive Suite*, Center for Creative Leadership, Greensboro, NC.

267 O'LEARY, Rosemary and Nidhi Vij. 2012. "Collaborative Public Management: Where Have We Been and Where Are We Going?" *The American Review of Public Administration*, vol. 42, 16 May, p. 507-522.

268 ____. 2012. "IBM CEO Study: Command & Control Meets Collaboration," Press Release, IBM, Armonk, N.Y., 22 May. Accessed at: http://www-03.ibm.com/press/us/en/pressrelease/37793.wss.

269 WOUTERS, Wayne. 2011. Speech to the Institute of Public Administration of Canada, Victoria, BC, 29 August.

270 RITTEL, Horst and Melvin Webber. 1973. "Dilemmas in a General Theory of Planning," *Policy Sciences*, vol. 4, p. 155-169.

271 SENGE, Peter, et. al. 2008. *The Necessary Revolution*, Toronto, ON: Doubleday, p. 369.

272 COLLINS, Jim. 2009. *How the Mighty Fall*. HarperCollins, New York, NY.

273 BLOCK, Peter. 1993. *Stewardship: Choosing Service Over Self-Interest*. Berrett-Koehler, San Francisco, CA: p. 6.

[274] ZANDER, Benjamin. 2008. *Collaborative Leadership: Awakening Possibility in Others*, address to the World Economic Forum Annual Meeting, Davos, Switzerland, 27 January.

[275] *op.cit.* PAQUET, Gilles. 2001.

[276] *op.cit.* BLOCK, Peter. 1998.

[277] *op.cit.* HAGEL, John 2010,

[278] GROVE, Andrew. 1996. *Only the Paranoid Survive*. Doubleday, New York, NY.

[279] LANE, David and Robert Maxfield. 1995. *Foresight, complexity and strategy*. SFI working paper #1995-12-106, Santa Fe, NM.

[280] TAPSCOTT, Don and Anthony D. Williams. 2007. *Wikinomics: How Mass Collaboration Changes Everything*, Portfolio-Penguin Publishers, Toronto, ON. p. 8.

[281] WESTLEY, Frances, Brenda Zimmerman and Michael Quinn-Patton. 2006. *Getting to Maybe: How the World Has Changed*, Random House Canada, Toronto, ON. p. 136.

[282] *op.cit.* BLOCK, Peter. 2008.

[283] VARELA, F.J., Maturana, H. R., and Uribe, R.1974. "Autopoiesis: The organization of living systems, its characterization and a model", *Biosystems*, 5, p. 187-196.

[284] Quoted in MEARIAN, Lucas "The next corporate revolution will be power to the peons", *Computerworld*, 4 June 2013

[285] RAYMOND, Eric S. 1998. *The Cathedral and the Bazaar*, first published 22 November 1998 at www.tuxedo.org

[286] STRUTHERS, Marilyn. 2012. "Of Starlings and Social Change", *The Philanthropist*, vol. 24(4).

[287] ROTHSTEIN, Bo. 2005. *Social Traps and the Problem of Trust*, Cambridge University Press, Cambridge, UK

[288] ARTHUR, W. Brian. 2013. *Complexity Economics: A Different Framework for Economic Thought*, SFI Working Paper: 2013-04-012, Santa Fe Institute.

[289] FERGUSON, Charles. 2012. *Predator Nation*, Random House, New York, NY.

[290] DE GEUS, Arie. 2002. *The Living Company*. Harvard Business Press, Boston, MA. p. 36

[291] *op.cit.* PATTON, Michael Quinn. 2010.

[292] *op.cit.* WILSON, Christopher. 2013.

[293] MUSGRAVE, R. A. 1959. *The Theory of Public Finance*, McGraw-Hill, New York.

[294] HOOD, Christopher. 1991. "A Public Management For All Seasons?", *Public Administration*, vol. 69(1), March. p. 3-19.

[295] PAQUET, Gilles. 1997. "Alternative Program Delivery: Transforming the Practices of Governance," in Robin Ford and David Zussman (eds.). *Alternative Service Delivery: Sharing Governance in Canada*. Toronto, ON: RIPAC/KPMG, p. 31-58; PAQUET, Gilles. 2014. *Unusual Suspects: Essays on Social Learning Disabilities*. Inveníre Books, Ottawa, ON. Chapter 6.

[296] GWYN, Richard. 1995. *Nationalism without Walls – The Unbearable Lightness of Being Canadian*. McClelland & Stewart, Toronto, ON.; PAQUET 2012: 56

[297] PAQUET, Gilles and Christopher Wilson. 2016. *Intelligent Governance: A prototype for social coordination*. Inveníre Books, Ottawa, ON. June

[298] de TOCQUEVILLE, Alexis. 1840/1961. *De la démocratie en Amérique*. Paris, FR: Gallimard, vols. I and II.1840/1961: vol. II, p. 144, 189

[299] FOSTER, G.M. 1972. "The Anatomy of Envy: A study of symbolic behavior," *Current Anthropology*, XIII (2): 165-202.

[300] BANG, Henrik P. 2003. "A new ruler meeting a new citizen: culture governance and everyday making" in H.P. Bang (ed.). *Governance as social and political communication*. Manchester University Press, Manchester, UK. p. 241-266.

[301] INTERNET WORLD STATS. 2015. Accessed at: http://www.Internetworldstats.com/stats.htm

[302] ____, 2013. *What will we make of this moment? 2013 Annual Report*, IBM, Armonk, New York. p.13.

[303] TUNG, Liam. 2017. "IoT devices will outnumber the world's population this year for the first time", *ZDNet* 7 February. Accessed at: http://www.zdnet.com/article/iot-devices-will-outnumber-the-worlds-population-this-year-for-the-first-time/

[304] WIKIPEDIA, 2014. *Fields of Knowledge*. Accessed at: http://www.thingsmadethinkable.com/item/fields_of_knowledge.php

[305] SHIRKY, Clay. 2012. "How the Internet Will One Day Transform Government", *TED Talks*, 25 September. Accessed at: https://www.youtube.com/watch?v=CEN4XNth61o

[306] PAQUET Gilles and Christopher Wilson. "Inquiring Systems" in *Stewardship: Collaborative Metagovernance and Inquiring Systems*, by R. Hubbard, G. Paquet and C. Wilson. Inveníre Books, Ottawa: 2012.

[307] MCLUHAN, Eric. 1996. "The source of the term 'global village'". *McLuhan Studies*, Issue 2. Accessed at: http://projects.chass.utoronto.ca/mcluhan-studies/v1_iss2/1_2art2.htm.

[308] HUBBARD, Barbara. 1998. *Conscious Evolution: Awakening the Power of Our Social Potential*, New World Library, Novato, CA.

[309] BOYD, Stowe. 2013. *Sociology: Interview with John Hagel*, 1 May. Accessed at: http://stoweboyd.com/post/49386411425/sociology-interview-with-john-hagel.

[310] HUBBARD, Barbara. *Conscious Evolution: Awakening the Power of Our Social Potential*, New World Library, Novato, CA, 1998.

[311] HEYLIGHEN, Francis. 2007. *Accelerating Socio-Technological Evolution: from ephemeralization and stigmergy to the global brain*, ECCO, Vrije Universiteit Brussels. Accessed at: http://pespmc1.vub.ac.be/Papers/AcceleratingEvolution.pdf

[312] WILSON, Christopher. 2011. "On Collaboration", *Optimum Online*, vol. 41 (1) March; ELLIOTT, Mark. 2006. "Stigmergic Collaboration: The Evolution of Group Work" *M/C Journal* vol. 9, Issue 2.

[313] *Ibid.*

[314] MCALPINE, Jill, and James Temple. 2011. *Capacity building: Investing in not-for-profit effectiveness.* PricewaterhouseCoopers Canada Foundation. Accessed at: http://www.pwc.com/en_CA/ca/foundation/publications/capacity-building-2011-05-en.pdf

[315] MANCE, Henry. 2016. "Britain has had enough of experts", *Financial Times*, 3 June. Accessed at: https://next.ft.com/content/3be49734-29cb-11e6-83e4-abc22d5d108c

[316] MEYER, David. 2012. "Finland is about to start using crowdsourcing to create new laws", *GigaOM*, 20 Sept.

[317] ____. 2011. "Iceland is crowdsourcing its new constitution", *World e-gov Forum*, 16 June. Accessed at: http://wegf.org/en/2011/06/iceland-is-crowdsourcing-its-new-constitution/

[318] ____. 2007. "NZ police let public write laws", *BBC News*, 26 September.

[319] IBBITSON, John. 2013. "We don't need politicians in charge. With technology, it's time to put citizens first", *The Globe and Mail*, 2 February.

[320] Quoted in, LOVE, Dylan. 2014. "A Conversation With Linus Torvalds, Who Built The World's Most Robust Operating System And Gave It Away For Free", *The Business Insider*, 7 June. Accessed at: http://www.businessinsider.com/linus-torvalds-qa-2014-6#ixzz34cksJobN

[321] HURST, Aaron. 2014. "Etsy is proof that our economy is experiencing a biological event", *The Guardian*, 6 June.

[322] CARROLL, Dave. 2009. *United Breaks Guitars*. Accessed at: http://www.davecarrollmusic.com/music/ubg/

[323] CARROLL, Dave. 2009. *United Breaks Guitars*, YouTube, 6 July. Accessed at: https://www.youtube.com/watch?v=5YGc4zOqozo

[324] Former US Surgeon General Jocelyn Elders, quoted in BACKER, Thomas. 2003. *Evaluating Community Collaborations*. Springer Publishing, New York. p.10

[325] *op.cit.* MEARIAN, Lucas. 2013

[326] LALOUX, Fredric. 2014. *Reinventing Organizations*, Nelson Parker, Brussels.

[327] LEONARD, Andrew. 2013. "Silicon Valley dreams of secession", *Salon*, 28 October. Accessed at: http://www.salon.com/2013/10/28/silicon_valley_dreams_of_secession/

[328] MALONE, Thomas. 2014. "How Is the Internet Changing the Way We Work?", *Open Mind*, 14 March.

[329] ____. 2013. *State of the Global Workplace: Employee Engagement Insights for Business Leaders Worldwide*, Gallup, Inc., Washington, DC.

[330] *op.cit.* MEARIAN, Lucas. 2013.

[331] FERENSTEIN, Gregory. 2014. "Zappos just abolished bosses. Inside tech's latest management craze", *Vox*, 11 July. Accessed at: http://www.vox.com/2014/7/11/5876235/silicon-valleys-latest-management-craze-holacracy-explained

[332] FELONI, Richard. 2015. "Here's how the 'self-management' system that Zappos is using actually works," *Business Insider*, 3 June. Accessed at: http://www.businessinsider.com/how-zappos-self-management-system-holacracy-works-2015-6

[333] *op.cit.* HARFORD, Tim. 2011.

[334] *op.cit.* BLOCK, Peter. 1998.

[335] BOILIER, David. 2009. "Elinor Ostrom and the Digital Commons", *Forbes*, 13 October. Accessed at: http://www.forbes.com/2009/10/13/open-source-net-neutrality-elinor-ostrom-nobel-opinions-contributors-david-bollier.html

[336] DELONG, J. Bradford and Lawrence H. Summers, 2001. *The 'New Economy': Background, Questions, and Speculations*, August. Conference draft accessed at: http://www.j-bradford-delong.net/Econ_Articles/Summers_New_Economy_2001.html

[337] RIFKIN, Jeremy. 2014. "Capitalism is making way for the age of free", *The Guardian*, 31 March.

[338] Quoted in Badger, Emily. 2013. "Share Everything: Why the Way We Consume Has Changed Forever", *The Atlantic's CityLab*, 4 March. Accessed at: http://www.citylab.com/work/2013/03/share-everything-why-way-we-consume-has-changed-forever/4815/

[339] *op.cit.* RIFKIN, Jeremy. 2014.

[340] *op.cit.* BADGER, Emily. 2013.

[341] DENNING, Steve. 2014. "Is The Creative Economy Also In Trouble?", *Forbes*, 9 May.

[342] PHILLIPS, Robin, Greg Cordell, Geno Church and Spike Jones. 2010. *Brains on Fire: Igniting powerful, sustainable word of mouth movements*, John Wiley & Sons, Hoboken, NJ.

[343] PAHLKA, Jennifer. 2012. *Coding for a Better America*, TED Talks, March. Accessed at: http://www.ted.com/talks/jennifer_pahlka_coding_a_better_government.html

and Don Tapscott quoted in TOSSELL, Ivor. 2013. "Let's crowdsource Canada", *The Globe and Mail*, 20 February.

[344] *op.cit.* PAQUET, Gilles and Christopher Wilson. 2012.

[345] PAQUET, Gilles. 1999. *Governance through Social Learning*, University of Ottawa Press, Ottawa, ON.

[346] WILSON, Christopher. 2011. *Collaborative Co-Governance: A checklist approach to networking and collaboration*, presentation to National Collaborating Centre for Public Health workshop, Niagara-on-the-Lake, ON, May 6.

[347] GIGERENZER, Gerd. 2001. "The Adaptive Toolbox" in GIGERENZER, G. and R. Selten (eds) *Bounded Rationality – The Adaptive Toolbox*. The MIT Press, Cambridge. p. 37-50.

[348] GIBSON, James J. 1977. "The Theory of Affordances", in *Perceiving, Acting, and Knowing*, eds. Robert Shaw and John Bransford, Lawrence Erlbaum & Associates.

[349] GOFFMAN, Erwin. 1959. *The Presentation of Self in Everyday Life*. Doubleday, New York; RHEINGOLD, Howard. 2002. *Smart Mobs*. Perseus, Cambridge, MA.

[350] NORMAN, Donald A. 1999. "Affordances, Conventions and Design" in *Interactions*, vol. 6 (3). p. 38-43; NORMAN, Donald A. 2007. *The Design of Future Things*. Basic Books, New York. p.68-69.

[351] DE GEUS, Arie. 2002. *The Living Company*. Harvard Business Press, Boston, MA. p. 36

[352] WILSON, Christopher. 2008. "Attention to Place" *Optimum Online*, vol.38 (1) March.

[353] PAQUET, Gilles and Christopher Wilson. 2011. "Collaborative co-governance as inquiring systems," *Optimumonline*, 41(2): 1-12.

Made in the USA
San Bernardino, CA
31 January 2019